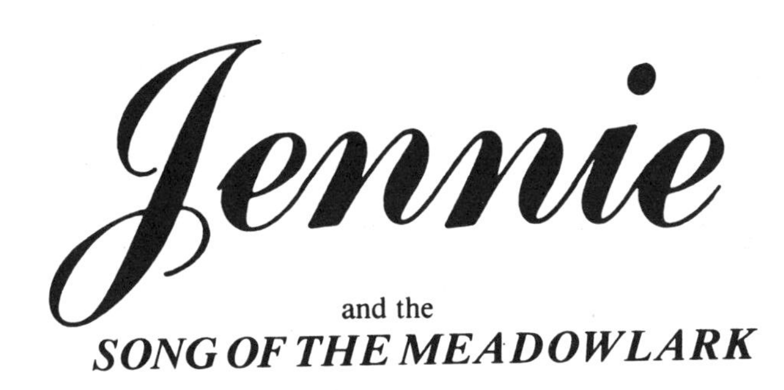

and the

SONG OF THE MEADOWLARK

by

Robert Bryant Mitchell

and

Marietta Mitchell Smith

with

Howard Hugh Wade

Open Bible Publishers

Des Moines, Iowa

Jennie
and the
Song of the Meadowlark

Scripture quotations are taken from the King James Version of the Bible.

First printing: September 1988

Second printing: March 1989

Another book by R. Bryant Mitchell: Heritage and Horizons

Book Design by Vesta Publishing Services, P.O. Box 5474, Eugene, Oregon 97405

Published by Open Bible Publishers, 2020 Bell Avenue, Des Moines, Iowa 50315

Western Distributors: Go-Ye Fellowship, P.O. Box 26405, Los Angeles, CA 90026

Library of Congress Cataloging in Publication Data:

Mitchell, Robert Bryant, 1905-

Jennie and the song of the meadowlark : the true story of one of this century's most beloved foreign mission pioneers--teacher, writer, radio evangelist, and citizen of the world--Jennie Clay Mitchell 1885-1978 / by Robert Bryant Mitchell and Marietta Mitchell Smith with Howard Hugh Wade.

p. cm.

ISBN 0-9608160-2-X (soft)

1. Mitchell, Jennie Clay, 1885-1978. 2. Christian biography.
3. Missionaries--Biography. I. Smith, Marietta Mitchell, 1921-
II. Wade, Howard Hugh, 1942- . III. Title.
BR1725.M49M57 1988
266'.0992'4--dc19
[B] 88-19661

CIP

Printed in the United States of America

Dedicated to

Jennie's twenty-six grandchildren
and sixty-plus great-grandchildren
who were influenced by her life and prayers.

With Gratitude

To my retired missionary wife, Lucille, who has "labored more abundantly" on her word processor for several years in the preparation and revision of the manuscript;

To my career missionary sister, Marietta Mitchell Smith, scholar and international student counsellor, who gathered much of the material for this book and whose close relationship to our parents has given theological depth and spiritual insight to the ministry of Mother Jennie;

To Howard H. Wade who spent many months in the final writing of the manuscript, conceiving and structuring the narrative, adding dialogue and drama to the exciting story of Jennie;

To the office staff, directors, and missionaries of the Go-Ye Fellowship of Los Angeles, California, whose vision for missionary evangelism has sent the light of the Gospel to many mission fields of the world; and to Fern Nelson, faithful homebase secretary for Go-Ye over a period of thirty-one years, who has handled correspondence and finances for the Fellowship, and gathered historical material and pictures for the preparation of the manuscript;

To Milton Stewart and Donald Bryan, Superintendents of the Pacific Division Open Bible Standard Churches, who have donated the use of their office equipment for the duplication of the manuscript;

To my brother, Hubert, and sisters, Helen, Jean, Marietta, and Esther, who with their spouses were all career missionaries in foreign lands, and who contributed their memories to the story of Andrew and Jennie Mitchell and the Go-Ye Fellowship

Authors' Introduction

Our family background is similar to the Latin words *e pluribus unum* embossed on the face of every USA coin, "Out of Many, One." This variety growing into unity is certainly a part of our heritage.

Our parents and grandparents were emigrants coming from Wales, Scotland, England, France, and Canada. The six children born into Andrew and Jennie Mitchell's family also chose spouses from diverse ancestral groups. In addition to the Americans, three married Norwegians, one spouse was born in India, and another was born in Ethiopia.

With differing educational backgrounds and religious affiliations these six children and their spouses served the Lord at home and abroad under several Christian banners. Their generic religious affiliations were Presbyterian, Brethren in Christ, Full Gospel, Methodist, and Inter-denominational. Even the family music was varied. We had a home-made orchestra with piano, violin, two harps, trombone, piano accordion, and a musical saw.

In spite of variety, our parents, Andrew, Sadie (deceased in 1919), and Jennie, emphasized the *unum* in our home. Diversity within Unity was the plan. The words "step-mother", "half-sister," or "half-brother" were never mentioned. A large aluminum plaque with golden letters over a deep brown background spoke to us daily from the wall of our front room: "O MAGNIFY THE LORD WITH ME, AND LET US EXALT HIS NAME TOGETHER." Together we would worship, and together we would proclaim the Gospel of the Lord Jesus.

All U.S. coins likewise carry the inscription "In God We Trust." This was also our motto from our earliest years. Faith in God and in the Everlasting Gospel were part of the milk of our spiritual diet. It was faith in God that enabled our parents to found a missionary organization in the midst of the depression of the thirties, to survive polio, smallpox, and the vicissitudes of world-wide travel in behalf of missions.

Jennie and Andrew with undaunted confidence translated "mustard seed" faith into "penny-on-the-Bible" faith to build mission stations, and send their own children and scores of other men and women to mission fields in foreign lands.

When our parents passed into glory, we felt their mantle descending upon us. Jennie had asked us to tell the story of her prairie experiences to the next generations. We were to pass on to them the Gospel heritage our parents had given us. This is the reason for writing this book.

In order to convey the impact of spiritual forces which enriched our lives, we have recorded the basic substance of many family experiences. They are building stones cut from a quarry of personal letters, diaries, interviews with those who knew them well, and many publications of the Go-Ye Fellowship. The narrative has been written in fictionalized story form with dialogue to give substance and living reality to the testimony.

The theme of the book is timely. In an age of fragmenting personal relationships, of divorce and single-parent families, it provides an example of how families can live happily and influence all whom come in contact with them.

Robert Bryant Mitchell and Marietta Mitchell Smith
Son and Daughter
Eugene, Oregon
April 1988

CONTENTS

Chapter 1

FRONTIER JUSTICE

On the northern border of Nebraska in August, 1889, the weather had been unusually dry. For weeks, four-year-old Jennie Clay had listened to her father Cassius talk worriedly about the possibility of a prairie fire, while her mother, Marietta, fretted about the family's field of sod-corn which was withered and brown.

A strong, chubby girl, with blond hair and freckles, Jennie spent nearly the entire morning of that August day riding stick horses and playing Indians with her older brother Tom. Around and around the corral they galloped, whooping and hollering. Once Tom went in among the horses where Jennie was scared to follow because her mother had told her never to go into the corral. So she stood looking over the mud wall, warning her brother, "Tom, you better come out. You better not go close to those horses. Mommy'll get mad."

Tom did not answer, but continued padding softly in a half-crouch like an Indian warrior until he stood almost beneath them. Softly he touched their flanks and bellies, speaking in the gentle voice his father used. To his pride, they continued standing sleepy-still in the warm sun, their only movement an occasional twitch. Cautiously, he stroked them.

After lunch, Jennie sat in the main room of the family's sodhouse watching her mother mix corn bread. She considered telling on Tom going into the corral, but then didn't, because he had made her promise. While the corn bread was baking, her mother mended Jennie's dress, the one made of left-over flour sacking which had "A-1 Flour" written in large blue and red letters across the front. Jennie couldn't read, but she thought the words pretty. In mid-afternoon, she fell asleep on her parents' bed.

After supper, as the sun was sinking beneath the far rim of the Nebraska prairie, blazing like the dying heart of a blacksmith's fire, it was Jennie who, standing in the doorway, her too-long, hand-me-down dress hanging in dusty folds around her bare feet, first saw the caravan of wagons and riders heading across the prairie toward their house. Behind her at the table, Tom, and Jennie's two sisters, Nellie and Bonnie, were quarreling over who would eat the last two corn muffins. The prospect of visitors excited Jennie. The family didn't get many, except for the men who sometimes rode up at night to talk with her father. He often rode off with them to be gone a day and sometimes a week—sometimes she lost count of the days he was gone. He frequently returned driving horses or cattle. Jennie thought that maybe he was going to ride off with these men tonight. Turning, she ran to her mother crying, "Mommy, Mommy! Some men coming for Daddy!" She tugged at her mother's dress.

Marietta Clay, a short dark-haired woman with a tired expression about the corners of her deep, dark eyes, did not immediately hear her youngest child. She was clearing the dinner dishes and trying to arbitrate among the quarreling youngsters. Only when Nellie, her oldest daughter, announced, "Whole bunch of wagons and horses comin', Ma," did she turn and peer through the narrow window, wiping her hands on a dish cloth. "Where's your father?" she asked.

"He and Ralph went to groom Peekaboo," said Tom. "Want me to fetch 'em?"

"No," Marietta said, "you children stay in the house. I'll get your father. Nellie, you hold Jennie."

"Yes, ma'am," said Nellie, taking the child into her arms.

The next instant Marietta was hurrying toward the stable, the dry dust of the yard swirling about the hem of her dress. Halfway, she met Cassius, walking back to the house, a grim expression on his unshaven face.

"Cassius...!"

"Yeah, I see 'em," his voice was sharp and low.

"We should have gone," said Marietta, turning to trail along after him. "Now it's too late...Cassius!"

"Hush, and get back into the house. Keep the kids inside." He walked out into the wide, dusty, unfenced yard, which was fringed with close-cropped buffalo grass. Marietta followed slowly, stopping by a corner of the house. The four youngsters stood in a tight knot in the doorway of the soddy, more curious than afraid.

While still a quarter mile away, three riders broke away from the wagons and rode up to the soddy. All were armed, two with side holster pistols, the third with a carbine slung sideways across his saddle. Tig, the family's lean, black greyhound, ran to challenge them, barking wildly, until Cassius motioned with a swift cut of his hand and the dog slunk back to the house.

The riders reined their horses into a semicircle around Cassius, who stood straight, almost defiant. The glare of the setting sun cast the riders' faces in shadow. The man carrying the carbine, after surveying the house and yard, raised slightly in his stirrups and nodded to Marietta. She did not respond, but strained to hear what one of the others—a tall, lanky man—was saying to her husband. She caught only the words "...a warning, Clay...," before a farm wagon and a buckboard together holding about ten men, pulled noisily into the yard, stopping to either side of the riders and reinforcing the circle around Cassius.

Marietta now became aware of several rifles aimed, if not directly at her husband, at least in his direction. One man's rifle was cocked and ready to fire. This so riveted her attention that she did not notice Ralph, her older boy, standing at her shoulder.

"You're nothin' but a double-crossin' thief, Clay," the tall, lanky man was saying in a harsh tone, "and folks 'round here ain't gonna put up with it any more. The plain fact is you been stealin' from everybody since you come. Not one man hasn't had somethin' taken – stock, horses, or both. We found the animals you been keepin' out in the Sand Hills. Ain't no secret any more."

He paused and gave the briefest glance toward the children standing in the door. "Now, since you've a family, we give you a warning. You should've left when the deputy come out. But you didn't, and that's too bad."

From the buckboard a man in a slouch hat and a black waist coat snarled, "You been playin' both ends against the middle, Clay, ridin' with us and stealin' from us at the same time. You ain't gonna get away this time."

Two weeks earlier a deputy sheriff from Springview had come to the ranch to arrest Cassius on charges of cattle and horse theft. Younger than Cassius by about ten years, the man had, when confronted by the entire family, lost his nerve. He had lamely suggested he could not arrest Cassius if "overpowered." The family had taken the hint. While Marietta and Nellie grabbed the deputy's arms, Ralph circled his chest with a bear hug, and Bonnie and Tom each a leg. Cassius escaped safely across the South Dakota border into the Rosebud Indian Reservation.

On the border between South Dakota and Nebraska, no law existed except what the settlers were willing to enforce themselves through vigilance committees – with whom Cassius himself had often ridden. The family had several times been awakened at night by some of these same men who had come to enlist Cassius in chasing horse thieves, rustlers, or desperadoes. Quickly, Marietta would help him with his clothes, boots, cartridge belt, and saddlebags. She would listen for the swish of his leather chaps as he mounted his horse and disappeared into the darkness.

Cassius loved the adventure. If no other excuse had existed to ride off, he would have invented one. Half the men on the Great Plains were just like him, infused with the same cunning, courage, and enthusiasm for danger. Even now, Marietta sensed his excitement at the threat of death.

"Since you didn't git out when you had the chance," the tall man continued, "we don't have no choice. You know the price for horse stealin'."

"Yeah, you're gonna git hung, Clay," growled the man in the slouch hat from the buckboard again. He slurred the words and appeared unsteady in the wagon. With a sharp stab of fear, Marietta realized that he was drunk. How many others were drunk as well?

The tall man turned abruptly in his saddle, "Some one o' you shut that fool up!" he shouted. "Can't you see the fam'ly standin' in the door?"

As if the words were addressed to her, Marietta stepped to the soddy, scooted the children inside, and closed the door, remaining outside herself. Ralph continued standing by the corner of the house.

"Ralph, go into the house."

When the boy made no move, she added, "I said, *now*."

"Do as your Ma says," Cassius added, turning his head slightly without altering his stance.

Silently, the boy disappeared around the side of the house.

Cassius said loudly, "So now what?"

"Let's move over to the stable," said the tall man.

"No trees over there," said Cassius.

"When we need a tree, we'll find one," growled the man in the slouch hat.

Slowly, Cassius, hemmed by the three horsemen, led the way toward the stable. Only the buckboard turned and followed. The men in the wagon climbed down and followed on foot.

The stable was a sod-walled enclosure about fifty feet from the house, roofed at one end with limbs and brush, and topped with sod. It held three horses, some pigs, and perhaps two dozen chickens, each separated from the other by low mud walls. Cassius stopped at the outer wall and turned to face the group. The men slowly gathered about. Marietta stopped at the back of the circle, near the buckboard.

For the next hour, the men recounted, in their capacity as judge, prosecutor, and jury, the evidence against Cassius. The principal allegation was that Cassius, in partnership with a Sioux Indian from the Pine Ridge Indian Reservation near their ranch, had been stealing horses for resale in Kansas and Oklahoma. Thus far, the two had collected more than one hundred horses which they were hiding in the Sand Hills southwest of the Clay ranch.

Although she had never known Cassius to steal, Marietta had to acknowledge that it was not an outrageous allegation. Their travels had certainly offered him a thousand temptations. It was easy to see how, as they moved about the country, he might have found ways to steal an animal. There was always a market for a good horse, if not to ranchers or farmers, then to immigrants traveling through the territory who needed a replacement for one that had broken its leg or worn itself out pulling a wagon. It accounted for Cassius' frequent absences from home which lasted anywhere from three days to three weeks—time away that Marietta had always attributed to his wanderlust and longing to explore the frontier.

Of course, not every horse Cassius traded was stolen. Most of his dealings were legitimate, complete with bills of sale identifying buyers and sellers. He had become, like most horse-traders, half-honest, half-crooked, depending upon the circumstance. A likeable man, he was generally welcomed. People enjoyed his yarns and appreciated his knowledge of veterinary. On the surface, he was honest and upright, a dependable neighbor and family man; beneath, he was, like many men on the frontier, easily tempted.

The blunt fact that he had been caught and would likely be hanged before the night was over, struck Marietta with both shame and fear. Stealing horses was almost the worst thing a man could be charged with, aside from murder. On the frontier in the 1880s, good horses were more valued than gold. They not only pulled wagons and plows, but constituted the only swift, reliable transportation. In a country where the dangers of Indian attack, foul weather, starvation, and injury from wild animals were ever-present, human life depended on the fact that when a horse was set to graze at night, it could be found in the same general location come morning. Its disappearance could well mean the loss of everything—land, house, family, even one's life. Moreover, many regarded a horse as the best company a man alone on the prairie could have—loyal, willing, ungrudging, good-natured. Unlike a mule or an ox, a horse could be loved, and rare was the man who did not, after a short time, form a strong bond of attachment and affection for his horse. Given all this, it was understandable that, for as long as anyone could remember, frontier justice had demanded that horse thieves pay for the crime with their lives.

Worse than shame was the icy dread in Marietta's heart of what would become of the family. They were six now, five children and herself. What would they do without him?

The men were but shadows dimly illumined by starlight when the tall man at last called for the vote:

"All who judge guilty, say 'Aye.'"

A strong chorus of ayes sounded in the yard.

"Nay?"

There was silence.

"You're guilty as charged, Cassius Clay," said the tall man. To Marietta, his tone held a disgusting note of self-righteous satisfaction.

"All in favor of hanging?" he asked.

A second chorus of "ayes" came out of the shadows, but spoken this time in low tones that made the men sound more guilty than Cassius. Only the man in the slouch hat, who had been drinking continually throughout the trial, now goaded both Cassius and the other men by loudly proclaiming his vote for hanging.

Three opposed the sentence. "Not me, I'm against," said one man. Another said, "I vote we take him to Springview. It's better the law do it." A third man argued, "He's my neighbor. If I didn't know him...."

"We *are* the law," snarled the man in the slouch hat. "He's a thief and that makes him no neighbor at all!" This opinion was seconded with grunts from several others. The men appeared to be working up the courage to actually carry out the sentence they had pronounced.

Presently, Cassius spoke up, "Well, for what it's worth, I vote this way." A crack sounded that made Marietta think he must have broken someone's jaw. Immediately, a dozen men lunged forward in the darkness, followed by a desperate sound of punches and scuffling in the dirt. Finally, she heard Cassius gasp, "All right, all right...."

"Tie his hands, for cryin' out loud."

"Here's a rope."

Marietta turned so abruptly that she bumped into someone standing in the darkness behind her. Mumbling an apology, he stepped aside to let her pass. Her thoughts now centered on one thing, the Winchester rifle by the head of their bed. Inside the soddy, the children were huddled in the darkness; she only sensed their presence in a corner. As she stepped quickly across the dark room, she said impatiently, "What're you children sitting in the dark for? Nellie, light the lamp. But stay in the house all of you, hear?"

Lifting the rifle, she went back out into the starlit night. Although she had seen Cassius use the Winchester a hundred times, she fumbled with the lever that cocked it. The black metal felt oily and cold. As she rounded the corner of the house, a hand reached out of the darkness and grasped the gun barrel.

"Sorry, Ma'am, but I'll take that," a voice said. With firm pressure the man twisted the weapon out of her hands.

The men had saddled Cassius' favorite horse, a gelding pony named Peekaboo, and hoisted Cassius upon it. In the dim starlight, Marietta could see him sitting upright and stiff, his hands tied behind his back. Even in the darkness, she could sense his defiance.

"Cassius!" she called, rushing over and leaping up to throw her arms about his waist to drag him off the horse. Startled, the horse wheeled in a circle, swinging her in a wide ark. Several men leaped for its reins. When the horse quieted, Cassius leaned down. Marietta whispered desperately, "Cassius, I tried to get the rifle but one of them took it from me."

"It's all right," Cassius said, "don't worry. Take care of the children."

"I love you, Cash."

"And I you, Etta."

The men stood watching the two embrace and whisper. When at last Cassius sat upright, the men mounted their horses and climbed into the wagons. Then the party headed out of the yard, a rider on either side of Cassius, the buckboard leading, the wagon following behind. Marietta continued walking beside Cassius for about half a mile, stopping only when the horses picked up to a trot. She stood looking after them until all sound had faded away, then returned quickly to the soddy, where, by now, Nellie had lit the lamp. From his corner Tom said, "Where'd they take Pa?"

"Never mind. He'll be back. The Lord'll bring him back." She sat down on the edge of the bed. "Come here to me – quick! Let us pray for him!" The children knelt around her in a small cluster, Nellie holding Baby Jennie, who was asleep. However, Marietta was so agitated that when she attempted to speak, no words came out. Instead, she saw Cassius as he had been twenty years before, black hair waving in long curls over eyes sparkling with love for her. Holding trembling hands about the children, she recalled her girlhood faith in God and His mercy to her during their years on the prairie. "Dear Christ, Oh my Lord God, deliver him!" she prayed. After a few minutes, she opened her eyes and said to the children, "Now go to bed."

It was a black, moonless night. The faint silvery tinge of waving grass transformed the prairie into a black ocean, a darkness broken only by swarms of fireflies winking on and off in the distance. The vigilance committee decided that Cassius should be hanged from one of the cottonwood trees bordering Keya Paha River, three miles north of the Clay ranch. The river ran southeast out of South Dakota. The Clays had hauled their water from the Keya Paha when they first settled the ranch.

During the ride to the river, no one spoke. Cassius knew the mood well: weighed by the finality of the act they were about to commit, each man had retreated into himself, hoping for something to interrupt the course of events. In the darkness, he was working to do just that. Twisting in the saddle, on the pretense of looking back for Marietta, he reached for the folding knife in his trouser pocket. A hundred yards from the river, he finally managed to get it out, only to have his numbing fingers nearly drop it. Barely did he catch it against the rim of the saddle.

As they neared the river, the horsemen separated to look for a tree, and two men leaped down from the wagon and took the reins of Cassius' horse. In the darkness, with as little movement as possible, Cassius slowly opened the knife blade.

"Here's one," someone called, "Bring him over here."

The tree stood near the river embankment and was surrounded by thick brush, which someone was pushing down to make room for the horse. In the darkness Cassius could see a rider standing on his saddle attempting to throw a rope over a heavy limb. After several tries he managed to get it over.

"All right, lead him under."

A horseman rode up beside Cassius and placed the noose over his head, cinching it snugly around his neck. On the ground, another man tied the loose end to the tree trunk, taking up the slack. Desperately, Cassius twisted the knife to begin cutting the rope that bound him. He felt the blade slice into his wrist.

Someone said, "Now, we're all agreed on this."

A number of low grunts sounded in the darkness, but not as many as in the stable yard.

"Anyone not agreed?"

"I'm not agreed," a voice said.

"Me neither."

"But is a majority not agreed?"

There was silence.

"That means the majority's for hangin'....Any last words, Clay?"

"I...I...want time to pray," Cassius said, his voice raspy and low.

"He don't need no time to pray," shouted the man in the slouch hat impatiently. "Let's get on with it!"

"Please...!"

"All right then, pray."

Cassius was silent a long time, until someone said, "That's enough. Drive the horse out from under!"

"Wait! Not yet!" Cassius screamed.

"Let me do it!" shouted the man in the slouch hat. The next instant a leather strap struck the horse's haunches. Startled, it moved sideways. Gripping it tightly with his legs, Cassius attempted to calm it, "Whoa, Peekaboo, whoa big guy!"

"HYAAAHHHH!! GIT, HORSE, GIT!"

"Hey, his hands are loose!"

The whip struck even more violently. Rearing twice, the horse finally plunged off through the brush, a great shadowy form in the darkness.

Back at the soddy, Marietta, who was lying awake in the darkness, sat upright in bed.

Chapter 2

EARLY PRAIRIE YEARS

Marietta Gibbs had met and married Cassius Clay in 1869, four years after the Civil War. On a trip for his father, an itinerant merchant, Cassius one day visited the hotel which the Gibbs family operated in Pittsford, Vermont. At dinner the first evening, Marietta, a shy, delicate, young woman, had asked if he were related to the famous Cassius Clay of Kentucky who published an abolitionist paper and was a representative in the Kentucky State Legislature.

Cassius was glad for the question. He thought Marietta just about the prettiest woman he had ever met. "Actually, I'm named for him," he said. "The Confederates, you know, burned his building in Kentucky and forced him to move across the line to Ohio. Later, President Lincoln sent him to Russia as an ambassador. My folks thought a lot of him. And you, Miss Gibbs, what do you do?"

"Marietta teaches school," answered Marietta's mother.

"Ah, they need teachers where I'm going," said Cassius, facing Marietta as he spoke.

"And where's that?" asked Marietta's father.

"Well, sir, as soon as I'm able, I'm heading to the western territories – the Dakotas, Nebraska, Kansas, the Great Plains. I've talked to people who've been there. You can't imagine what a wide-open country it is!" He leaned back from the table, throwing wide his arms. "Why, it stretches from one end of the sky to the other. There's all the land you'd ever want, just for the taking."

"Sounds exciting," Marietta said.

"I can't wait," Cassius said. "I want to be a rancher." Glancing at Marietta, he added, "What I hear, they need teachers out west, too. Lots of new schools going up."

Although her glance did not linger, Marietta was observing Cassius closely. She thought him handsome: his sharply cut chin, his wavy black hair, his deep-set, sparkling blue eyes. His zest and enthusiasm excited her. Most young men in Pittsford had no greater ambition than to clerk in the mercantile.

The next day, Cassius left. A week later she received a letter thanking her for the pleasant evening. A week after that he wrote again, inviting her to go with him to the local fair.

"I believe that young man is courting our daughter," said Mrs. Gibbs to her husband.

"Seems like a fine young man," replied Mr. Gibbs. "I've known his father for years."

In the late 1860s the West was beckoning a whole generation of young people yearning to escape the confines of conventional Eastern society. The Lewis and Clark expedition in 1806, Marcus Whitman's historic wagon train migration of 1843, the building of the first railroad bridge across the Mississippi River in 1856 – all these had excited the imaginations of men and women dreaming of travel, exploration, and settling new country. When the Civil War ended, they began streaming westward by the thousands.

Cassius was indeed courting Marietta. An enthusiastic and persuasive suitor, he filled her with visions of challenge and opportunity on the western frontier. Like so many, she imagined herself pioneering in the wilderness, teaching school in the New West. When finally he asked her to marry and go with him, she hesitated only a moment before saying yes.

For a dowry, Marietta's parents provided a set of fine linen sheets and towels, a few pieces of china and silverware, and a portable pump organ. Soon after the wedding, the two started westward. For a living, Cassius peddled farm and household implements to the farmers and settlers. They followed the canal routes across New York and along the shores of Lake Erie. Their progress was slow. It took two years to travel from Vermont to Michigan. In 1872, in a log shanty in central Michigan, their first child, Ralph, was born. Three years later, in 1875, in the small town of De Pere near Green Bay, a girl, Nellie, was born.

From Wisconsin, Cassius plunged into frontier travel in earnest. He outfitted a Conestoga wagon. This large, high wagon was built watertight like a clumsy flatboat, to float while crossing rivers. The rushing water lifted the front like the prow of a boat. Its upswept ends jostled cargo toward the center, while the canvas top flared at both ends to protect the driver and passengers from sun and rain.

Crossing the upper Mississippi River, Cassius and Marietta travelled to Minnesota and then into South Dakota, eventually moving south into eastern Nebraska, where Cassius began trading horses, and where, on a farm near Albion, their second daughter, Bonnie, was born in 1880.

Never during this time did the family remain in one place longer than a year. Often, their home was a hastily-built sod shanty or dugout with a dirt floor and a roof that leaked muddy water in winter and sifted dry dust in summer. It was meant to last only a season, or until Cassius could think of where to go next. For a short time they owned the farm near Albion where Bonnie was born. However, Cassius impetuously sold it in the middle of winter, moving them into a large corn-crib to finalize the sale, because the buyer wanted immediate occupancy of the farmhouse.

Two years later, on a farm in Bone Creek in northwestern Nebraska, their second son, Tom, was born in October, 1882. The birth was not an easy one, and the midwife cautioned Marietta to remain in bed. Two days later, Cassius rode off to sell some horses, leaving Marietta in the care of Nellie and Ralph.

In 1879, Cassius added a second Conestoga wagon to accommodate the growing family. He drove one and Marietta the other. The cows and horses followed behind. On the move, the family ate off the land. Rabbits, desert turtle soup, and chickens kept in cages provided protein. Corn pone took the place of wheat bread. In treeless areas, the children gathered buffalo chips for fuel. Water was carried along in barrels strapped to the sides of the wagons.

Prairie travel was dangerous. Unexpected floods might rush down a wash or riverbed without warning. One day, while washing her fine linen sheets and towels by a stream, Marietta left briefly to walk to the wagon. When she returned, her linen, her laundry basket, everything, had vanished, swept away by a flash flood.

Even the most ordinary accidents could endanger one's life. One day, Marietta's wagon hit a deep, water-filled hole and almost tipped over. The shotgun hanging on the side of the wagon fell to the ground and discharged, hitting Marietta in the hip, arm, and head. Although she was not seriously injured, the buckshot remained lodged in her body, eventually gathering in knots in her arm, under her scalp, and in a lump on her knee.

The buckshot in the knee might have developed into a crippling infirmity, had it not been for another accident. Marietta had always been afraid of horses, whose skittering, unpredictable manner coupled with their enormous size, made her regard them as unmanageable and dangerous. Horses sensed this fear, and one day, as she was walking behind a team, a horse kicked her. The hoof landed on her knee, bursting the lump and scattering buckshot across the ground. After that, her knee slowly healed.

The endless prairie was as flat and formless as a table top. Fondly, Marietta remembered her childhood home of Vermont with its gently wooded vales and hills, watered by meandering streams. How beautiful had been the change of seasons, the spring with its blossoms, the autumn with its kaleidoscope of color. On the Nebraska prairie, the seasons were as harsh and unforgiving as iron. In the winter came blizzards; in the spring, dust storms, floods, and cyclones; in the summer, grasshoppers and drought; in the fall, prairie fires.

Through it all, the wind did not cease to blow, sifting dust into everything she possessed.

Efforts to tame the prairie were pitiful and short-lived. Houses were but hovels shovelled out of the ground. Fields, cultivated by an effort of strength and will that often killed the people who "owned" them, were barely distinguishable from the surrounding prairie. One might ride past without recognizing a crop had been planted. Even the best "roads" were mere wagon ruts which, if not continually travelled, soon melted again into the ocean of grass.

To Cassius, intrepid adventurer, horseman, wanderer that he was, the dust storms, blizzards, floods, and howling winds of the Great Plains were the very stuff of pioneer life, feeding and nourishing his spirit. To the polite, gentle-mannered Marietta, charged with the care and rearing of children, wandering ceaselessly about in the wilderness was a trial beyond enduring.

Thus, she welcomed his announcement in 1884 that they would file for land under the Homestead Act of 1863. In October, 1884, Cassius moved the family from Bone Creek to a hundred and sixty acres near the northern border of Nebraska, just a few miles south of the Keya Paha River.

A house was their first order of business. They had two choices, a dugout or a sod house.

Dugouts were quick and easy to build. Carved into the sides of gullies or ravines, and fronted by a single sod wall holding a door and perhaps a window, dugouts were, in Marietta's estimation, little better than caves. The walls oozed dampness and mud in winter and sifted fine dust and dirt in summer. The roof was usually level with the surrounding embankment, often giving no sign that a house existed, except for a stovepipe poking out of the ground. Care had to be taken that livestock did not stray onto the roof and fall in upon the family.

A sod house, on the other hand, looked like a real house. It sat on level ground, and although it might appear ramshackle, was often quite cozy and comfortable. With a sod roof and walls three feet thick, it was well insulated—warm in winter and cool in summer. Of course, there were disadvantages. Despite all one could do, the walls harbored mice, while the roof, usually a thatch of brush, straw, and sod, provided a breeding place for insects, particularly bedbugs, which emerged at night to feed upon the occupants. Bull snakes often nested in sod roofs, or crawled during the heat of the day into the dark, cool recesses of the house. Once, a bull snake had dropped into Marietta's arms as she was carrying a basket of clothes through the door.

Cassius argued for a dugout. "Just till spring," he coaxed. But Marietta refused. "A real sod house," she said.

On a slight rise that gave a view of the prairie, Cassius staked off a house roughly sixteen by twenty-four feet. In an adjacent low-lying patch of ground, he located the thick, claylike gummy soil called "gumbo," which was the least likely to crumble. Using a breaking plow, he and Ralph turned furrows of sod eighteen inches wide and four to five inches thick. Marietta and Nellie, using a hoe and shovel, cut these into three-foot slabs, which they pulled on a skid to the building site and laid end to end, layer upon layer, with joints overlapping. The stems and roots of the grass bonded the slabs together.

Cassius had purchased in Springview a framed door and two casement windows, which he now inserted as the clay walls rose. Marietta insisted that they have a gabled wood roof that would shed water. Accordingly, over rafter poles, Cassius nailed planks covered with tar paper, overlapped and sealed with tar. On this he laid thin slabs of sod, which Nellie and Bonnie carefully packed with fine soil. Although it might grow weeds, this roof would be warm in winter, cool in summer, and fairly resistant to water.

To finish the interior, Marietta slaked a mixture of lime, water, sand, and hair combed from the milk cows. It resembled thick, if slightly lumpy, cake frosting. Smeared over the walls, it created a smooth, white, stuccoed surface that kept the walls from crumbling and gave the rooms an airy and pleasing aspect. The floor was sprinkled with water, stamped smooth with bare feet, and swept. As a final touch, Ralph trimmed the exterior walls with a spade to make them square and neat.

This sod house, which took a little less than a week to build, was, in Marietta's opinion, as fine a house as any prairie settler could have. It needed a few things, of course, like a muslin ceiling to keep dirt from sifting down, gingham curtains to dress the windows, and board shelves for the deep window ledges on which she would set her potted geraniums. But it was snug. Its two south-facing windows would admit the winter sun, while its windowless back would shield against the northern winds.

The following June, 1885, Jennie was born. Her blue eyes seemed to recognize them all.

"New baby!" exclaimed little Tom, standing on his toes to peer over the coverlet. "Hi, baby! Hi, baby!" he called attempting to touch her face.

"Don't touch!" Nellie scolded, slapping his hand away. "Your hands are dirty! She's only a day old!"

From the beginning, ten-year-old Nellie was strongly attracted to her baby sister. At every opportunity, she sought to hold her, reluctant even to give her to Marietta for nursing. One day, about a month after the child was born, she asked Marietta, "Can I have Jennie?"

"What on earth are you talking about?" said Marietta.

"I mean...," Nellie struggled with the idea, obviously a difficult one, "can I have her to take care of, like my own, like my baby."

"Sweetheart, Jennie is not a doll," Marietta chided.

"I just want to do the things you do, like wash her, change her, and watch out for her. 'Course, you'd still feed her, but later, when she started eating real food, I'd feed her...."

"I'll think about it," said Marietta.

Nellie, a determined girl, argued her case at every chance, until Marietta finally agreed. As it turned out, Marietta found the arrangement a great help. Nellie proved herself a good "mother," exhibiting caution and good sense in the child's care. By Jennie's first birthday, the two had begun sleeping together on the same bedtick in a corner of the main room, across from Tom and Bonnie, who slept on a low cot in the opposite corner, and Ralph, who slept by Tig along the front wall. In the winter, while the other children shifted closer to the stove, the two girls moved onto the table to escape the cold and damp of the floor.

In the spring, Cassius plowed a garden where Marietta planted squash, onions, tomatoes, beans, watermelons, pumpkins, potatoes, and strawberries. They also planted five acres in sod-corn, which was easy because sod-corn did not require plowing. When the ground was just beginning to thaw, they simply chopped holes in the sod with an axe and dropped in corn seeds, stamping them down with their heels.

The family was not completely alone on the prairie. The Van Kennisons lived on a homestead about four miles east. Their place, known as "Enterprise," was the official address for the Post Office. However, Marietta didn't see much of them, except when Mrs. Van Kennison drove over in a buckboard with her two smallest youngsters, a girl Nellie's age, and a boy, six.

In the second year, Marietta decided they must have a well. It was inconvenient hauling water three miles from the Keya Paha River. Settlers all around had dug wells, getting all the good water they needed. Considering their elevation relative to the Keya Paha, she calculated that in the low spot south of the house they might not have to dig more than twenty feet.

They began in late April when the ground had thawed but not yet dried out. Ralph and Cassius took turns with a pick and shovel, digging a hole four to five feet in diameter. It took two hours to dig through the top-soil and "loess," the clay-like earth resembling river sediment. When the hole got too deep for the earth to be thrown out with a shovel, they set posts on either side and attached a windlass hung from a cross-tie. Using a bucket, they winched the dirt out.

Although most wells were no deeper than twenty or thirty feet, Marietta had heard of some that were two hundred feet deep! As each bucket was hauled up, she called down to ask if there was any sign of water. The men would call back, "Not yet."

At twenty-three feet Ralph struck through to the sandy soil containing the underground waterflow. In a few minutes he was ankle deep in cold water. Tying the rope to a horse, they pulled him out. The rest of the day they celebrated by hoisting out buckets of water and splashing it on the ground. Cassius boxed the bottom to maintain a free space for the water to collect. He also covered the top to keep out dirt, rocks, and inquisitive youngsters.

That summer the region was plagued with locusts. From afar, they appeared silver-grey like glinting fog, eventually becoming so thick they blotted the sun. Anything left outside was devoured – garden, sod-corn, the wash line that hung from the house to the stable, Cassius' leather harnesses, even wood implements like the plow handle and hoe. At the height of the infestation, the creatures covered the ground several inches deep, a crawling, writhing mass. At first, the family tried to fight them, beating them against the ground with boards. The creatures flew against their faces, tangled in their hair, crawled into their clothes. Eventually, they could only retreat into the house until the creatures rose up and moved on. Afterwards nothing was left but bare earth. In the garden, finely sculptured holes remained where vegetables had been.

But even worse was the blizzard which struck in January, 1888. To Marietta, it was a perfect example of the prairie's savage, unpredictable nature. The day dawned mild with a south wind, a light mist, and a comfortable forty degree temperature. About two o'clock, a cold wind suddenly began blowing from the northwest. Marietta glanced out the window to see thick snow driving nearly level across her field of vision. In a short time, the grass was covered with snow. Soon, it was impossible to see anything beyond thirty yards.

Cassius was somewhere on the range, and Ralph had left early that morning to collect firewood at the river. Stepping out into the already blinding storm, she called their names. The howling wind smothered her words. Checking the animals, she hurried into the house to stoke the fire, wait, and pray.

An hour passed. The snow drove more fiercely, covering the windows with a thick crust. "When's Pa and Ralph gonna get back?" Tom asked.

"Soon. They'll be here soon," she answered, fear at the edge of her voice. "Why don't you children play some games? Nellie, play with them. I'll make some corn bread."

For a time Marietta considered saddling a horse and riding out to search for them. Although she had no idea where Cassius might be, she knew the general direction Ralph had taken. She pondered this a long time, finally reaching for her coat.

"Where you goin', Ma?" Nellie asked quickly.

The children, sitting in a circle on the floor, were staring at her wide-eyed. Marietta hesitated. If she too perished, they would be alone. "Just to get some wood," she said.

By late afternoon it was dark. Marietta put a kerosene lamp in the window and another outside behind the house. Although the wind was blowing hard, the lamp burned brightly.

The children were getting bored and hungry. Marietta began fixing supper. Food always brought cheer.

"Shouldn't we wait for Pa and Ralph?" asked Bonnie, as they gathered round the table.

"They'll be late tonight," said Marietta. "Eat your food." She tried to avoid Nellie's anxious look.

Finally, as she was putting the plates away, Marietta heard the clatter of the wagon pulling into the yard. Throwing on her coat, she ran out the door.

"Is Pa back?" Ralph called, climbing stiffly down from the high seat, his entire figure crusted with snow.

"Not yet."

"I'll go look for him...."

"No...."

"I know pretty much where he might be...."

"I said no! Get in the house...I'll unhitch the horses."

Unlike others who lost both family and friends to this storm, Marietta's prayers were answered. Cassius came in two hours after Ralph. They didn't hear him ride up. The door suddenly flung open and he stepped into the room. "Whooeee!" he slapped his hat on his leg, scattering snow. Marietta threw herself around him.

"Thank Peekaboo!" he said, as they hugged him. "I gave that horse his lead and he found the way home!"

The storm blew for two days. For months after, Marietta heard horrifying tales of youngsters let out from school to make their way home only to become lost in the storm and die, and of husbands and sons going lightly clad into the field, losing their way and freezing to death; of families starting out to visit neighbors, only to be found dead in a ravine weeks later.

Ralph was as big now as his father. They could rely on him to do almost anything. He could plow, dig, cut wood, and manage the horses. Weekly, he gathered firewood along the Keya Paha River, north of their house. He also hunted rabbits and prairie chickens using a small caliber rifle which Cassius gave him.

Nellie, a staunch, cheerful girl, with a practical sense, helped Marietta however she could. Besides caring for Jennie, she staked the cows to pasture, milked them, and fed the hogs and chickens. She helped with cooking, washing, sewing, and housework. In every way she sought to guard and preserve the family. She could be a soft and tender mother caring for Jennie, or a tough young woman ready to defend their lives. One autumn, word came that the Sioux Indians on the Rosebud Reservation were planning to attack the settlers. With Cassius and Ralph away, she saddled a horse and carried the alarm to the next homestead. Although the Clays were not attacked, other lives were saved by the warning.

Bonnie, a shy girl, kept close to Marietta. Kind and mindful, she got along well with everyone and did whatever her parents or Nellie asked.

Tom, from his earliest years, was the most confident and aggressive. He was boastful and swaggering and liked to imitate his father's language and manners. Physically reckless and daring, he jumped from the roof and played among the horses in the corral. He loved the prairie and seemed perfectly at home in all seasons. The snug soddy, with its cozy warmth, appeared at times to stifle him, and he derived a special exhilaration in running about half-naked in the most bone-chilling weather. He had an uncommon fascination with horses and riding, and took every opportunity to observe Cassius with the horses. He bragged to Nellie that Cassius "had all the horses in the world."

As did Nellie, Tom regarded young Jennie with special affection. Cutting two sticks which he fit with cords for bridles, he demonstrated how they could ride these "stick horses" about the yard. Together, they galloped barefoot around the sod house and corral and down the narrow road, leaving zigzag trails in the dirt.

From her earliest years, Jennie was cheerful and good-natured. To her, the world was filled with excitement and wonder. She loved the farm and prairie animals, the cows, chickens, hogs, rabbits, prairie dogs, ground squirrels, meadowlarks, killdeer, and mourning doves. She took particular pleasure in lingering alone on the road, barefooted, feeling the cool dirt between her toes, and listening to the wind rustling through the tall, clean grass. Everyone contributed to spoiling her, even Cassius, who frequently took the child on his lap and hugged her, defending her against the unjust accusations of the other children.

Marietta regretted nothing about the prairie as much as its lack of schools. She had a few textbooks and tried to teach the children the basics of reading, writing, and arithmetic. Nellie gave her the best cause for pride. The child was a good reader and could figure numbers well. She had a keen, logical mind, and a willing spirit.

Religious teachings were another matter. Marietta's parents had been keenly interested in spiritual matters. She remembered the white, steepled clapboard church in Pittsford, where a minister in a black frock coat had preached to the congregation sitting attentively in carved oak pews. Even now, she could hear the bell ringing them to service, could see the polished wood floor, the white walls, the cross hanging behind the minister's pulpit.

She had sung in the choir, had even learned the organ, which she still played to accompany her own singing. She particularly liked "Nearer My God To Thee," "Onward Christian Soldiers," and "The Battle Hymn of the Republic." The children often joined with her. Cassius didn't sing, but he appreciated the music.

Cassius was indifferent to any discussion of God, perhaps because he saw it as unreal. The prairie, his cattle and horses, the wind and rain and snow—these were real. God, angels, and the hereafter were nothing but wishful thinking. Life was a struggle. One survived by one's own strength and cunning.

When Marietta talked about God to the children, her explanations were sketchy and vague. After twenty years in the wilderness, her spiritual insights had dimmed. Strangely, it was Nellie who reinforced her. Where the girl had learned about such things, Marietta didn't know.

It was the morning after the vigilance committee had taken Cassius to be hanged that Tom asked, "Ma, does God answer what you ask Him?"

Marietta, who was preparing their breakfast, did not answer. She was thinking that she would have to drive the wagon alone to the Keya Paya to recover and bury Cassius body. The thought made her feel a thousand years old and very tired. When Tom repeated the question, she sighed and said, "I don't know. I guess sometimes."

"Will He help Pa?"

Tears suddenly welled in her eyes. She hadn't yet told the younger children that their father would never be returning. "Yes...He will."

"How do you know?"

"I just know."

"Well, when?"

"I don't know, but He will."

After a moment, Tom said, "I don't understand why we can't see God."

"Because He's spirit and you can't see spirit," Nellie spoke up.

"If you can't see Him, how do you know He's there?" asked Tom.

"You have faith," said his sister. "You have to believe even if you can't see Him."

"Is God as big as the whole world?" Tom continued.

"Bigger."

"But if he's so big, how come we can't see him?"

When Nellie didn't answer, Marietta said, "No one has ever seen God, Tom."

"Does He have more horses than Pa?"

"All the horses in the world," said Marietta tiredly.

"He owns every horse? Even Pa's?"

"Yes, even Pa's."

"Is that why those men took Pa, because he took some of God's horses?"

"Hush up, Tom!" said Nellie.

Suddenly the door flew open, and Ralph, thrusting in his head, shouted, "Somebody's comin'!"

The single horseman sat on his horse before the door. The family stood in a cluster looking up at him suspiciously. He spoke in a voice that Marietta recognized as belonging to one who had voted against hanging Cassius.

"I've come to tell you, Mrs. Clay, that Cassius escaped and that, as far as we know, is still alive. But I'm to tell you that if he comes back, he'll be hanged for sure."

"Oh, thank God!" said Marietta, collapsing back against the door, sobbing. The younger children, alarmed, crowded about her.

The man touched his hat, wheeled his horse, and rode away.

Two weeks later, a letter arrived from Cassius. After his escape, he had ridden two hundred miles south to Beatrice, a town below Lincoln near the Kansas border. Would Marietta load up the furniture, the kids, and as much stock as she could manage, and come south to meet him? He had a buyer for the ranch.

Chapter 3

A DISPLACED FAMILY

With the help of neighbors, the family prepared the two Conestoga wagons. Only one still had the white canvas top, which Ralph now struggled to fasten over the iron hoops. Into this wagon, they loaded the table, chairs, cupboard, pump-organ, pots, pans, dishes, personal clothing, and bedding. Into the open wagon went Cassius' tools, harnesses, saddles, farm implements, including the plow, and finally the cook stove. The stove was so heavy they had to load it in pieces.

Ralph rounded up all the stock he knew to be theirs. Two teams of the strongest horses were hitched to the wagons, while the remaining horses and cows were tethered behind. The chickens were hung in cages on the sides of the open wagon. Since pigs couldn't be herded in hot weather, Marietta sold all except three of the youngest, which they penned in the second wagon. Marietta drove the lead wagon and Ralph followed in the second.

It had been a fine homestead, this little sod house on the northern border of Nebraska, the only place Marietta had hoped to live the rest of her life. Now, at forty-six, to think that she must give it up and start over in a new place in a distant part of the country, well, it was almost too much to bear.

The bitterness was that they had just that year "proved up" their claim on the land, having lived on it five years. Under the provisions of the Homestead Act, the entire quarter section of land, 160 acres in all, now belonged to them free and clear. The deed had been signed and sealed by President Benjamin Harrison himself! Compared to her time on this ranch, the twenty years of moving here and there, from Michigan to Wisconsin to South Dakota to Kansas and back to Nebraska, blurred in her mind like a dream.

Early that morning Nellie and Bonnie had picked all the edible vegetables in the garden. Before walking over to the wagons, where her children watched from the high seats, Marietta now made one final pass to see if anything had been overlooked. She looked old and very tired. In the last week the ache from the old knee injury had returned, and she walked with a limp.

Ralph, Nellie and Bonnie were almost as dismayed at leaving the ranch as their mother. Only Tom and Jennie did not realize they would never see the soddy again, or walk down the road, or play stick horses near the corral. They thought riding away in the wagons a great adventure.

The two-hundred-mile trip to Beatrice took three weeks. They travelled slowly, eight to ten miles a day. Several times they camped near settlers. Alone on the prairie, people were eager to talk with folks travelling through. The wives, especially, were anxious to visit. On the prairie, women shared a special loneliness. After only a few hours together, they felt such natural affection for one another they often cried and embraced upon parting. The second night Marietta cautioned the children: "We don't say anything about your father, or why we are really going, because, well, folks just wouldn't understand. We simply tell them that we are going south to join him at a new place. That's all. It's all right to tell them about the Keya Paha where we lived. People want to know that."

One day, Marietta began talking optimistically about their new circumstances. "I just know it's going to be better," she said. "I'll bet your father has found a place already. A good place. It'll be better, I know it will."

Reaching Beatrice, they camped outside of town and sent Ralph to find Cassius. When the two returned, Cassius was smiling broadly. He wore a dash and charm that none of the children had seen before. He kissed and embraced Marietta and hugged each of the children in turn. That night around the campfire he sat among them like a prince out of exile, talking enthusiastically of his plans for their new life. No one mentioned the near hanging, not out of embarrassment or shame but because it was even now too frightening to speak of.

At one point Tom said, "Pa, when are we going back home?"

"We're not going back, boy. That's all over. We're going to a new place!"

In the dim firelight, only Nellie, sitting close to Tom, saw the uncertainty and dismay which clouded the boy's face.

The new place was a three room, single-walled frame house in very poor repair. The wind whistled through broken windows. The door hung on rusty, broken hinges. Trash littered the floor. Marietta stood in the middle of the main room a long time, looking about, while the children explored the other rooms cautiously, as if wary of ghosts. Cassius walked about like a salesman. "Few nails in the door, some boards over the windows.." —he nudged the trash with the toe of his boot— "...a little sweeping out and it'll be just fine."

"Yes, a little sweeping out...." Although Marietta worked to make the house tidy and comfortable, she did not suggest any long term improvements. They were hauling water again, but when young Tom suggested digging another well, she said nothing.

The place had one advantage: it was close to other folks. They now saw more people in one week than they had in a year on the ranch. Nearly every day, neighbors from other farms dropped by to welcome them and offer help.

Marietta and Nellie visited with the women and Cassius talked horses, arranging several trades. One day about a month after their arrival, Marietta announced at supper that a neighbor had invited them to a Methodist service given by an itinerant minister holding meetings in a Presbyterian Church. "I thought we might all go."

Cassius was not interested. He shrugged indifferently.

Nellie looked at Marietta with pleading eyes.

"Well, then," said Marietta, "perhaps Nellie and Bonnie could go...?"

"Fine," said Cassius.

Arrangements were made for the two sisters to ride to the meeting in a small horse cart which Cassius had recently acquired in a trade. By the time the two girls arrived, the church was crowded. They parked the cart at the perimeter of a wide circle of wagons.

Nellie had never before attended a church and was very excited. Despite having to sit in a rear pew, they had a good view of the service. The minister was a short, fair-complexioned man from Missouri, with a strong, resonant voice. He was dressed in a black coat and held a Bible in one hand. The service began with a hymn the girls knew, "Onward Christian Soldiers." As Nellie sang, an expectant feeling welled in her that almost took her breath away.

For his Gospel message, the preacher selected Matthew 1:21, in which an angel appears to Joseph and foretells the birth of Jesus and His purpose on earth: "....He shall save His people from their sins." For some reason the import of this passage struck Nellie with such clarity and force that her lips trembled. At the final hymn, she was flushed and weak, and it was all she could do to stand. The service ended with an invitation:

"Come forward," the minister said, "to confess to the One who died for you."

"Let's go up there," Nellie whispered to Bonnie.

"What?" said Bonnie, who had been minding the crowd more than the service. She was completely unaware of the emotion surging in her sister's heart.

"I said, 'Let's go up there.' He's inviting us to come up and confess to Jesus."

Bonnie's eyes widened with alarm. She did not answer.

"Then I'm going," whispered Nellie.

Quickly, Nellie walked to the front where the preacher was acknowledging perhaps a dozen other men and women who had come forward. "Speak with me now to Jesus," he said to them in a low voice. Speak with Jesus! The thought drove the breath from Nellie. Uncontrollably, tears started from her eyes. Deep inside, a single thought intoned: "Jesus does love me! He came to save me!"

On the way home, Nellie could only think: "Jesus is with me now. I am saved." Wherever she looked, the world was somehow different.

That evening, she took out Marietta's small Bible and, carrying it behind the house, found the passage in Matthew that had been the minister's Gospel message. She read it aloud. Unable to control her emotion, she began jumping up and down.

Tom, who sometimes spied upon his sisters when he thought they were up to something, and who had followed Nellie outside, called, "What ya doin', Nellie, an Indian dance?"

"You git, Tom Clay!"

The next April, just after Nellie's fifteenth birthday, the family moved from Beatrice to a farm north of Lincoln. At the same time, Marietta announced that Nellie would become a school teacher.

"What?" said Nellie, alarmed.

"You will go to Teachers' school this summer, where you will take an examination that will let you teach school."

"But I've never even been to school. What if I don't pass?"

"You will pass, and then you will teach school this winter. It will work out." Marietta talked as if she were foretelling the future.

In Lincoln, Marietta bought a history of America and two textbooks on geography and mathematics. For the next two months, she worked with Nellie. In mid-June of 1891, Nellie found herself preparing to ride the twenty miles on horseback to Ashland to the Teachers' Institute north of Lincoln. Suddenly, she began worrying about her long gingham dresses and high prairie boots. How would they appear in the polite society of the Institute? Marietta, although she sighed away the concern, nevertheless agreed to buy her daughter new shoes and a dress with a high neck and long sleeves. Young Bonnie and Jennie thought their sister also needed a new hat with flowers, lace, and ribbon. Knowing what wind and rain could do to a lady's hat while riding a horse, Nellie chose instead a man's broadbrimmed, black buckskin hat.

Two days later, wearing the new black hat and a freshly pressed gingham dress—the new shoes and dress were safely packed in a homemade saddlebag—she rode off. About noon, she passed a threshing crew working in a field. One of the men called, "Hey, come take a look at this girl in a man's hat. Ha!" The dozen men and boys stopped their work to watch her ride by. As the boys whistled, one of the men called, "My, aren't you pretty!" Blushing, Nellie whipped the horse forward.

At the Teachers' Institute, she joined seventeen other aspiring teachers, three men and fourteen women. Most were her own age, though a few were in their twenties. The men lodged in a room next to the headmaster's office, and the women slept in a dormitory on the second floor. Nellie found the company of so many other young ladies fascinating, if not slightly intimidating. She was acutely conscious of the difference between her habits and manners, and theirs: how they sat at table, how they ate, how they talked. She listened with envy to their naturally correct pronunciation of "-ing" words, how they never used "ain't."

The six subjects – literature, history, geography, arithmetic, grammar, and essay writing – were presented more as a review than an introduction. While Marietta had, over the years, attempted to teach Nellie a little of everything, Nellie now became aware of the gaps. Grammar was the most difficult, and although Nellie wrote passably well, she could not always identify the parts of speech.

In August, as the final examination approached, Nellie grew increasingly nervous. Although she had studied hard, what if she failed? On the day of the examination, she was so nervous she could not even drink tea.

The examination consisted of nine essay questions. Nellie answered every one, although later, at home, she couldn't recall what she had written. She told Marietta, "I failed the grammar part."

"But you passed the examination?" asked Marietta.

"Yes."

"Wonderful!" cried Marietta, hugging her daughter. "That's my girl!"

Immediately upon Nellie's return, Cassius loaded the wagons and started the family south. For months he had been thinking of joining the land rush in Oklahoma which had started in 1889. He thought they might do again what they had done in Keya Paha.

They stopped for the winter in Greenwood County, Kansas, south of Emporia. Here, Nellie got her first chance to teach school. The first term she had ten girls and nine boys, ranging in age from 6 to 15, the three oldest boys being only one year younger than she. In return for teaching all the subjects she had studied at the Teachers' Institute, she received $30 a month, a salary which greatly impressed Marietta and Cassius.

On winter mornings, Nellie got to school early enough to build a fire in the small heating stove. There was a single chalkboard and a desk with a bench for nearly every student. The windows had no shades or curtains, and the only decoration on the wall was a picture of George Washington. A water bucket carried twice a day from the nearest farm, provided the class with drinking water. At the end of the school day, the students took turns sweeping the floor and cleaning the chalkboard. Twice a term, everyone pitched in to give the room a thorough scrubbing.

Young Jennie, now six years old, was proud to sit in the first row with the other young students. The respect paid Nellie impressed Jennie tremendously, and she worked hard to get her lessons just right.

Life was providing Jennie with surprises. One afternoon, as she stood watching her father mend a fence, he said, "Jennie, run to the house and get me a hammer." Immediately, she started off. Watermelon stained the front of her pinafore, and she licked her fingers as she walked. In a low place where the road was sheltered from the wind, a meadowlark lit on a fence post and began singing. It had a grey wings and a yellow and black topknot.

Jennie stopped to watch. The bird's high, clear song was more beautiful than any she had ever heard. As she listened, a strange, new feeling stirred in her heart. The bird's song seemed to speak of freedom, peace of heart, and exuberant joy in the midst of suffering and toil. And yet with it was a message: You need somebody besides yourself.

As if a veil were lifted from before her eyes, she suddenly perceived a glory, hidden yet revealed, in everything about her, in the high grass, in the deep well of sky and white clouds, in the cool, powdery dirt beneath her feet, in the watermelon stain on the front of her dress. The perception, which lasted only a moment, remained vivid in her awareness for long afterwards. Once or twice she tried to tell Nellie, but couldn't. Thereafter, she thought of the meadowlark as her "fencepost preacher."

At the end of the school year, Cassius loaded the wagons and moved the family closer to the Oklahoma border, stopping in Clark County just south of Dodge City. In 1892, although Dodge City, Kansas, was no longer a wide-open frontier town, and the gunfights and lawlessness were now legends, the town was still wild enough to negatively impress the Clay children. While the prairie had challenged their spirit, the drinking, gambling, swearing, brawling, and sometimes killing, only frightened and depressed them. That year, Nellie had a number of frightening experiences with young ruffians in her school. Bigger than she, with impulses to violence, they intimidated her in ways that Indian attacks and prairie fires never had.

Since her conversion two years earlier, Nellie's awareness for things spiritual had been growing. She attended church every Sunday, prayed every night, and regularly read the Bible. She discussed religion with Marietta. To young Jennie and Tom, she boldly declared: "Jesus came to save us from sin. He has cleaned my heart and I know that He is Lord of my life."

When the school year ended, Cassius began packing for the move into Oklahoma Territory. On the eve of their departure, however, both he and

"The bird's song seemed to speak of freedom, peace of heart, and exuberant joy in the midst of suffering and toil. And yet with it was a message: You need somebody besides yourself." 1891.

Marietta were arrested and detained by the authorities in Dodge City. Ralph, Nellie, and the other children were bedded in a livery stable.

"Why do they want 'em?" Tom kept asking Nellie.

"They just want to ask them some questions."

"About what?"

"About things," said Nellie, not daring to reveal her suspicion that Cassius had again been arrested for trading stolen horses. Late the next morning, however, Marietta and Cassius were released. As soon as the wagons were hitched, the family headed south toward the Oklahoma border.

Oklahoma Territory was a shattered dream, despite Cassius' continual encouragement that things were going to be just like on the Keya Paha. The unbounded frontier that Cassius had known twenty years before was gone. The territory was filled with wagonloads of people looking for land, among whom lawlessness and violence were the rule.

They stayed only three months, Cassius trading horses and stock, the family living out of the wagons. In August, Cassius suddenly proposed they go to California. "Why, the ocean is so blue and big, you can't imagine," he told Marietta. "And there's opportunity, too. The weather out there is fine. All we have to do is grease the kids and turn them loose." He laughed. Looking into her eyes, he added, "I admit it, Etta, Oklahoma was a mistake. This is no place for a family."

"So much has been a mistake, Cassius."

"But we can still make do, Etta. We have one more chance, and it's California. What do you say?"

They sold their farm equipment and started westward across the Oklahoma Panhandle to Clayton, New Mexico, a crossroads town that was a rail terminus for the Denver, Texas, and Fort Worth Railroad, running up to Denver.

It took six weeks, to the end of September, to reach Clayton. The red Oklahoma dust sifted into every corner of the wagons. After a rain, the clay stuck to the wheels like thick bread dough, and the horses sank up to their knees. In Clayton, they sold everything except Marietta's pump organ, which they crated for shipment. Cassius found a wealthy cattleman who paid $2000 in gold and silver for two burros, three cows, and fifty horses. It was more than enough to get them to Denver and from there to Los Angeles.

The night before they were to leave for Denver, Cassius, having lodged the family in a hotel, took the money and went down to the saloon. There, in a poker game lasting nearly four hours, he lost $600 – "cheated out of it" he shouted at Marietta as he burst back into their hotel room and began rummaging for his Colt revolver.

"Cassius, No! We're on our way to a new life. The money doesn't matter. We have enough. Please!"

Spinning the cylinder to check the cartridges, Cassius slammed out the door without answering, clambering down the hotel stairs two steps at a time. Tom, lying on a mattress in a corner of the room, suddenly recalled the fateful night when vigilantes had come to their house near the Keya Paha. For the second time in his life he thought he had seen the last of his father.

One hour later, however, Cassius was back, carrying his pistol and the $600.

Without exception, the train was for all of them the greatest adventure yet. They had seen trains in Dodge City, had watched them pull in and out of the station, had stood beside the great iron wheels and closely inspected the puffing engines. However, no one had yet ridden one. For Marietta, sitting in a fancy paneled coach, on padded leather seats with velvet curtains on the windows, watching the countryside float by, was a luxury beyond describing. Only a slight swaying and a steady click, click of the iron wheels spinning smartly along the track, gave indication that they were moving at all. Outside, plumes of black smoke from the engine blew past the window.

Until they reached Denver, the younger children, Tom in the lead, did not stop marching up and down the aisles from one car to the next. Accustomed to the flat prairie, the family marvelled at the mountains, the forests, the frothing white rivers.

Eight-year-old Jennie, her nose pressed to the window, sighed to her mother, "I hope they have horses and meadowlarks in California."

None of them had ever imagined a town as large as Denver. So many people! Unbelievable! With a population of sixty-five thousand, Denver was one of the largest cities in the West. A major rail terminus, through which travellers bound for all points in the country daily arrived and left, the city was exploding with growth. Situated along Cherry Creek, it had, by late 1892, paved streets, streetcars drawn by cables, and buildings over seven stories high.

They stayed in Denver two weeks, in two rooms on Larimer Street. They bought new pants, dresses, shoes, hats for everyone – so that, when they finally boarded the Union Pacific train to Los Angeles, no one could have suspected that only days before they had traded in their horses and covered wagons to leave forever a life of twenty-three years on the Great Plains.

Chapter 4

NEW LIFE IN CALIFORNIA

For the Clay family, Los Angeles was the Golden Pot at the end of the rainbow. In 1893, the "City of Angels" had a population of 65,000 and was rapidly changing from a sleepy Spanish settlement of low adobe buildings to a bustling city intoxicated with developing riches from oil, sunshine, and tourists.

Despite this, Cassius, at first enthusiastic, soon became disillusioned. City life was suffocating. Living day after day in a cluttered rooming house jammed among a hundred other identical houses stretching block after block, nosey neighbors ten feet away, the unceasing din of city traffic, the sun and wind blocked by rooftops, was an impossibility he could not endure. A wanderer, he needed at least a thousand square miles of unsettled land just to draw breath.

As Cassius saw it, the city was for merchants and clerks, secretaries, prissy people dressed in waistcoats and polished shoes, carrying umbrellas and walking sticks, reading newspapers and books, trading over counters, riding in carriages and streetcars. Even laborers – masons, carpenters, machinists, blacksmiths, teamsters – somehow lacked spirit here, content to live their lives doing other people's work. Cassius knew one thing: horses. The only job he could find was grooming horses and cleaning stalls at a local stable. But appearing for work day after day, following orders given by an authority other than his own inclination, quickly became intolerable, and he quit.

Within a few months, the money from the sale of the stock in Clayton was gone, and the family was forced to take in boarders to meet expenses. For a time Cassius sold chickens door to door, an occupation he found too demeaning even to mention. Increasingly, he turned to sitting despondently about the house.

In the large fenced yard behind their house, he kept several horses. One day, saddling a horse, he rode out of town. He was gone a week and a half, and when he finally returned, he offered no immediate explanation of where he had been. Marietta, anxiety showing in her face, made no attempt to question him. However, he eventually explained that he had ridden out into the valley looking for work as a cowhand, but had turned up nothing. Two weeks later he was gone again.

From that time on, he was frequently away from the family. They were not always sure whether he was working or not. Although he had money when he returned, it was never very much and was soon spent. One day, about a year after their arrival in California, he rode off and did not return. As the weeks passed, Marietta and the family did not know what to think. Had he been killed? Had he left the state? Was he in jail? Three months later, a letter arrived postmarked Panama, saying that he was working as a mechanic on the Panama Railroad and would return when the job ended.

Early the next spring he actually did return. However, by now the family had adjusted to life without him. Marietta baked and sold pies and took in washing. Ralph worked as a machinist's apprentice in a tool company. Tom sold newspapers after school in downtown Los Angeles. Since Nellie's credentials were not adequate for the Los Angeles public schools, she clerked in a dry-goods store. Together with what two boarders contributed, the family was getting by.

Cassius stayed only a month before disappearing again. Jennie returned from school one day to find him gone. This time the family did not hear from him again, and it was speculation what became of him. Years later, a report came that he had perished in the Galveston Flood of 1900, where he was employed as a construction worker, driving teams of horses, but no one knew for sure. Marietta continued to speak fondly of him.

Despite continuing economic worries, life became easier for the Clay family. Marietta could not quit exclaiming over Southern California's mild winters and the lack of wind. With little effort, she could keep the house almost dust free. With double walls, a wood floor, a separate kitchen with a sink where water issued from a tap, two bedrooms upstairs and one downstairs, a parlour, and a dining room, their house was a far cry from the little two-room soddy. Outside the back door next to the stoop, she had not one potted geranium, but a whole bed of them!

Unlike Cassius, Marietta and the children appreciated the closeness of people in the city. Nothing had so terrified and depressed Marietta as the loneliness of the prairie. For the first time they had neighbors they could visit without having to ride half a day in a wagon. With a population of 65,000, Los Angeles had gas lights, some paved streets and, after 1900, electric street cars on which, for a quarter, one could ride clear to Santa Monica. On Sunday afternoons Marietta, Nellie, and the younger children would ride to the beach. Jennie and Tom would play all afternoon splashing in the waves and running in the warm sand.

The children often rode horses through the middle of downtown. Young Jennie and a school friend would ride down Main Street from 21st Street to

Marietta Clay, Jennie's mother from Vermont.

City Hall. They rode bareback, and boys on bicycles would ride alongside and cluck to the horses till they were almost trotting, and the girls just hanging on.

For the first time in their lives, Jennie, Tom, and Bonnie were attending large public schools. They had some difficulty at first, not only with lessons, but socially. From the isolation of the prairie, where their only companions had been each other and assorted farm animals, they now confronted crowds of children, many of whom were contemptuous of their dress, their speech, their innocence. "Hey, hick, your feet hurt? No? Mine would if I'd never worn shoes before!" The teasing and derision continued the entire first year. The second year, other newcomers took their place and things got easier.

After visiting a number of churches, Marietta eventually settled upon a nearby Methodist Church, attended by neighbors that made her feel welcome.

She and Nellie enjoyed every aspect of the service, the worship, the sermon, the hymns, the praying, and the visiting with friends and neighbors.

In the spring of 1898, Nellie, now twenty-three, began volunteer work with the Peniel Mission, a Christian missionary foundation in downtown Los Angeles that held Gospel meetings to reach unconverted people coming into the mission off the street. The mission fed the hungry, visited the sick, sent missionaries to other countries, and served as a service center for military personnel.

Jennie, now thirteen, was helping Marietta prepare supper the afternoon Nellie announced she was going to San Francisco to manage one of the mission's shelters for soldiers returning from the Philippine Islands.

"Oh, Mother," Nellie hurried to explain, "When they asked for volunteers, I just said yes."

"I think it's exciting," blurted Jennie, her eyes alight with excitement.

"How long will you be there?" asked Marietta.

"Everyone commits for a year," said Nellie.

"Who will you live with? Do we know any of them?" Marietta had a hundred questions, which Nellie spent all of supper answering. "I don't know...." Marietta said finally, "It's so far."

"Mother, San Francisco's only a day away by train. I can visit every other month. And I'll write, two...three times a week. Why, you'll get more words out of me than you ever did before....Mother, I'm grown up now...."

Later, alone with Jennie, Nellie said, "A chance might open to go to the Philippines and work in a real mission."

Jennie pictured jungle islands, hot and tropical.

"It's too early to know," said Nellie, "but I'd probably be helping in a clinic with the injured soldiers, and distributing food to the hungry and teaching people to read....but also establishing churches – missions....Oh, Jen, I want to do this!"

Nellie left for San Francisco three weeks later. As she promised, she wrote several times a week, letters which Marietta, with ceremony, read to the others at suppertime. A year later, Nellie was in Manila working in a small mission hospital.

The other children were growing up and leaving, too. Ralph had moved out of the house the year Cassius left. In 1906, after completing school, Bonnie married Will Slater, a young farmer who owned a tidal-basin farm in the "peat lands" near Huntington Beach. A hardworking man, he made a good living raising lima beans, sugar beets, celery, and seed for onions, tomatoes, and peppers.

Tom worked after school selling newspapers in downtown Los Angeles.

Jennie Clay, graduate of Normal School, 1907.

One afternoon he wandered into the County courthouse and, finding a trial in progress, sat down to observe the proceedings. Thereafter, his principal amusement, aside from baseball, was watching lawyers arguing cases in the Los Angeles County Courthouse.

In 1906, Nellie, back from her missionary work, married George Murdock whom she had met while working in the Peniel mission in San Francisco. Like Bonnie's husband, Murdock was a farmer near Huntington Beach, raising onions and seeds, where he had built a large thirteen room house.

Jennie finally completed public school in 1905. It was a proud day for Marietta. Hurriedly she began prompting her daughter to become a school teacher, the only respectable profession she could think of for a woman. The next fall, Jennie began the teachers' course at the Los Angeles Normal School which sat like a castle on West Fifth Street, not far from the Civic Center.

At Normal School Jennie gave herself to organizing clubs, meetings, and social events. She enjoyed working with people and usually had a sensible opinion about how things ought to be done. Her enthusiasm for projects was contagious. People naturally gravitated to her and sought her advice. She directed the school's YWCA program, and in her last year was elected a class officer. In 1907, she graduated and took her first job as a teacher.

From the beginning, Jennie liked everything about teaching. It challenged her ingenuity, inspired her, and filled her with energy. She arrived at school early and left late. At home she constantly thought about how to make the class more interesting. As the year progressed, the fourth grade became like her family. She regarded each child with an affection that made them feel special. She counselled them, worried about them, took their problems home to discuss with Marietta over supper.

Although she could appear stern when necessary, she was by nature good-humored, which instilled in the children more of a willing obedience to her authority than a grudging compliance. She could enjoy a good joke one minute and be guiding the students soberly through a lesson the next. At the end of the first year, the principal, a tall, thin, bespectacled man, who scarcely smiled ("for discipline"), and who was careful to see that his teachers at least control the children, if not teach them, rated Jennie "outstanding in all areas." He noted that "her firm control in classroom situations is tempered by a rollicking sense of humor, aided by her size and strong physique. Young people are attracted by her wit and sincere interest for their welfare."

Toward the end of her second year, Jennie, with financial help from Tom, Nellie, and Bonnie, moved Marietta into a comfortable two-bedroom cottage on Coronado Street, just south of Sunset Boulevard. It was their third house since coming to Los Angeles. Marietta cried and hugged her daughter when Jennie showed it to her. Walking slowly from one room to another, favoring the leg with the old buckshot injury, she asked, "You bought this house?"

"We own this house, Ma," said Jennie.

Jennie found a new church, the Echo Park Methodist Church, which was located nearby on Reservoir Street, overlooking busy Alvarado Street. It was a cozy, family church with a homey air. It had a social hall below the chapel which was used for Sunday School, social events, and youth gatherings. On the surrounding hillside grew California pepper trees with their green and red clusters of hard little berries and small narrow, green leaves. Several tall eucalyptus trees shaded the rear of the lot. On Sundays, most of the families who lived in the surrounding neighborhood walked to church. The few families that drove parked their cars – Model-T Fords, shiny black Dodges, and a few classy Hupmobiles – facing head-in at the curb.

Jennie quickly involved herself with activities at the Echo Park Church. She longed for something to influence her life in a way that teaching public school did not. She volunteered to lead worship groups and counsel children, and soon various church committees were enlisting her aid. Before long, she was at the church more than she was at home, prompting Marietta to remark, "Aren't you doing too much, dear?"

"I'm all right," Jennie reassured her. "What else should I be doing?"

In 1914, a new couple joined the Echo Park Church. Jennie noticed them almost immediately, as if an invisible finger directed her glance: the woman, slender, beautiful, with dark brown hair, her husband, short, straight, and dignified. After the service, Jennie approached them.

"Andrew and Sarah Mitchell...recently arrived from Denver," someone introduced them.

"I'm sure you'll enjoy the church," said Jennie. "The people here are warm and very friendly. Do you have children?"

"Four," said Andrew Mitchell, "Two boys and two girls. The youngest is six weeks." He seemed stiff and reserved.

"And you?" asked Sarah Mitchell, her brown eyes filled with warmth and sincerity.

"Oh, I am...unmarried," Jennie blushed. "I'm a teacher, and my students are my children, I guess."

The Mitchells were longtime, experienced evangelists, who for years had preached in mining and lumber camps throughout the Rocky Mountains. Recently arrived in Los Angeles, they quickly became active at the Echo Park Church.

In the next few months, Jennie became close friends with the Mitchells. As she came to know them, she saw that in religious matters they exhibited a strength and resolve that made Jennie's own life appear frivolous and empty. Difficult as it was, their presence forced her to face a fact about herself that no one suspected, not even Marietta. Sometimes, alone in her room, gazing at herself in the mirror, Jennie had to acknowledge the loneliness and fear she felt. Compared to the Mitchells, she was adrift, without direction, going nowhere. Not an hour passed that an emptiness did not gnaw at her. To escape it, she pushed herself among people and kept busy.

One Saturday, in the room behind the sanctuary, where she and Sarah were sorting music for the choir practice later that afternoon, Sarah said, "It's too bad that so many people come to God's house and go away empty, like children in a candy shop, who take the wrappers and leave the candy. Outside they feel cheated and disappointed. I think they just don't know the power of God. They don't see how real He is. They think worship is just socializing, and that all you have to do is show up at church, like someone turning out to vote. The more active you are, the more blessed you are. But of course that isn't what God wants at all. God doesn't care a fig about all our activities. He wants only one thing."

"And what is that?" said Jennie in a guarded tone, thinking that her friend had somehow glimpsed her most private feelings.

"He just wants our hearts surrendered to Him."

When Jennie replied, she tried to sound disinterested, but her tone revealed more emotion than she intended. "Yes, but how do you surrender? How do you turn your heart to God?"

"Well, that can be difficult," Sarah said. "Sometimes we get hardhearted, because we're having too good a time. We enjoy things not of God, like the scripture says, 'and men loved darkness rather than light'. Or maybe we're afraid, filled with doubts, having no faith. Whatever it is, we have to take the first step. We surrender our life to God. This may not be much at first. But God helps us, and the next time, it's easier, and we give more. It's like opening a rusty, creaky door. You open your heart even a crack, and God sticks in His foot. From then on, He helps you push it open."

For a few moments, there was only the sound of the music sheets being sorted. Presently, Jennie found herself turning away and crying.

"Jennie, what's the matter?" Sarah said, stepping over to her friend.

"Oh, I'm so unhappy, I'm so lonely! I do want God, but I just don't know how!"

Sarah embraced her. "Just trust God," she said. "That's all. Just trust God."

"I try, I do try...." Jennie said, wiping her eyes. "But I don't know how...!"

"Just trust God," Sarah repeated.

In the days and weeks that followed, a loneliness more powerful than Jennie had ever experienced, engulfed her. Emptiness filled every action. If she were praying, a voice in her mind commented how futile it was. Expect anything of God? Certainly a waste of time! Why, He didn't even exist! Although she continued teaching evening Bible classes, the stories and parables appeared flat and pointless. In her room alone, she would burst out crying for no reason. A few times, dark longings for the end of life came to her, which scared her very much. One night, returning from church, she felt such weariness and despair she thought, "I am just going to give it up. It is just too much."

While Marietta may have noticed that her daughter was troubled, she did not know what to do about it. After making a few attempts to comfort Jennie, she retreated and said nothing.

Finally, one Saturday morning, after a particularly hard week at school, a week filled with tedious class preparations, rowdy students, disagreements with parents, Jennie rose from bed and hurriedly scribbled a sign "DO NOT DISTURB," which she hung outside her door.

For a long time she sat on the bed staring at the covers, her mind considering every subject except the one that concerned her most. She examined her students and every member of the Echo Park Church. She pondered Nellie and Bonnie and their families. Finally, her mind focused on Sarah Mitchell. Sarah was right, of course. It was difficult to get down on your knees and pray to the Lord from your heart. Easy enough to bow one's head in church and mumble along with everyone else, but hard to kneel alone. How she finally slipped down, she never remembered, but presently she was beside the bed. A great rush of shame boiled up through her. "God, help me," she said. "If this is all there is to life, I am really not interested. Where is the meadowlark? I want my heart's rest."

She stopped, wondering again if anything would make any difference. She felt strange, as if she had stepped outside herself and was momentarily suspended from the circumstances of her life. With this feeling came a wonderfully easing sense of relief, and she thought, "Oh, things will work out. Somehow, they will work out." She didn't know exactly how they would work out, but that didn't matter. Having petitioned God, she was curious to see what would happen, because for the first time she knew that an answer would come.

Presently, she found herself thinking of Mr. Miller, who lived across the vacant lot from their house and whose wife had died that year. She had been a very religious woman, a regular member of the Echo Park church. Mr. Miller had never attended and made no secret of his disinterest toward God, treating his wife's beliefs with disdain.

"What a shame," thought Jennie, "maybe I should go talk to him."

She started as if slapped in the face. "Why, I can't go and talk to that man," she thought. "What would he think of me?"

Suddenly, the detachment was gone, replaced by the old feelings of dread. A heaviness closed about her again. She shut her eyes tightly. No, she couldn't go see Mr. Miller. There was no way in the world she could do that. However, aloud, she heard herself saying, "I will. I will...go and see Mr. Miller...I will."

While fixing her breakfast, she decided to put the visit off until after church the next day. She hoped to tell Sarah of what she had decided. However, on Sunday Andrew Mitchell reported that his wife was ill and in bed.

Returning home, she went immediately to Mr. Miller's house and knocked on the door. He was not home. "Mr. Miller isn't sick, is he?" Jennie asked at lunch.

"He went out to the Valley yesterday to see his daughter and her husband." Marietta said. "He'll be back tomorrow."

At school the next day Jennie was distracted and nervous. She tried to think of what she would say. Should she take her Bible? Try as she might, she could not remember one thing from all the sermons she had ever heard. On her way home that evening, she muttered, "Oh Lord, let him be on the porch!"

And he was, just as always, rocking in his chair, watching the traffic go by. Rushing into the house, Jennie threw down her purse and books and quickly combed her hair. In the kitchen she passed Marietta scraping carrots at the sink. "Be back in a minute," she said and slammed out the back door.

Jennie had decided to discuss Christ's Sermon on the Mount, which, if she could bring the discussion around to it, would afford several good points. Approaching the porch, she glanced up at Mr. Miller, who seemed to be gazing at the floor and didn't notice her. Perhaps he is dozing, she thought; Marietta often dozes.

"Hello!" she called, as she climbed the steps.

"Well, hello, Jennie, hello," the old man exclaimed, rising out of his chair. He seemed delighted to see her.

"Just dropped over to say hello."

"Oh, well, come up, Jennie, come up."

A stout, balding man in his seventies, Miller wore soiled, grey pants and had tobacco stains on the front of his shirt. A white, two-day stubble of beard covered his chin, and a ripe smell of garlic hovered about him. "Very nice evening," he said, resuming his easy rocking back and forth.

"Yes, very nice," Jennie agreed.

"'Bout done with school now, aren't you, Jennie?"

"Almost. Just another month."

"That'll be a relief, for you and the kids! I always liked the end of school – that and the first week! In between...!" he made a discarding motion with his hand.

"Yes," said Jennie, laughing, too. Suddenly, all the words she had rehearsed went out of her head. For the next forty-five minutes, she sat and talked in a friendly way, answering yes or no to his questions. Finally she said, "Well, I have to go fix dinner. I'll drop over and see you again, Mr. Miller."

The old man rose stiffly to his feet, "Please do, Jennie. And say hello to Marietta for me."

The next evening, she returned, but again, as she sat on the porch, rocking, the words she had planned would not come.

The third evening, after she had been sitting about twenty minutes, he suddenly leaned forward in his chair and said, "My, Jennie, you're getting very neighborly."

She felt a prodding inside her. She said, "Mr. Miller, it's about you. God has brought me here to talk to you about your soul."

"Oh," he said, falling back in his chair.

Her heart racing, Jennie began talking. Later, she would not remember anything, only that when she looked at him, he seemed to be listening. "God is somehow saying all this, not me," she thought.

When she finally stopped, he said, "Jennie, I appreciate that, and I'm sure you believe it. The problem I see is that most Christians don't practice what they preach. You talk about being hungry for God, but most Christians I see don't make you hungry for God."

Jennie sensed that this was a tired old argument he had used all his life. She brushed it aside.

"What others do, or don't do, doesn't matter. You don't judge God by the weakness of the people around you. It's *your* relationship that counts, not theirs. It's what you do, not them."

She had been talking for twenty minutes. She said, "Mr. Miller, I know it may not be your custom, but would you join me in prayer before I leave?"

He cleared his throat. "Well, all right, Jennie, if you like." He started to rise, but Jennie put her hand on his arm and he settled back. Closing her eyes, she quickly said a short prayer. He continued silently for some time after she finished. When he finally looked up, she was standing ready to leave. He jumped up and took her hand.

"I do appreciate you coming over to talk, Jennie," he said. "Mrs. Miller often railed at me, and I guess I never understood what she was talking about until...well, until she died."

Jennie walked down the steps. At home, preparing dinner, she felt light and almost giddy, as if she had just completed a difficult exam...as if she had pried open the door of her heart, and God had thrust in His foot.

A month later Mr. Miller died. Jennie never saw him again.

In June, 1917, Tom Clay came to the house on Coronado Street to tell Marietta that he had volunteered to serve with the YMCA, one of several American service organizations attached to the U.S. Army in Europe.

"You're going to the war?" she exclaimed. For three years now she had been reading of men dying in France.

"I won't be fighting, Ma. Anyway, the war won't last long now with America getting into it. It'll be over in a year, and then I'll be back."

A month later he was in France. His first letter said he was working in a Red Cross unit, which, in cooperation with the Salvation Army, coordinated

Tom and Jennie Clay at train station as he leaves for war service in France.

entertainment and recreational activities for injured soldiers at the Army hospital outside Paris. The family sighed with relief.

In 1917, Marietta was 73 years old. She walked with a stoop. The old knee injury bothered her more now. Stiff with rheumatism, she had difficulty performing even simple chores. In the evenings she sat in the parlor and massaged her hands. Two months after Tom left, she began to experience blurred vision. She complained of dizziness and weakness. All day she sat in the parlor, and though she didn't want to, she began declining church on Sundays. She did not always hear or understand what Jennie said. She complained of thirst, but had little appetite.

When Jennie offered to call the doctor, Marietta waved away the suggestion. "I'm all right, just a little tired."

One evening while Jennie sat correcting papers by the light of a small desk lamp in the parlour, Marietta suddenly complained of nausea. "I think I'm going to throw up," she said.

"You didn't hardly eat anything," Jennie said.

"I just feel a little sick to my stomach."

"Maybe I should call the doctor."

"Just help me to bed, dear." Attempting to rise, Marietta suddenly collapsed. Jennie half-carried, half-dragged her mother into the bedroom. By the time she got her into bed, Marietta was delirious. Running to the phone, Jennie rang the doctor. "She's barely conscious," she told him. "Please hurry!"

By the time the doctor arrived, Marietta was unconscious and breathing with difficulty. He examined her for half an hour, checking her heart and breathing. He questioned Jennie about symptoms. Finally he said, "Miss Clay, your mother has diabetes. I'm afraid she's dying. She will probably continue unconscious until death, which, in my guess, will occur before morning." He began repacking his few instruments.

Jennie was stunned.

The doctor continued. "I'll stay, of course. Is there someone else you can call?" While the doctor retreated to the parlor, Jennie phoned Nellie, who promised to drive up from Huntington Beach immediately. By the bedside, Jennie, unable to believe what was happening, proceeded to watch and wait, praying that the whole process would somehow reverse itself.

Shortly after midnight, Marietta's breathing suddenly became labored and irregular. Alarmed, Jennie ran to the doctor, who had fallen asleep in Marietta's rocker in the parlor.

Jennie had been unable to pray earlier, but now, tears streaming from her eyes, she fell to her knees and sobbed, "Bring her to heaven, dear Lord. She is a good woman whose heart was ever filled with love for her family and for Thee." To think that the soul who had raised them with love and patience all during the long hard years on the prairie was now departing, broke Jennie's heart.

Marietta's funeral was attended by family and friends from the church. After the service they drove to the Los Angeles-Hollywood Cemetery. It was a particularly hot, windless day. As Jennie watched the casket resting over the open grave, her memory floated back to the times on the prairie long before. She saw the soddy, the wagons, the horses, and Marietta's garden. Once again, she saw the meadowlark, as clear and brave as if the fence post on which it perched stood at the end of the open grave. Singing to her across the years, it filled her not with wonder, but with sadness. At the end of the brief service, the family huddled together on the lawn. Jennie embraced each person in turn. Three weeks later Tom's letter arrived from France. "We Clay children were blessed," he wrote. "We may have had a horsethief for a father, but we had a saint for a mother."

In late 1919, Sarah Mitchell, the woman to whom Jennie had confessed her sorrow, and who had comforted her, died following a hospital operation, leaving her husband, Andrew, and four children. For years the woman's health had been precarious, progressively deteriorating after the birth of her last child. Recently she had been unable to come to the church, and Jennie had seen her only on occasional visits to their home. The news of her death shocked Jennie.

Shortly after this, another terrible blow struck. Jennie's sister, Bonnie, pregnant for the fourth time, died suddenly of a tubal pregnancy. Jennie immediately took leave from her school and went out to the large rambling farmhouse at Huntington Beach. Will's eyes held a despair that wrung Jennie's heart. A strong, decent man, he had stood helplessly by and watched his precious Bonnie die. Immediately Jennie took charge of the family, cooking the meals, managing the children.

Bonnie had been a kind, sweet, loving woman, who cherished her husband and family. At the funeral, Jennie stood looking down at the face she had loved since her earliest awareness. Again, the meadowlark sang: How quickly the world passes away! How brief our lives!

Jennie was now alone in the house on Coronado Street. At thirty-four, she had begun to think she would remain unmarried. She had never thought about men in the same way that other women did. While she occasionally met a man she considered attractive, she had never fallen in love. She wondered what it was like. At Normal School, while she had several close male acquaintances, none had ever approached her romantically, perhaps because they thought her indifferent to it. Was she indifferent? She didn't like to think so. Perhaps her unceasing activity—superficial when she thought about it—was just a way of avoiding intimacy.

She knew that men did not find her physically attractive. Like all the Clay women, she was big-boned, and though not fat, was stocky, with heavy upper arms and large hands. Her face was plain, its principal feature a strong, square jaw, which suggested determination. Did that frighten men, she wondered? She dressed neatly, but did not fret over fashion, changing her dress three or four times a day, or styling her clothes to achieve a particular charm or sexual appeal that might attract men.

And yet, increasingly, her thoughts turned to men and marriage. She thought of Nellie's and Bonnie's families, of the rich happiness they shared. The prospect of returning to an empty house day after day for the rest of her life, with no one to talk to, no one to love—hug, kiss, hold, talk with—well, that was depressing, even scary.

One night a week, Jennie taught a Bible study class at the Echo Park Church to a dozen young men and women. The flirtatious glances they exchanged sometimes disconcerted her. After class, Jennie saw them in the ice cream parlors, talking and laughing. She envied them. In church, she caught herself scanning the congregation for eligible men. She couldn't help it. Did other women do that? Unfortunately, the men she might have liked were already taken!

Marriage, home, family seemed to her a remote and unattainable prospect. In her worst imaginings, she saw herself a talkative, lonely spinster, overweight, fluttering about an empty house cluttered with the bones of her dead dreams, filling her days with school teaching and church functions. Relentlessly, time was nudging her forward. Today she was thirty-four, tomorrow she would be forty, the day after that her life and youth would be gone. Although, as she often told others, there was nothing too small to pray about and nothing too hard for God to do, she had never voiced the matter in prayer. For some reason she didn't think it proper, or worthy enough.

One morning, toward the end of 1919, while walking down the steep hill to the Echo Park Church on Reservoir Street, she saw Andrew Mitchell, the husband of her dead friend Sarah, coming up the hill. Eight years older than Jennie, he walked with a purposeful, confident step. A slight man with a spare frame, he nevertheless gave the impression of being bigger and more solid than he was. Hair receding on a high forehead, he had a fair countenance which reflected his Scotch-English-Canadian heritage. His blue-grey eyes held a friendly, honest look.

Jennie knew him principally through the Church, to which he devoted much of his time, singing, teaching, and doing personal witnessing. Professionally, he worked as a commercial artist for the Times Mirror company in Los Angeles, drawing business logos and commercial illustrations. His chalk drawings, illustrating popular biblical scenes, decorated the basement room of the church where Jennie taught her Bible study classes. A capable musician, he frequently played his small autoharp at church functions. Despite his friendly manner, the death of Sarah had left him saddened and morose. He was obviously struggling to comfort and hold together a grief stricken family.

Today, Jennie thought he altered his step as she approached. "What shall I do now?" she thought, focusing her gaze and preparing a smile. As they met on the narrow sidewalk, he stepped aside, inclined his head, and, touching the brim of his hat, said, "Good morning, Miss Clay."

"Good morning, Mr. Mitchell," Jennie answered.

Exchanging no other words, the two paused only a moment before walking on. She hadn't gone very far before she just *had* to turn and look at him. To her surprise, Andrew Mitchell turned also and looked at her.

In the weeks after, Jennie, following a mystic sense of propriety, stayed clear of Andrew Mitchell. If she noticed him coming up one aisle of the church, she'd choose another. If he volunteered for a committee, she would decline to serve. In her conversations with God, she said, "If You want me to marry this man, You'll have to arrange it all Yourself."

Chapter 5

SHAPING A FAMILY

Martha Kinney was barely five feet tall, with small delicate hands and a face prematurely lined, as if covered by a thin veil of lace. A widow at twenty-three, she had nursed her first husband through a long siege of tuberculosis, the "white plague," as it was called in 1870, a disease few survived and which had finally taken his life. Shortly after her husband's death, she had lost her one-year-old daughter to the same illness.

In the Canadian town of Elora, fifty miles west of Toronto, Ontario, on the Grand River, vocations for women were limited mainly to housekeeping and marriage. To earn a living, Martha cleaned and washed for families and for Elora's small hotel.

In 1876, at the age of thirty, she married again, this time to Robert Mitchell, a widower with six children, who had, five years before, emigrated with his family from Portsoy in the District of Banff, northwest of Aberdeen, Scotland, on the North Sea. From there, one could look out across the Firth towards Norway. Mitchell and the men of his family, back as many generations as anyone could remember, had worked in the great, deep, green-marble quarries. It was a life that had made him, and all the Mitchells, serious and a bit stern.

Andrew, their first son, was born March 10, 1877, eight years before the prairie birth of Jennie Clay. In the next ten years, Andrew was followed by five other brothers and sisters, which might have added considerably to the Mitchell household had not the children from Robert's first marriage grown up and left home.

When Andrew was ten, and shortly after the birth of Martha's last child, Robert Mitchell died suddenly from what a doctor described as "congestion of the brain." His death left Martha, now a widow for the second time, with six children, a few pieces of furniture, and two hundred dollars.

Neighbors and friends advised her to give the children away. A wisp of a woman, now even smaller than she had been, she replied, "Never. Not while I have a crust of bread to share with them." It was a streak of stubborn courage, inherited most likely from her English Churchill ancestors.

Taking ten-year-old Andrew aside, she said, "Son, we must form a team if we are to get by." Andrew replied he was willing to do anything, try anything, to keep the family together.

Borrowing money from neighbors, they rented a small space on the main street of town, actually a converted alley between two larger buildings, which was barely wider than Andrew was tall. This "store" they stocked with school supplies, candies, and notions. During the day they left Andrew's sister, Bessie, to watch over the family while they "kept store."

Since early childhood, Andrew had exhibited artistic talent, sketching pictures of birds, animals, flowers, and mountains on whatever scrap of paper or cloth he could find. He now pencilled designs on plain cloth which Martha embroidered into colorful doilies and hangings. The two peddled these and simple children's garments, which Martha cut and sewed, from house to house in Elora and surrounding towns.

Besides drawing, Andrew liked music, which he learned on an old harmonica traded from a friend. While Martha sewed, he played tunes. Once, after a fruitless day of tramping the streets of a neighboring town, he secured a night's food and lodging by giving an impromptu concert at a small inn.

Their house was situated on the Grand River. The back porch, supported by pilings, extended out over the water. The children fished by letting lines down through holes in the flooring. The river froze in winter, and one spring morning the ice broke loose and swept the porch completely away.

Young "Scat," as his schoolmates called Andrew, was industrious, and eagerly sought any employment. At twelve, when his mother could be assisted by one of his sisters, he began work in a stove factory in Elora. It was a filthy, bone-wearying job. All day, in a lamp-lit, windowless room, he crouched on a cold, damp floor, polishing iron castings. That winter, he never saw the light of day, walking to work in the snow before daybreak, returning home after sunset.

The next year, Andrew got a job building sewing machines, at slightly higher pay. The factory was a great noisy place crammed with whirring equipment that cast, drilled, and assembled sewing machines. One day, while working at a grinder, he caught his hand in a steel pulley, instantly severing his right little finger at the first joint.

Despite their meager existence, Martha Mitchell had great compassion for anyone in need, and was forever taking homeless people into her house. One winter morning, not long after his father died, Andrew awoke to find a small, gray-haired woman in bed with him. Raising up quickly, he stared at her as she lay with the covers up to her chin, snoring faintly through open lips. She had come to the door during the night asking for food and shelter. Martha had no place to put her except with Andrew. A deeply religious woman, she never let anyone leave the house without first speaking to them about Jesus "who loved them and could save them from their sins."

When Andrew was fifteen, his sister Bessie contracted tuberculosis. He knew that Martha's first husband and child had died of it, but now to watch it slowly consume his own sister struck Andrew with horror. At night he would lie awake listening to her ceaseless cough. In the morning, before leaving the house, he would gaze in fear upon the bloodstained cloths. She died in February, shortly before his sixteenth birthday, leaving himself, his younger brother, Loren, and his three sisters, Eva, Elinor, and Suzanne.

In the fall of 1895, a crisis confronted the family. Andrew was abruptly dismissed from work when the sewing machine company experienced a decline in sales. Martha's small store was not producing enough to feed them, and the family found itself facing financial disaster. Consulting with Martha, Andrew decided that their best chance depended on him finding work in Detroit, just across the U.S. border. He would send money back to help them.

In Detroit, he tramped from one manufacturing company to another, but found nothing. Funds low, he began to despair he might have to return to Canada. Then one afternoon, passing the J.L. Hudson department store, which was holding a large sale, he sensed an opportunity. For years he had been drawing simple pictures, and some thought his work was good. His designs for Martha's embroideries had always been popular. Back in his room, he quickly sketched on rough note paper a cartoon depicting the store festooned with banners, bulging with merchandise, and besieged by crowds.

Returning to the store, he told a secretary at the general manager's office, "I'm looking for work."

"Sorry, no clerk positions open right now," the woman said.

"I'm not a clerk. I'm an artist," he said and laid the sketch on the woman's desk. "This is the work I do." In the well-lit office, the drawing was even more eye-catching than it had been in his room.

"Just a moment," the woman said, taking up the drawing and stepping through the door behind her desk. A few minutes later, a stocky man in a grey waistcoat walked out carrying Andrew's sketch. "You did this?" he said.

Andrew nodded.

"What's your name?"

"Andrew Mitchell."

"Well, Andrew, would twenty dollars a week be enough for more of the same?"

"Yes, sir!" said Andrew.

Andrew sent half his salary back to Martha in Elora. Besides producing advertising for the J.L. Hudson Company, Andrew began receiving, after a year, piecework from an engraver, as well as jobs from other businesses in Detroit. In autumn, 1896, Martha and the other children were able to move to Detroit.

Although raised as a Presbyterian, Andrew had experienced a spiritual conversion during a Methodist revival in Guelph, Ontario, several years before. Now, in Detroit, he regularly attended a Methodist church, where he served as the Sunday School Superintendent. He also ministered in the Murray and Tracey McGregor Rescue Mission, continuing his mother's tradition of helping the less fortunate.

In late 1898, Andrew became ill. He began coughing just as Bessie had and Martha's first husband before that. It was a prolonged, hacking cough, that frequently culminated in the spitting up of mucous. At first, Martha hoped it might just be a lingering cold, but when it continued, and he experienced fever and began losing weight, she knew it to be the same "white plague" come to claim another of her children. Although he continued to work at home, he grew worse with each passing day. By spring, he was almost too weak to leave the house.

Martha knew that if he spent another winter in the cold and damp of the Great Lakes region, he would die. "You must leave here," she told him.

"Where will I go?" asked Andrew.

"To Denver," said Martha.

"Denver?"

"Yes, and there God will cure you."

"But what about you and the others?"

"We will somehow make do."

Denver, the "mile high" city, with its cold, dry climate, was, in 1900, considered to be ideal for victims of respiratory ailments. The town boosters, hoping to attract citizens, advertised the city's salutary climate throughout the Eastern seaboard. Accordingly, Andrew, taking a carefully hoarded bit of family savings, boarded a train west, arriving in Denver in early summer, 1899.

Denver was beautiful: clear blue skies, warm bright sun, an adventurous city filled with life and activity. Behind it to the west, rose the Rocky Mountains, a great, pristine, snow-covered backdrop that appeared slightly unreal.

Within a few days, the grim reality of his condition swept over Andrew. Jobless and alone, with savings running low and loved ones far back east, lungs hemorrhaging daily from the advanced stages of tuberculosis, he had little hope of surviving. Even if he could find work, how could he possibly do it? One evening in a Denver park, he became so tired, so overcome with despair that he could not go on. Concluding that God had indeed forsaken him, he lay down on a bench and buried his head in his arms. "Oh, God," he thought,

"I cannot live much longer. I've tried hard, but now I have no health and no hope. I can't help my family any longer. Just let me go to sleep and die on this bench." He imagined the police finding him in the morning.

This thought had just passed through his mind, when a mountain canary lit upon a bush nearby and began to sing. Stirring, Andrew looked up. *"Andrew,"* the bird seemed to say, *"you are precious to God. Your heavenly Father loves you and wants to heal you. He will give you a song. Trust Him to help you now."*

"Surely, God is speaking to me through this bird," thought Andrew.

Thinking of Christ's miracles of healing, Andrew recalled something the Methodist minister in Elora had said. "God has promised to heal us of all infirmity. We need only claim His promise earnestly from our hearts." Like a subterranean wave rising from the depths of earth, the thought now surged in Andrew's mind: *Then I claim it, dear Lord, I claim it!*

A consciousness of God suddenly filled his mind, so powerful and compelling that tears started from his eyes, and he felt he must bury his face in shame at his own unworthiness. In anguish and despair he cried out, "Oh, dear Lord!" Presently, the deep pain in his lungs which had for so long filled him with unspeakable anguish, rapidly diminished and disappeared. The constant, terrible itch to cough, to clear his throat of blood and mucous, was suddenly gone. In its place he tasted only the sweet, clean, mountain air. A moment later, Andrew was again alone in the soft, summer, Colorado night. He lay very still, feeling in his body a sense of quiet and peace so infinitely deep he thought he must have died. Rising up, he looked about. Next to the bench sat his suitcase, a shabby thing of pasteboard tied with cord. Filling his lungs, he cried, "I am healed! Lord God, I am healed!" The next instant he was running and shouting to startled persons strolling in the park: "Praise Jesus, I am healed! I am well!"

"Hallelujah, brother!" a voice replied from the darkness.

The next day, filled with the same trust and hope that had infused him the previous night, he went searching for work. Almost immediately he found employment with an engraving firm, earning thirty-five dollars a week, ten dollars more than he had made in Detroit. At the end of the first week, he made a down payment on a large golden harp, although he already possessed a small autoharp which his mother had given him in Canada. As soon as it was delivered, he set the harp in the middle of his small apartment and, plying its strings, began a hymn of praise and thanksgiving to God, which he sang over and over until dark. Early the next year, he sent for his mother and the rest of the family.

Shortly after this, Andrew began attending the newly constructed Trinity

Methodist Church. He immediately joined the choir, because more than ever now, he wanted to sing. The choir participated in the church's evangelistic outreach program, in which young men and women ventured into the skid-row areas near the railroad station, where, crowding together on sidewalks and street corners, they sang and preached to passersby. Each took turns testifying to the people. One evening, Andrew stepped forward. He hadn't planned on saying anything, but something was urging him.

"I have not lived a long time in Denver," he said, speaking slowly, but in a firm voice that commanded attention. "Three months ago, I came west from Michigan. At that time I was dying, and would have died, had God not saved me." In a voice faltering with emotion, he related the circumstances of his healing. Perhaps fifty people stopped to listen.

Riding the electric car home, Andrew noticed a young woman, a member of the choir, smiling warmly at him from across the aisle. At a stop, she rose and took a seat beside him.

"Your talk was very inspiring," she said.

Andrew blushed. Already, a reticence had overcome him, so that now he could hardly believe he had spoken in public of such a private, intimate experience.

"It was a mistake," he said, "I shouldn't have told about it."

"Oh, no!" she exclaimed. "It is your duty to speak of those things! You are not boasting or bragging. You are testifying to the power of God! Christ used miracles as a sign of his divinity. People must hear it!"

"You think so?" said Andrew, feeling his heart quicken as he looked into her brown eyes, which sparkled with enthusiasm.

"Oh, yes! We can do no greater thing! How else can we convey the truth of God's existence except that we speak from our hearts of our own experience. Only then will others hear us and open their hearts."

Her cheeks and lips had a rosy flush. Andrew was watching her closely. "I'm happy to hear you say that," he said.

Aware of the intent look in his eye, she straightened in her seat. A moment later she said, "You also sing well, Mr. Mitchell."

"Well, thank you Miss...."

"My name is Sarah Bryant," she said.

"I'm happy to make your acquaintance, Miss Bryant."

"And I yours, Mr. Mitchell."

Andrew had noticed Sarah Bryant within ten minutes of the first day he had joined the choir. His eyes, passing circumspectly from one person to another, as they always did when he came among people, had locked upon her. She was a slim, beautiful girl with dark brown hair and soft brown eyes.

Andrew with his golden harp. Denver, 1902.

Slightly older, but nearly the same height as Andrew, she walked with the same straight dignity and sense of purpose.

The youngest in a family of five children, Sarah was born in Flintshire, Wales, on Christmas Day, 1872. Her French Huguenot ancestors had fled to Wales during the Revolution in 1789, taking the name "Jones" to hide their French identity—Chevalier Du Bowen. By 1850, several Welsh blood lines had mingled with the family. Mining engineers, the family had emigrated to the United States after the American Civil War, settling first in the east, but then moving in 1875 to Colorado. In 1880, both parents had died of pneumonia, leaving the children to be divided among adoptive families. Eight-year-old Sarah had been adopted by the Frank Bryants of Greeley. Several years later, Sarah moved to Denver to attend school, where she lived with the Curtis Chamberlains, who acted more or less as her godparents. She had a strong soprano voice, a token of her Welsh ancestry. For the last five years she had sung in the choir of the Trinity Methodist Church. Bright, attractive, and friendly, Sarah experienced no want of companions. Young men, both in and out of the church, sought her acquaintance. Despite this attention, she remained unspoiled, neither conceited nor with any social ambition.

One Sunday afternoon, shortly after their conversation on the street car, Andrew approached her and said, "You know, Miss Bryant, I also play the harp."

"Do you?" she answered, smiling warmly. "I think there is no more beautiful instrument than a harp."

"Perhaps you would like to hear me play," he said.

"That would be wonderful," she replied.

The next Sunday afternoon Andrew transported his harp in an open carriage to the Chamberlain home. For an hour, he played for Sarah and the Chamberlains. Afterwards, they talked over tea. Andrew felt himself under the scrutiny of Mrs. Chamberlain, and, sitting stiffly on the parlor chair, he answered her questions as politely as he could.

Church activities drew the two young people closer together. They began singing regularly together in gospel teams at orphanages and missions. They travelled together by street car and wagon to meetings throughout the Denver area. Frequently, Andrew escorted Sarah home after an evening meeting. One Sunday afternoon, he took her to meet his mother and sisters.

Martha embraced the girl warmly. "You are every bit as beautiful, dear, as Andrew claims."

While Andrew fidgeted, his three sisters, Eva, Elinor, and Suzanne, laughing gaily, crowded about Sarah.

Their acquaintance continued for nearly two years, deepening and becoming more intimate. Finally, on a spring morning in 1902, as they sat on a park bench looking westward to the snowy peaks of the Rocky Mountains, Andrew, turning slowly, swallowed, cleared his throat, and said, "Sadie, we have both given our lives to the Lord, and now I think we should give our lives to each other. Will you marry me?"

After a respectable pause, Sadie grasped his hand with both of hers and replied, "Andy, God has put a beautiful love in my heart for you. Yes, I will marry you and love you the rest of my life." Andrew was twenty-five and Sadie thirty when they married in Denver that year.

By now Andrew's career as a commercial artist was in full bloom. Caught up in the fever of western expansion, he regularly travelled by stage and narrow gauge railway throughout the state, plotting and sketching survey maps for lumber, mining, and real estate interests. He created advertising materials for promoters and worked as an artist for the Denver Post.

Both he and Sadie continued with the Trinity Methodist Church. Their mutual love of music and desire to preach to others about God led them very naturally into pioneer evangelism. On weekends, they travelled to the mining towns around Denver—Boulder, Golden, Leadville, Cripple Creek—where they preached and sang together. When journeying by train, Andrew always took along his concert harp, shipping it in the baggage car. A slight man, barely one hundred and twenty-five pounds, he sometimes struggled to carry it. One night, a miner emerging from a saloon saw him staggering under the huge load and cried out in surprise, "Well, for Christ's sake!" Quick to seize an opening to testify, Andrew retorted, "Yes, it is for Christ's sake!"

Sadie soon proved a stalwart advocate, leading many a rough miner and mountain man to repentance. Standing on a small stool, she testified to all who would listen, speaking with a passion and conviction that few could ignore. One man, the owner of a string of saloons and brothels across Colorado, after listening to her speak outside one of his establishments, experienced a profound conversion, whereupon he immediately closed his saloons, poured the liquor into the street, and dismissed the prostitutes working for him.

Andrew and Sadie began each day with prayer and scripture reading. They felt an urgency about their ministry. They not only believed the Word of God, they sought to live it each minute of the day. One day, Sadie, peering over Andrew's shoulder as he sat designing a label for a distilling company, said, "Andy, tell me, can a person walk upstairs and down at the same time?"

"Well, I don't think so," he answered.

"Then how can you draw whiskey ads to the glory of God?"

Thereafter, although he was in great demand as a creative artist, Andrew never again accepted advertisements for alcoholic beverages.

In March, 1905, while on a trip to California, Sadie gave birth to their first son, Bryant, whom they named after her foster parents. On returning to Denver, they moved into a large house on South Penn Avenue, where, two years later, Hubert was born, and in 1909, Helen Elizabeth. In their large dining room they held youth meetings in the evenings, inviting young people for Bible study, singing, and art work, which Andrew supervised. Andrew also began counseling at the Denver home for delinquent boys.

Although healed of tuberculosis, Andrew still suffered severe hay fever attacks in the late summer and fall. Hoping for relief, the family moved first to Salida, then to Rifle in western Colorado, and finally in 1913, to Grants Pass, Oregon, where they spent the summer at the pear orchard and turkey farm of Sadie's sister, Elizabeth Heller. In the fall they travelled on to Los Angeles, where Jean, the last of Sadie's children, was born in December, 1913.

A few weeks after the child's birth, Andrew purchased the house that was to be the Mitchell family home for the next sixty-six years. Like many houses on Waterloo Street, 1307 had a large palm tree in the front yard and pepper trees in the back. It was located just north of Sunset Boulevard on the crest of a hill overlooking Hollywood. The large lot, which sloped steeply down behind the house, offered plenty of room for expansion, and in the first two years the family added a small cottage in the rear and rooms beneath the house, creating a two-story home.

In 1913, Southern California was the Mecca of the west, and once again Andrew found himself in a bustling city where business was booming and his

Sarah Bryant Mitchell with baby Bryant, 1905.

advertising art in great demand. His first employment, found easily the first week, was with the Riley Moore Engraving Company. The next year he accepted a position with the Times-Mirror Publishers. Within a few years, he was working largely on his own as a commercial artist.

In the days before aerial photography, his gift for making survey maps and miniature plaster models of cities and countryside brought him numerous contracts for modeling and designing. Sitting atop Point Fermin hill, he sketched a survey panorama of the San Pedro-Los Angeles Harbor and Shipyards. He modeled clay figures of monks for the Spanish Missions. One of his most lucrative tasks was designing logos and product labels for companies headquartered in Los Angeles, including the famous Del Monte shield for the giant California packing corporation. However, remembering Sarah's rebuke over the whiskey ad, he extended his ban on advertisers to include tobacco companies and the Hollywood movie producers.

Del Monte shield redrawn by Andrew Mitchell. Courtesy California Packing Company.

Early in 1914, the family joined the Echo Park Methodist Church on nearby Reservoir Street. It was a small church, with friendly people who satisfied their desire for community and fellowship. The first Sunday, Sadie met a young woman for whom she immediately felt a great love and kinship. She told Andrew, "I can tell the poor girl is troubled in her soul. For all her involvement in the church, she has not yet truly surrendered to God." One Saturday, this woman, who was as drawn to Sadie as Sadie was to her, confessed her great sorrow of heart.

"Jennie Clay," Sadie answered, taking the younger woman in her arms, "even now God is knocking at the door of your heart. Believe me, He will not let you suffer long for Him."

Several months later, Sadie remarked to Andrew, "I knew Jennie would do it. Have you seen her? There is no mistaking it. I don't know how or when it happened, but she has opened her heart to the Lord! She is a fine person...Do you hear me, Andrew?"

In the years following the birth of Jean, Sadie's health deteriorated. She developed a "racing heart" and goiter trouble. An old hip injury incurred as a child, began bothering her anew. Andrew, using a crude chiropractic technique, learned to manipulate her thigh back into place, and so provided some relief. But it was not enough, and often she was in such pain that she had to be pushed in a wheelchair.

Throughout the war years, the family took Sunday afternoon walks with Andrew and the boys pushing Sadie in the wheelchair, Helen and Jean riding on their mother's lap. Strolling the streets, they greeted friends and neighbors. Occasionally, they walked the two and a half miles to the city jail where Andrew and the boys sang hymns, and the two parents spoke to the prisoners.

After the war, Sadie's health declined rapidly. Confined to bed, she saw less and less of the children, a circumstance which affected them no less than her. One day Andrew returned home to find that nine-year-old Helen and five-year-old Jean had disappeared. Tracing the children by phone, Andrew located them at a neighbor's house several blocks away, where they had made their way along sidewalks and across boulevards, Helen pulling young Jean in an apple-crate coaster. Collecting the girls, he brought them home. Sensing that the escapade was not just naughtiness, but the act of love-starved children yearning for their mother, he placed them in bed with Sadie. "I think they just wanted to be with you," he told her, "and didn't know where to go."

In early March, 1919, Andrew moved Sadie to an apartment below the kitchen, where she could see the garden that was just then breaking into green. But the move seemed to inflame her condition and the goiter condition deteriorated. The doctor recommended surgery. She entered the hospital on Andrew's forty-second birthday. Waiting outside the operating room, Andrew feared he would not see or speak with Sadie again. Early the next morning, Andrew called Bryant and Hubert, then fourteen and eleven, to his room and told them of their mother's death. Later, he knelt beside the girls' bed to pray with them.

Sadie left a pencilled note to the children:

"Never give your heart to an unsaved one.

Take care of precious Jean.

I will meet you, bringing in your sheaves."

"And she will," said Andrew. "She will be there waiting for each of us."

The family buried Sadie in Evergreen Cemetery in East Los Angeles, "among the poor, the neglected, and the disadvantaged," as she had requested. A few days after the burial, he took the children to the grave site. First, he told them the story of the Rapture of the Saints and then of the Resurrection of those who died in Christ. Into the spiral opening of a specially prepared sea shell, he tucked the printed resurrection scriptures from I Corinthians XV and I Thessalonians IV. Securely sealing the shell with some modeling clay, he buried it in the green earth of the grave. It was a "planting" that went deep into the hearts of them all.

For a long time after Sadie's death, nothing seemed clear to Andrew. Troubles descended upon the household. The family suffered illness of every kind – headaches, earaches, fevers, scarlet fever, adenoids, and tonsillitis. Not a day passed when one or another was not sick or depressed. If there was not too much bluing in the wash, the toast burned, the tea kettle boiled dry, frying grease caught fire, and dishes broke. It took all of Andrew's patience to get the four youngsters fed, dressed, and off to school.

In April, his three maiden sisters, Eva, Elinor, and Suzanne, arrived from Denver to help with the family. Their mothering of Helen and Jean was most welcome, and Andrew gladly relinquished responsibility for family tasks that were crumbling about him.

For Andrew, nothing now held the same joy and fulfillment it once had. Everything reminded him of Sadie. In church, while singing the familiar hymns, the absence of her voice left a void. During the sermons, a vision of her standing on a boardwalk in some Colorado mining town, earnestly prying at the hearts and minds of rough miners, would drive into his heart like a spear. Now, as he looked into the faces of the children, he saw only bits and pieces of her, the color of an eye, a straggle of hair covering a cheek, a smile prying at young lips, consternation furrowing a brow. Everywhere he looked, he saw Sadie, and yet she was not there.

One day in January, nearly a year after Sadie's death, Elinor took him aside and said, "Andy, you have to get on with your life! You can't be all the time thinking of Sadie! It's no good for you or the children."

That night he prayed long and earnestly. "Dear Lord, You rescued me once before, and now my heart has fallen into an abyss of sorrow. Lift me up and set me upon a new direction, for I cannot find it on my own!"

The next morning he felt better, filled with an expectant hope and lightness of heart he hadn't known for months. Yes, Sadie was gone, but her separation was only temporary. They would meet again, in a higher place.

He recalled the day he passed Jennie Clay on the steep hill near the church. A strange thing that encounter, how they had turned and looked at each other. Even stranger was how from that time on, he kept running into her. Suddenly, wherever he turned, there she was! He had always liked Jennie, although while Sadie was alive, he had not paid her much attention. Having lost her mother two years before, Jennie lived alone. She had never married. Sadie had mentioned a spiritual crisis that Jennie had undergone. From her healthy pink cheeks, golden hair, laughing blue eyes, he thought she must have triumphed mightily.

Jennie Clay was not a designing woman, he could tell that, but plain, honest, and good-natured. Although not as physically beautiful as Sadie, she was attractive in other ways. Never had he heard her speak a negative word, nor anyone speak badly of her. She was always cheerful. How the Mitchell family could use some of that just now!

He couldn't remember exactly when he first spoke to Jennie Clay at length, or when he consciously began seeking her out. However, he did remember the first time he called at her house. It was a Saturday afternoon in March. He invited her to ride the Red Car out to Santa Monica. The entire way out and back they talked of God and what it meant to serve Him. Jennie had said, "With God's help, I can do all that He puts in my hands to do."

It occurred to Andrew that Sadie must have had a premonition before her death that he would marry Jennie Clay. She had never said as much, but she had often talked fondly of Jennie, listing her qualities, praising and admiring her to him. One day, shortly before her death, Sadie had regarded him serenely. "God is even now preparing a new life for us," she told him. "It is very near."

One evening in April, little Helen came into his studio to show off a new dress that her Aunt Elinor had sewed. A year after her mother's death, the girl was finally beginning to smile again. As she turned to leave, Andrew caught her round the waist.

"Wait, Sweetheart, I want to ask you something," he said in a confidential tone that brought a sober look to her face. "How would you like to have a new mother?" he asked.

"A new mother? How could that happen?" she asked, puzzled.

"It could happen," said Andrew. "Tell me, who do you think would make a good mother?"

Frowning thoughtfully, the girl reviewed all the maiden ladies she knew at the Echo Park Church, but evidently without finding a suitable mother.

"I don't know, Papa," she said, "who do you think?"

"How about Jennie Clay?"

"Jennie Clay! To be our mother? Oh, Papa, yes!" She threw her arms about his neck. "But will it happen?"

"Well, I don't know. For now it's a secret. We won't tell anyone."

"All right," said Helen, running out of the room.

A week later, Andrew asked Jennie. The question did not surprise her. For the past four months, since that memorable meeting on the hill, she had thought about little else. However, she didn't answer immediately. She couldn't. It was not that she didn't want to marry Andrew Mitchell. She did. It was just that, well, she saw problems. For one thing he was so much older, so much unlike her...reserved, dignified. In contrast, she was a boisterous, talkative, joking school girl. He was a commercial artist, a Bible scholar with a philosophical turn of mind, she an elementary school teacher, with only a prairie child's understanding of God. His wife, Sadie, now gone almost a year, had been a beautiful singer; Jennie could barely stay on tune. He was the father of four children, the oldest a high school boy. Experienced teacher that she was, she knew the skill and love it would take to assume the role of mother and homemaker to such a large family. One couldn't just walk in and say, "Good morning, my name is Jennie and I'm your new mother!" as if they were a new class.

"But I'm thirty-four years old," she objected.

"Well, I'm forty-two," he said.

"I've never been married, and I don't know anything about families."

"Neither does anyone until they have them."

"The children might not accept me."

"They'd love you."

"How do you know?"

"I asked them."

"All of them?"

"Actually only one, but she speaks for all of them."

Jennie was silent a long time. Finally she said, "I knew and loved Sadie very much."

"And she loved you."

"Even though she's gone, I'm not sure there would be enough room for me...in everyone's heart, I mean."

For answer, Andrew took out the pen and small pad he carried in his coat and drew a simple sketch, a triangle, closed round by a circle.

"We are here," he said, pointing to the corners of the triangle, "You, me, and Sadie, the family between us. One mother bearing the children, the second nurturing them."

"And the circle?" Jennie asked, although her eyes, brimming with tears, said that she knew, but wanted him to say it.

"The circle is God," Andrew said, "closing 'round us all, protecting us, loving us, blessing us."

Two weeks later, Andrew and Jennie were married in a simple early morning ceremony in the living room of the house on Waterloo Street. Pastor Barton of Echo Park Methodist, a thin, tired-looking man with stooped shoulders and black hair combed straight back over his head, performed the ceremony. The couple stood in front of Sadie's piano. Behind Jennie stood Nellie, her husband, George, and Tom and his wife, Jennie T. Behind Andrew stood his sisters, Elinor, Eva, Suzanne, and the children. Early morning sunshine poured through the bay window. The only decoration was a vase shaped like a log, filled with pansies, which Jean, Helen, and Aunt Elinor had placed on the piano the evening before.

Jennie was surprised at how short the ceremony was. Immediately after Pastor Barton pronounced them husband and wife, the children rushed out the front door to school, still dressed in their Sunday best. Their kisses and hugs were hurried, almost perfunctory.

For a wedding breakfast, Nellie and Elinor cooked eggs and pancakes. For an hour the wedding party sat about the kitchen table talking and laughing. The newlyweds outlined their honeymoon: three days at Huntington Beach, with travel provided by the big, red Pacific Electric streetcar.

Pastor Barton was just rising to take his leave, when a knock sounded at the door. Rose Davis, the Logan Street elementary school principal, escorted a tearful and obviously injured Hubert into the house, his arm wrapped in a makeshift sling.

"He's broken his arm, I'm afraid, Mrs. Mitchell," the woman said to Jennie, who stood in the middle of the room in her white voile wedding dress sewn just the week before. "He didn't quite make the 'big drop whirl backwards' on the horizontal bar."

"Oh, my goodness!" exclaimed Jennie, kneeling and receiving the boy into her arms, while Andrew stepped to the phone to call the doctor.

Looking about, the school mistress asked, "Am I interrupting?"

The honeymoon was postponed and the next week Jennie resumed work at the Atwater School near Glendale where she had been teaching since Marietta's death.

Having lived alone for so long, housekeeping for a family of six did not come easily to Jennie. For a time, the sustained level of chaos that reigned in the house, as the children darted about, pursuing their lives, made her feel rather like a turnstile in a train station. Although she tried, meals were not always perfect, and the house not always orderly. However, the family was understanding, and several times everyone pitched in to help her pick up the pieces.

Years of teaching had taught Jennie that while some short term obedience might be gained by reprimanding or scolding a child, love and enduring respect were best engendered by regarding them with high esteem and making them feel their contribution was valued.

Helen and seven-year-old Jean ("Snooks" to Jennie) were the easiest and quickest hearts to win. Although it was not Jennie's most avid interest, she regularly scheduled sewing and homemaking activities to share with the two girls. Together, they made ruffly dresses and petticoats, and several times Jennie arranged for them to meet her at school, or to ride on the streetcar to a downtown department store for an afternoon of shopping. On Fridays, to celebrate the end of the week, she purchased bakery sweets or peanut brittle.

She was careful to honor the memory of their mother, for she had truly loved Sadie, with whom she felt a deep and mystic bond. Her wedding ring had been inscribed "1, 2, 3," symbolizing her inclusion in the triangle of love that was Sadie and Andrew's family.

Jennie saw that Andrew Mitchell was indeed old-fashioned in his concept of family life, deriving and projecting his authority from a strict interpretation of God's Word. Like Abraham, whom God had selected to father the nation of Israel, Andrew attempted to command his children in love: "He will command his children and his household after him," the Lord had said of Abraham, "and they shall keep the way of the Lord." (Genesis 18:19)

In what amounted to a "spiritual huddle," he daily counselled the children on the spiritual values they needed to get through life. At the breakfast table, after the dishes were taken away, the Bibles were brought out. As soon as a child could read, he or she began reading Scriptures. Andrew would ask questions about the verses – simple "milk" questions for the younger children and harder "meat" questions for the older.

Following scriptural dictums, he sought to erect boundaries of behavior for the children. "Correct thy son and he shall give thee rest," believed Andrew. These were not unthinking or unreasonable, but in his view, simply right action commanded of God, good for the individual, for the family, and for "Christian witness," which is to say, they exemplified proper Christian life.

Love in the family was a quality to be learned, and once learned, never allowed to lapse. "The Lord make you to increase and abound in love toward one another, and toward all men...." (I Thess. 3:12)

Knowing that "we have different gifts according to the grace given us...serving, teaching, encouraging, contributing to needs of others...." (Romans 12: 4-8), Andrew encouraged the children to develop their inherited abilities and creative inclinations. He encouraged Bryant to experiment with chemistry, even though this involved mixing strange solutions, igniting dangerous explosive powders, or melting nails in a homemade electric furnace that frequently blew a fuse, plunging the house into darkness. Surprisingly, a crystal radio set the boy constructed was powerful enough to receive a signal from as far away as Santa Barbara. Hubert, like Andrew, had a talent for music, and quickly learned to play the piano. One afternoon he played so long and loud that a neighbor rushed into the house and handed him a dollar bill to make greater use of the soft pedal.

Andrew taught the Biblical view of humanity, that all human beings, irrespective of race or color, were one family under heaven. Every human being was created in the image of God and is "my neighbor."

Nevertheless, there were unwholesome elements in society which must be guarded against. Hollywood was just blocks away. Youngsters all around were infected with lewd, licentious, and unwholesome preoccupations, from smoking and drinking to soliciting sex from each other. The home and family were sacred institutions where nothing impure or divisive must be allowed to enter. The family was God's laboratory where a child's character was molded in righteous patterns of living. As father, Andrew's duty was to launch the children upon a trajectory toward God: "As Christians," he said, "we are not supposed to copy the evil examples of the world around us. The Lord expects us to stand on our own two feet, and resist doing things we know are wrong." "Speak evil of no man," he instructed them.

To the boys, he said "When you encounter smutty literature – and you will – dirty jokes, or unlawful situations, don't just say 'My father won't let me do this', but resist it from your own convictions!" He was particularly strict that they treat girls respectfully and regard them with purity of mind.

While these guidelines may have been well-intentioned, they nevertheless served to make the Mitchell children feel somewhat different than the other neighborhood children. "Why can't you stay overnight with me?" a friend would ask. "Why don't you get the Sunday funnies?" "Why do your parents always make you play in your backyard all the time?" To these questions, the Mitchell children had no ready answers.

Jennie contributed balance. She saw that while growing children needed orderly rules, they also needed relaxation. Thus, very soon she began to arrange the weekends so that the Saturday clean-up – the sweeping, dusting, window-washing – was completed in double-quick time, thus leaving an afternoon free for a family outing – a picnic into the nearby hills.

From her teaching experience, she realized that play and humor were just as much a part of a child's normal Christian life as prayer and Bible reading. Frequently she played stick-hockey with the children on the street in front of the house. Arms wielding a broomstick to whack the tin can puck, she rushed up and down the asphalt street, hairpins and combs flying, brushing all opposition aside on her way to the goal. Even big boys could seldom withstand her hilarious and boisterous advance.

During evening dinner, Andrew and Jennie would encourage the children to tell what had happened during the day. Following dinner, Jennie would say, "I'll wash the dishes if you play the piano and sing me a song!" The parents seldom went out in the evening, reserving the time for family activities, practicing music lessons, studying or playing games, and story telling. Hubert would play the piano while the girls and Bryant would sing. Or, they would all crowd in a semi-circle around Andrew while he played the harp.

Laughing and acting like a silly teenager, Jennie often found herself the life of the party. One evening, a woolly caterpillar captured in a small bottle was, for fun, dumped onto the table to hump along on its many legs. Mischievously eyeing the children, Andrew said, "Ten dollars to the one who swallows it!"

"Yuk!" Helen and Jean drew back.

"Not me!" echoed Hubert, also recoiling.

"That's not so much," said Bryant, "I swallowed a fly once! Didn't even know it, either."

"Yeah, but that was by accident!" corrected his brother. "Try this – on purpose!"

"Ten dollars!" Andrew challenged them again.

"I'll do it!" Jennie exclaimed. With a whoop, she snatched the caterpillar from the table, popped it into her mouth, and washed it down with a gulp of water. It was gone before anyone had time to blink. The kitchen erupted in screams and laughter. Smiling and smacking her lips, she calmly held out her hand for the ten dollars. Snapping the crisp bill in her hands, she said, "This should buy just enough material for two new dresses for you-know-who!" Helen and Jean screamed and jumped up and down.

The house on Waterloo Street was larger than Marietta's cottage and had a splendid view. From the glassed-in bedrooms and kitchen on the west end, Jennie could see, in one panoramic sweep, the Pacific Ocean fifteen miles away at Santa Monica Beach, the low skyline of Malibu, and the sometimes snow-capped Sierra Madre Mountains beyond Burbank. At the top of the Hollywood mountains, she could almost touch the giant letters spelling "HOLLYWOOD", which Andrew pronounced "Follywood".

Only a few things needed improvement. One day, she suggested they landscape the steep hillside lot behind the house, which was covered with weeds. The project appealed to Andrew's artistic inclination, and he set about designing a terraced rock garden. Piles of boulders and buff-colored flagstone, purchased from a quarry and dropped in front of the house, were carried by Hubert and Bryant down to the back of the lot. Working with picks and shovels, Andrew and the boys created an elaborate garden of retaining walls, walks, and terraced flower beds. Beneath a spreading fig tree they excavated a miniature lake with a grotto and a castle at the end of a causeway. A copper pipe dripped water down through green foliage into a pool. Shrubs, trees, and flowering vines were planted amid winding walks to create shady arbors. The lower part of the property offered space for a playground in which was erected a horizontal bar over a sawdust pit. A one-inch knotted manila rope hung from a tall pepper tree provided a giant swing for the children.

Jennie sought every occasion to celebrate – the Fourth of July, Easter, Christmas, Valentine's Day, Thanksgiving, and, particularly, family birthdays. Every child needed to be annually authenticated as one dearly loved by his family. Birthdays provided the opportunity.

About a year after the wedding, Jennie encountered Bryant, the older son, returning from school. She fell into step beside him as they walked up the hill to the house. At a street intersection overlooking the hills of Hollywood, she stopped and put her hand on his arm. "Bryant," she said, "I thought you should be the first to know. Your father and I are going to have a baby."

His reaction was greater than she had expected. Impulsively he threw his arms about her. "A sister? I'm going to have a new sister?"

"Well, I don't know what it will be. But a sister, I hope, if you like!"

It was a difficult delivery for the thirty-six-year-old mother. Finally, after twenty-three hours of labor, Marietta Mitchell was born at 5 a.m. on a Monday morning in October, 1921. The child was named for the Vermont grandmother who had reared Jennie on the Nebraska prairie. Two years later, also in October, a second child was born. Gathering the children at the supper table, Andrew informed them of the birth and conveyed a message from Jennie at the hospital. "This time Mother wants you to name your new sister. We haven't named her because we want all the family to share in it."

The children looked at each other. Andrew could sense the responsibility and honor they felt. The discussion began. Names came thick and fast: Anna, Laverne, Lorraine, Barbara, Elaine, Christine, Heather, Patricia, Sharon. As each name was suggested, Bryant carefully listed it on paper.

Presently, Hubert observed, "Most of these are just girls we know."

"So what!" said young Jean.

"Well, I don't want to name our sister after just some other girl at school."

"You're right," said Bryant. "We should name her after someone great. How about 'Esther' after Queen Esther?" The children all knew the Bible story and nodded agreement.

"Yes," said Helen. "But maybe also for someone we love, too. I think she should be 'Eva', for Aunt Eva, who took care of us when Mother Sadie died."

"Esther Eva!"

The two girls, Helen and Jean, helped Jennie to care for their new sisters. They took turns rocking them to sleep. Helen sang lullabies. Watching them, Jennie recalled Marietta's stories of how Nellie had cared for her as a baby. She could see that in some subtle way, God was preparing these girls to one day care for their own families.

Thus was Jennie catapulted up the sheer face of a mountain that only a short time before she had seen no way of climbing. From a single woman, she had become the wife and mother to a family of seven.

Chapter 6

MARCHING TOGETHER

The Mitchell family was gathered around the kitchen table for breakfast. The boys, who knew that they were not supposed to chew gum at mealtime, had parked their gum under the ledge of the window seat that surrounded the table on three sides. Andrew sat in his chair at the open end of the table. He had a faraway look in his eye. As Jennie served the steaming cornmeal mush, he blinked, focused his eyes on the family around him, and proceeded to say grace.

Andrew was a dreamer and a creator. Jennie often observed him striding up the steep incline of Elsinore Hill lost in thought, or lying quietly during an afternoon's siesta, his lips forming whispered, but unvoiced thoughts and prayers. It was during these times that his imaginative and artistic creations were developed.

He was drawn as much to the physical world as to the spiritual. While he could contract with business men, romp with his children, draw a rose that looked like a rose, one eye was always turned toward transcendental realities. Early in life, he had discovered the Biblical guidelines, and was now using his artist's gifts to extend and apply them. Although largely self-taught, he was widely read. His lack of formal education had merely stimulated his investigative nature. The clutter of the world's ideas were not entanglements, because God's Word provided a true measure by which to evaluate them.

Fascinated with the physical universe, he closely examined the world around him. On a hike with the children, he explained natural phenomena, the life cycles of plants and animals. While painting, he would search patiently for just the right combination of pigments to achieve the color of sea or sky in a landscape, the tint of skin and hair in a portrait. Patiently, and with a kind of reverence, he explained aspects of the human form to the children – "God's greatest work of art." His investigations sought to substantiate God's Written Word.

One night, a month or two after Marietta was born, he said to Jennie, "What do you think of enrolling in BIOLA?"

BIOLA was the Bible Institute of Los Angeles, an institute of theology in downtown Los Angeles, a center for the training of Protestant ministers and missionaries, which emphasized the practical aspect of preaching the Word of God.

"You?" asked Jennie.

"No, both of us."

"Well, I don't know. When?"

"The beginning of the next term."

"How could we do that? I teach school full time."

"Well, the course of study runs from eight till noon. My work will allow it. You can begin teaching at Atwater part time. We'll hire a housekeeper to help with things around here."

"Why this all of a sudden?"

"Well, it's what I've always wanted to do. And I believe it's what you want, too. If we are going to do it right, we must be properly trained."

It was just like him, Jennie thought, to discern the goal, and with firm decision propose the direction they must take. "All right," she said. Although a veteran student, Jennie felt trepidation at pursuing a course of Bible study at the Institute. She had always been in awe of scriptural scholars. Would she be able to do it?

Two months later the two enrolled in BIOLA's morning Bible theology classes. One professor was Dr. R. A. Torrey, a noted theologian from the Moody Bible Institute of Chicago and the author of the class text, "What the Bible Teaches." This course presented the central teachings of the Bible, including doctrines of God, Jesus Christ, the Holy Spirit, Man, Angels, and Satan. The professor first cited Scripture, then summed up its contents in a proposition. Discussion was encouraged.

Aside from academic studies, the program included practical aspects of ministry and preaching the Gospel. All students were required to attend church regularly and participate in preaching the Gospel in street meetings and in churches and schools.

Andrew plunged into the program eagerly, relishing particularly the discussions of theology and philosophy. Jennie brought to it her own particular style. Although her academic achievement was sometimes not as solid as Andrew's, she made up for it with a high level of enthusiasm. While Andrew sometimes appeared too scholarly, too stern and philosophical, Jennie was light-hearted, her jovial good nature charming everyone they met.

Visiting the skid row missions on Main Street in downtown Los Angeles, they spoke to the vagrants, the alcoholics, and the homeless. Andrew took his autoharp and the two sang and spoke, urging their listeners to make "their decision for Christ." Following the service, they talked with people individually, often staying to share a meal.

They had no illusions their message changed the hearts of every person they met. Many attended only for the free food. One evening at the Midnight Mission, as they sat down to a meal of bean sandwiches and stew, Andrew asked his son Bryant to bless the supper. Nearby, a grizzled man in ragged clothes prompted the young man, "Make it short, Bud, we're hungry!"

In churches throughout the Los Angeles area, they preached, sang, and gave "chalk talks," sermons accompanied by impromptu drawings. If the topic was Calvary and Christ's death, Andrew quickly sketched on a piece of newsprint thumbtacked to a folding easel the hill with its three crosses, Christ between two thieves. His skillful artistry captivated audiences.

For years Andrew had been molding olive-green art clay into designs for his illustrative photo-art work. His roses in bas-relief were so lifelike, they resembled flowers freshly plucked. He now conceived creating decorative Gospel art inscribed with passages from Scripture. Using plaster and clay molds, he cast small wall plaques, which he called the "Mitchell Art Mottoes." They carried sayings such as, "Be Not Afraid, Only Believe," "Prayer Changes Things," "Jesus Never Fails," and "I Will Never Leave Thee Nor Forsake Thee."

Facsimiles of wall plaques designed by Andrew printed on stationery.

Mitchell family, 1924-1925. Top left to right: Helen, Bryant, Hubert; Bottom: Andrew, Esther, Marietta, Jennie, Jean.

Soon he was creating before audiences, inviting people to come forward to help. While a volunteer stirred the water, he poured in the dry plaster of Paris. Another gingerly placed a copper hook into the still soft plaster. Others peeled the clay mold away. Finally, after preaching a short sermon on the motto, Andrew presented it to someone in the audience.

Jennie dedicated herself enthusiastically to Andrew's "art ministry," organizing their appointments and lightening his presentations with homey stories and anecdotes.

Jennie's public ministry developed from her personal prayer life. Since her "first errand" to Mr. Miller, prayer had become the answer to her every problem, every need. As Dr. Torrey had explained: "Jesus Christ was a human being, with a human parentage and human ancestry. Like all men he was subject to weariness, hunger, thirst, agony, and death – to the physical limitations of human nature. As a man, He was subject to human conditions for obtaining what He desired. He obtained power for work and for moral victory as other men do, by prayer."

Jennie was instant in prayer. When a situation needed mending, she stopped, closed her eyes and began praying. Some of her intercessory praying went on by telephone. In the midst of a conversation, she would say, "Let's stop and pray about this right now." She often surprised those on the other end of the line.

On one occasion a very serious-looking woman came to the house seeking advice. Alone with Jennie, she proceeded to pour out a long list of grievances: unthoughtful husband, disobedient children, no understanding from friends, no visits from her pastor, not enough money for furniture, constant headaches – the list went on. Jennie suddenly interrupted: "Now darling, that is enough. We'll stop right here and pray about each one of these problems and ask the Lord to show you what you can do about them with His help." Grasping the woman's hand so tightly that escape was impossible, Jennie prayed fervently for each problem. Ending, she kissed the woman on each cheek and said, "Now, we have called a halt to all these things. Put your trust in the Lord and leave these problems right here, right now."

Jennie's praying was original. A frequent strategy was to "clear the devil out" of an unsavory situation so that the Lord would have "free space" in which to act. She didn't take all day to do it. She dismissed Satan quickly. "All hell out! All heaven in!" she commanded. When she prayed, it was to recall the Lord's promises. Seldom did she keep praying over and over about the same matter. Once was sufficient. The Lord could hear well enough.

Jennie's and Andrew's habit and manner of prayer had a profound impact on the family, imparting a sense of the reality of God, and modeling what a family's relationship to God should be. Jennie prayed in the front room by the davenport near the bay window. If one of the children accidentally intruded upon her, she might glance up but would continue praying. Although the child might leave quickly, it was not without feeling that Jennie was bringing God's presence down into their home.

Jennie never ignored an opportunity to enlist the children in prayer, a habit that did not always delight them. If she were preparing to pray with a visitor, and one of the children happened to enter the room, she grasped their hand, saying, "Help us pray, Sweetheart."

The children often saw Andrew and Jennie praying together. Moving around the house in the morning, getting dressed, preparing for the day, they would take turns talking to God. First one and then the other would take up the subject, praying about it in a kind of three-way conversation: husband, wife, and their Lord.

Besides the family, the house on Waterloo Street was crowded with other guests, some temporary, some permanent. Shortly after their wedding, old Auntie Segar, a friend of Jennie's mother, moved in with them. A quiet, gentle, white-haired woman who shuffled about the house minding her own business, she occupied the middle bedroom next to Helen and Jean. "She just has no place else to go," Jennie explained.

Following a family tradition of helping individuals who had stumbled in life, Andrew one day requested the Los Angeles municipal court to probate men to him for rehabilitation, not violent men, but harmless incorrigibles, petty thieves, con men, and alcoholics. The parolees, dressed in faded clothes smelling of disinfectant, with pallid, unshaven faces, ate with the family, joined in family prayers, and helped Andrew around the hillside property. Accustomed to the clanking of steel doors and the rattle of brass keys, they were often surprised at the treatment accorded them in the Mitchell household.

McGrogan, a wily confidence man, could, while smiling and looking one straight in the eye, tell the smoothest lies ever conceived. Unknown to the court, he was an Army deserter and a longtime fugitive. After several months in the Mitchell home, and after continual exhortation from Andrew and Jennie, he finally repented, was converted, and went with Andrew to surrender to the authorities. After hearing his case, the magistrate released him to the Mitchells for a final period of probation.

Pauley, a secretive man who stood shyly in doorways, consumed every intoxicating liquid he could find, from bay rum, to canned heat, to witch hazel, to vanilla extract. One day he died in his bed in one of the lower apartments

– too much raw alcohol. Andrew, searching among his belongings, discovered a leftover cache of whiskey. To Bryant and Hubert he said: "Let's see what killed this man." Going to an empty lot, they broke the bottles on a rock. Igniting the liquor with a match, Andrew said, "That's how it burns inside of you, too."

Hennessy, on the other hand, stole anything he could lay hands on, rings, pens, watches, silverware, any gimcrack he could sell for a quarter. He was a practiced thief who could slip the ring off a lady's finger while holding her hand. One day Auntie Segar made the mistake of displaying to him her gold and silver heirloom jewelry. The next morning it was gone, along with Hennessy. Jennie made a quick call to Andrew at Riley Moore Engravers. "Hennessy's gone," she exclaimed, "and Auntie Segar's jewelry is missing. We think he's stolen it. I'm taking the next streetcar. I'll meet you at the corner of 4th and Main Streets."

On Main Street, the Mitchells began checking the pawn shops, Jennie on one side of the street, Andrew on the other. At the third shop, Jennie found Hennessy bargaining to sell the jewelry. "Hennessy!" she called out, charging at him with the same energy and determination she had often shown playing street hockey. Batting and shoving him into a corner, she grasped him firmly by the collar. "Now, Mrs. Mitchell...," Hennessy said, meekly raising his arms. Hauling him to the door, she called across the street to Andrew. Without summoning the police, the three took the next streetcar home, where they resumed the process of Hennessy's rehabilitation.

Although not every parolee gave himself up to genuine repentance, over the years – years filled with toil and prayer – Andrew and Jennie witnessed the conversion and rehabilitation of many. To Jennie and Andrew, it was not just "good works," but God's long arm of love and redemption reaching out to restore the weak and stumbling. It was a special ministry that God had assigned to them. The older children could not always understand why their parents continued to bring these derelicts into their home. Once, in exasperation, Bryant exclaimed, "Why don't you just let them go to hell?!"

"We will NOT let them go to hell!" Andrew replied emphatically. Not until later years did this answer make sense to the children.

Cycling around the neighborhood, the Mitchell boys one day brought back news that a new church was going up six blocks away on Glendale Boulevard just north of Echo Park Lake. "It's huge!" said Bryant. Indeed, it was – a large semi-circular building of concrete and reinforced steel with a glistening white dome that rose above the tall palm trees of the park. A few days later, Andrew read that a woman evangelist from San Diego was building this "temple," which would seat five thousand people. "We'll have to go and see what this is all about," he said to Jennie.

On New Year's Day, 1923, the Mitchells joined thousands of curious people from all over Los Angeles thronging to the newly constructed Angelus Temple at Echo Park. Entering the great glass doors, they were awed by the lofty auditorium, with a stage, tiered balconies, and a sky-blue dome painted with clouds overhead. At the rear of the stage was a baptismal font and a mural of the river Jordan. An orchestra pit held musicians, an organ, and a Steinway grand piano. On the high walls loomed great canvas-covered openings for as yet unfinished, two-story-high stained glass windows. On the front wall, dominating the entire auditorium, a mural depicted the Second Coming of Christ. Frescoed angels on the concrete walls beamed down upon the crowd.

Andrew, Jennie, and the children were ushered to seats in the top balcony by a young woman in a white uniform and a blue cape. As the audience continued to fill the hall, the family gazed about, excitedly anticipating what was to come. Presently, down a side rampart strode a young woman in a flowing white gown. She carried a white Bible and an armful of red roses. It was Aimee Semple McPherson, the renowned gospel evangelist. She walked eagerly, as if bearing joyous good news.

What followed utterly overwhelmed the Mitchells. Never before had they experienced such a service. What singing! Heaven seemed to join the voices raised in worshipful chorus to God. Aimee McPherson, radiantly beautiful, spoke with a dynamism, an intensity and conviction which captivated the audience.

When she invited the audience to receive Christ, people throughout the vast auditorium rose from their seats. In the third floor balcony, Helen Mitchell jumped up. The family made way for her to join the throngs of people filling the stairs and aisles. At the stage, Helen was surprised to find a group of gypsies kneeling around her, arrayed in bright clothes and sparkling jewelry. Converted on the East Coast, they had devotedly followed Aimee McPherson to Los Angeles. When Helen returned to her seat, her face was suffused with a radiance, her eyes held a new confidence and peace. She whispered to Jennie, "Jesus belongs to me and I belong to Jesus."

The experiences at Angelus Temple were so moving and profound, that after a short time, Andrew and Jennie decided to join. The change resolved a problem the older children were having with the more staid and traditional program at the Echo Park Methodist Church. Sunday, far from being anticipated as a day of celebration in the Lord, was dreaded. Hubert complained, "You have to sit in church and look holy." By contrast, the orchestra and the large concert organ at Angelus Temple nearly lifted one out of the seat. How grand was the pianist at the Steinway! How moving the sight of thousands of white handkerchiefs waving in unison as the congregation sang, "Wave the Answer Back To Heaven." How captivating the illustrated sermons, tableaux in which the Gospel message was enacted using costumes, props, scenery, lights—all the equipment of the theatre. What might have been a dry narration, became a living pageant that illustrated the Bible's spiritual message in ways few had ever appreciated.

In a collective act of devotion that was to continue for nearly eight years, the Mitchell family threw themselves into the activities of Angelus Temple. The family had always enjoyed singing together. Before long, they were singing as a group at the Temple services. Using the knowledge and training received at BIOLA, Jennie and Andrew volunteered for professional duties. Andrew joined the Temple's Foursquare Bible Institute as a full-time faculty member, teaching classes in Bible Doctrine, Philosophy of the Cross, and Gospel Art. After two years, he began writing pamphlets on Bible doctrine, addressing such themes as the essence and being of God, creation and evolution, the deity and humanity of Christ, and Satan and the question of sin. These were followed by "The Philosophy of the Cross," a series on the centrality and significance of the cross in Bible doctrine. Initially conceived as teaching aids for his students, these pamphlets became so popular he formed the A. E. Mitchell Publishing Company to produce and distribute them.

Jennie joined the City Sisters Movement, a women's outreach program to needy families. Eventually, she became the director of the group. She counseled delinquent teenage boys and taught a spiritual "prep course" for young people, as well as a course on "Missions" in the Bible Institute. She organized a Sunday School class of senior adults called the "Never Too Old Class." Every Sunday afternoon in the Temple's first balcony, the members polished up their musical talents, eventually organizing a band and choir. In 1924, when the Temple opened its own radio station KFSG, she gave regular devotional talks over the radio.

The older Mitchell children became active in the Temple's youth program called "The Angelus Temple Foursquare Crusaders." The Crusaders' "Covenant" defined the group's spiritual standards:

> "We now band ourselves together as the Angelus Temple Crusaders and enlist in the army of the King of Kings, and declare war against Satan and sin in all of its forms. We will go forth and win others....We will carry the banner of King Jesus and His righteousness in our homes, our neighborhoods, our businesses, our every walk of life....Furthermore, unless sent there as a messenger for our King, we will not at any time be found in the camp of the enemy such as the theatre, moving picture show, dance hall, pool room, or the card table....We will keep ourselves free from

Jennie Clay at the beginning of her radio and missionary ministry, 1930.

> tobacco, from swearing, from giddy talk and idle gossip, from immodest dress, from vulgar stories, and from backbiting and criticism....We will go forth under the bloodstained banner of the cross, to win other souls into the Kingdom of the Lord."

No one in the Mitchell family could fail to recognize the spiritual transformation happening to them, as if an inner fountain of joy had opened in each one's heart. A loving spirit characterized their relationship to each other.

One day in 1924, little Marietta fell ill with smallpox. An agent from the Los Angeles City Health Department tacked a sign to the front door proclaiming in large red letters: DANGER, QUARANTINE, NO ADMITTANCE. At school, Helen and Jean were told to gather their books and return home.

While Jennie and Auntie Segar nursed the sick child, the rest of the family moved to the detached bungalow in back of the house. For three weeks, the two kept a watchful vigil over the child, monitoring her fever, feeding her, changing her linen, washing her body, wrapping her hands to resist scratching. The ugly pustules on the child's face terrified Jennie. She could not bear to think her child might die. She proclaimed, "It will not happen! Death will not claim this child!" She began praying almost nonstop. On the ninth day, when it appeared that Jennie might collapse also, Marietta's fever broke. Her features suddenly cleared as if a wind had blown away the contagion. "Hi, Mommy!" she said in a weak, pure voice.

"Hello, my Sweetheart!" Jennie exclaimed, tears streaming down her cheeks.

"Mommy, I'm tired of being in bed. Can I get up now?"

Four years later, Marietta became ill again. Following a Memorial Day celebration at the beach, the child became strangely nauseated. Her legs crumpled beneath her and she fell to the floor. Andrew, realizing it was no child's pretense, carried her to bed and called the doctor. The diagnosis was infantile paralysis – Polio. "Dear Lord!" Jennie exclaimed.

Again, a quarantine sign was tacked to the front door. When it became apparent Marietta might never walk again, Jennie marshalled her courage and strength to fight another battle for her daughter's health. Unwilling to surrender Marietta to leg braces and crutches, she began a strict regimen of hot, soaking baths and long, soothing massages, rubbing Marietta's leg with hot olive oil. As soon as the child's strength allowed, Jennie began training her to walk again. She taught her to keep her foot pointed inward and to swing and flex the knee. Her constant affirmation of faith was, "This child shall walk again, she shall not be a cripple." Years later, Marietta would write: "With what patience my mother taught me....I remember pleasant times in the midst of misery, love in the midst of fear, and gratefulness along with pain. Today, I walk very well and praise God and Mother's tender nursing for my healing."

Each summer the family loaded blankets, groceries, and camping equipment into two old Model-T Fords and left for a week of camping. Jennie, an experienced camper, took delight in training her city-born family in the art of making comfortable beds under the stars.

Bryant constructed a cabinet for storing the family's food on the running board of his Model-T Ford. A hinged cover dropped down to make a table where Jennie could prepare the meals. One evening in Yosemite National Park, the family returned from a camp meeting to find that a bear had torn the box open and scattered their provisions.

"We'll have to hang everything in a tree," said Andrew.

"What if it comes back anyway?" asked young Jean.

"Well," said Andrew, "if we awake to find bears in or near the camp, we will turn on the car's headlights to frighten them away." To Bryant, he said, "I will keep a lookout during the night, and if a bear comes, I will alert you and you will run to the car and turn on the headlights."

The family's bedrolls were lined up together in front of the car. Bryant and Hubert slept at one end. Above the trees the Milky Way glittered in the night sky. For a long time, some scary speculation by Hubert, directed at his sisters, about the feeding habits of black bears, kept everyone laughing.

About three in the morning Bryant heard his father's loud whisper, "Bryant...bear! The headlights! Bryant!" Bryant opened his eyes to see a tremendous black shape looming in the darkness beside him. The blankets which had seemed substantially more heavy and protective earlier in the evening now felt as thin as tissue paper. Stealthily, Bryant ducked his head beneath them and lay as still as possible, holding his breath. What if the creature began pawing him? Should he fight back? Presently, the car door opened and the headlights came on. When Bryant poked his head out of the blankets, the bear was gone and Andrew was standing in front of them. Seeing the bear had been too close for Bryant to move, Andrew had jumped up, raced around the car, and turned on the headlights himself.

"We almost had one less mouth to feed for breakfast," he said to Jennie.

At the other end of the line, Bryant was breathlessly explaining, "That bear was right next to my head!"

"Next time give it a kiss," said Hubert. "That'll scare it off!"

By 1929, nearly all of Sarah's children—Bryant, Hubert, Helen, and Jean—had grown up, and, like branches on a tree, begun reaching to fulfill a separate destiny. As early as 1922, when Jennie and Andrew were graduating from BIOLA, eighteen-year-old Bryant had enrolled in the same two-year course of study. Subsequently, in 1925, he had entered UCLA as a pre-medical student. However, two-and-a-half years later he had changed institutions again, joining Hubert and Helen as a student in the Foursquare Bible Institute (L.I.F.E.). Here he met and later married Lola Lee Raney, a fellow student. In 1929, the young couple left Los Angeles to establish a new church in Kansas.

In the same year, Hubert met and married Helen Pomeroy at the Institute. They became Foursquare evangelists, later traveling as musicians with Evangelist Paul Rader.

Graduating from the Bible Institute, daughter Helen Mitchell began holding children's revivals in the Eastern states, eventually assuming co-pastorship of a church in Wooster, Ohio. In March, 1935, she married a young evangelist from Minnesota, David Morken.

During the years with the Temple, the Mitchells had been exposed to the ministries of such renowned preachers as Doctor Lillian B. Yeomans, author with a gifted ministry of praying for the sick; evangelist Smith-Wigglesworth from England; and Paul Rader, former pastor of Moody Church in Chicago and President of the Christian Missionary Alliance. In 1931, the Mitchells joined Paul Rader's Tabernacle program of evangelism and foreign missions, which was just then beginning in Los Angeles.

The change could not have been more drastic, from the grandeur and extravaganza of Angelus Temple to an unadorned wooden auditorium, a tabernacle, with folding chairs and wooden benches. In the pulpit, however, was one of the most electrifying evangelists in the country. A former pugilist and coach, Paul Rader had been converted during a campaign in Denver by D. L. Moody years before. He had become pastor of a Congregational church in Boston and, subsequently, pastor also of the D. L. Moody Church in Chicago. From there he had established the Chicago Gospel Tabernacle, and pioneered several Christian radio broadcasting stations.

As the Mitchells saw him, Paul Rader was attempting big things – the founding of tabernacles, foreign missions, salvation for the masses. Having established two tabernacles in Chicago and Fort Wayne, he was now beginning his third in Los Angeles. Rader didn't require elaborate programming, illustrated sermons, or spotlights – only his own strength, faith, and conviction in the Word of God.

At Rader's Tabernacle Jennie and Andrew received what was to mark their future life together: a vision of foreign mission evangelism. For years Rader had been championing indigenous foreign missions, the establishment of native churches in foreign nations. It was not enough for missionaries to travel to a country and establish a church which they administered forever after. The church had to produce trained national pastors, so that when the foreign missionaries withdrew, it did not collapse. Throughout the twenties, Rader had been sending and supporting such foreign missions.

In the early thirties, one of his final efforts was the creation of a program called "The Worldwide Couriers," in which selected young men travelled to remote locations – Burma, Sumatra, Southwest China, Borneo – seeking out the native tribes that no one had reached before. Rader had just launched this program when the Mitchells joined his group. Immediately, Andrew was asked to prepare Bible study materials which the missionaries could use in the field.

At the Tabernacle, Jennie organized a Sunday School Bible class for young married couples. Following Rader's emphasis on missions, the class called themselves the "Go-Ye Bible Class," after the scripture "Go ye therefore, and teach all nations...." (Matthew 28:19.) In addition to weekly Bible study, the class undertook practical projects related to the support of foreign missions. Missionaries, wherever they were serving in the world, needed one thing: support, spiritual as well as monetary. The class' first project was a pledge of $50 per month for missions, which was routed to Rader's Couriers. Gradually, the group began undertaking other tasks. If a missionary needed clothing, literature, medicine, a boat, they attempted to send it. They wrote letters of encouragement. How welcome these were to a man or woman living among strange peoples in a town or wilderness thousands of miles from home.

Above all, the Go-Ye Class prayed. Weekly, the group met to provide intercessory prayer for each missionary by name. Praying was no small matter. It was the most valuable help the group could offer. Prayer secured God's mercy and aid, and released His power.

From her earliest school years, Jennie had been directing and organizing people – in schools, homes, the YWCA, churches, Angelus Temple, and now Rader's Tabernacle for missions. She had taught Bible classes and counseled both young and old. However, she had never experienced anything quite like this Go-Ye Class. Watching the people work together, she marvelled at the changes occurring in them. They exhibited a loving closeness, a joyful gladness of heart, energy and enthusiasm! What was going on? Were they, by taking practical action to fulfill the letter of the Lord's command, unsuspectingly enlivening God's grace among themselves? If so, had Jennie at last found the instrument she had been preparing for all her life, an organization that would get people working not only for themselves and their world, but for their God?

Chapter 7

LAUNCHING the GO-YE FELLOWSHIP

One Sunday morning at the Tabernacle, George and Mabel Berryhill, welcoming the arrivals, noticed that Jennie Mitchell seemed unusually preoccupied as she hurried past them on her way upstairs. George acted as the Go-Ye Class president, and today as the class gathered in its upstairs meeting room, his curiosity rose another notch when Jennie, the teacher, whispered, "George, if you don't mind, would you cut the preliminaries short today? I need extra time to tell the class what is on my heart."

At forty-nine, Jennie was a popular teacher at the Tabernacle, loved for her good nature and warm heartedness. She spoke with lively humor and a jolly manner. One could not sit long without smiling with her. Today, as she rose to speak, the class was quiet and curious.

"We have enjoyed many months of studying God's Word together," she said, "and we all know that God has called us together for a high purpose. We are doers of the Word, we don't just sit and listen. With God's help we have sent money and support to various missionaries, and have written and received letters from them. We have also put our fingers on the map and prayed for them. But now I think it is time for us to become more than the Go-Ye Bible Class. Our vision should become a reality. I feel that the Lord would have us do something daring."

"Do we," she scanned the upturned, attentive faces, "have the faith to send a missionary couple – a qualified couple – out from our class?"

At last it had happened! They had speculated upon it before, many of them speaking in wishful, dreamy tones about journeying to other parts of the world to evangelize, but now the challenge had actually been given. For a few moments, the members looked silently at one another. They were like soldiers trained to "go over the top," but when the time finally came, they hesitated.

"Do we have that faith?" Jennie mused quietly.

Forrest and Mary Esther Forbes were consulting each other with deep looks. They rose together. "Yes," Forrest said, "we can and we should do it." Mature and zealous witnesses, the Forbes had often expressed a desire to go abroad as missionaries, even specifying the Lhisu Tribe along the borders of China, Tibet, and Burma.

"Yes, I agree," said George Berryhill, "We can and we should."

"We think so, too," said Bob and Rena Williams, rising.

"Yes," said the Van Meters.

"Yes!"

"Yes!"

Around the room, the young people rose to their feet. In less than a minute, all were standing, signifying their accord.

"We can do it!"

They laughed nervously with disbelief as they realized what they were proposing.

"But who...?"

The Mitchells greet George and Mabel Berryhill, leaders of the Go-Ye Sunday School Class. 1954.

George Berryhill said, "The Lord has taught us to co-labor with Him in the financial part of any program like this." Taking chalk, he wrote on the small blackboard, "One thousand dollars, Lord, to send Forrest and Mary Esther Forbes to China."

Laughing excitedly, the class crowded around the blackboard, pushing Forrest and Mary Esther forward, who were smiling proudly.

"But how will we get the money...?"

"When Jesus fed the multitude," Jennie said, "which numbered over five thousand, he started with a little boy's lunch!" Opening her Bible, she turned to Matthew 18:18. Laying a copper penny on the page, she read: "Whatsoever ye shall bind on earth, shall be bound in Heaven, and whatsoever ye shall loose on earth shall be loosed in Heaven."

And with that, hands clasped, some with tears on their faces, the members of the newborn "missionary society" prayed together.

Within a few weeks, funds began coming in. The Go-Ye group provided the first donations. Spreading the news to friends and acquaintances, they secured additional support. Paul Rader mentioned the new mission on his radio program. His audience, accustomed to supporting missions, readily promised support.

Forrest and Mary Forbes began a thorough investigation of the tribal conditions in Yunnan Province in Southwestern China. By 1935, they were ready to sail. In a moving farewell service, their friends prayed them off as the Go-Ye's first missionaries. Jennie thought of the church leaders in Antioch two thousand years before, of Paul and Barnabas departing on their first missionary journey (Acts 13). She had laid a penny on the Bible, which, multiplied by faith, was now taking two missionaries to China.

Months later, Forrest wrote to the Go-Ye from Yunnan: "We are staying awake guarding our very lives these horrible nights as evildoers seek to burn the mission. We are printing and binding the first volume of the Grace Book this week. We know beyond a doubt that there is a principality of demon power in Western China, but God has His people here, too. Thanks be unto God who giveth us the victory." This letter filled the Go-Ye with some apprehension. Earnestly the group prayed for the Forbes' safety. Eventually, the trouble dissipated and subsequent letters from the Forbes spoke of success.

Other couples in the Go-Ye Bible Class now stepped forward to be missionaries. Lester and Bea Van Meter, the sister of Mary Esther Forbes, were also sent to Yunnan Province in Southwestern China, while Bob and Rena Williams left for Borneo in the Dutch East Indies.

No missionary left without a grand send-off banquet held at some well-known church cooperating in the effort, such as Hardy Mitchell's Central Tabernacle, Paul Rader's Tabernacle, and the Bethel Temple of the Assemblies of God. These interdenominational banquets amounted to inspirational rallies to generate enthusiasm and support for the missionary effort.

Jennie was the center of the organizing effort. She invited missionary leaders living in or visiting the area to speak. Her buoyant manner usually brought a positive response. Among the many who visited were Norman Grubb, Bob Bowman, and Paul Rader. She spent hours phoning friends and supporters, organizing food, transportation, and music for the rally. In her most attractive cursive handwriting, she composed posters and pamphlets to advertise the meeting, which Andrew decorated with sketches of flowers, ferns, and rocks, reminiscent of the garden behind the Mitchell house.

By the early 1930s, several of the older Mitchell children had left Los Angeles and settled in the Midwest. Hubert and his wife, Helen Pomeroy, had been travelling with Paul Rader for almost two years, holding evangelistic meetings in many churches. One day Hubert wrote to Jennie and Andrew: "We are going to Sumatra."

They were going under the auspices of Rader's missionary society and the Christian and Missionary Alliance (C&MA), which had established comity relationships in Sumatra. The Go-Ye Bible Class immediately volunteered their support also. In the fall of 1934, Hubert and Helen, with their child, David, sailed on the SS Silver Walnut for Sumatra. "I shall never forget the look in my father's eyes," Hubert wrote, "as our little family sailed off. I think he had the feeling we would never meet again."

Reaching Sumatra, the Mitchells began studying the Malay language, while testifying and preaching to the Chinese and Muslim population in the small cities. As expected, they met resistance. Hard-core Muslims petitioned the authorities to expel them. Yielding to the pressure, they left the cities and began preaching to the aboriginal Kubu tribes in the jungles.

Now that one of their own children was a Go-Ye missionary, and as more missionary letters were arriving at the Sunday School class, Jennie and Andrew saw the need for a stronger home-support base. Within the year the Go-Ye Bible Class became the "Go-Ye Fellowship." Interdenominational, its guiding motto was: "No divisions in Christ, no unity out of Christ." Any Christian worker could participate without compromising his or her denominational membership.

In addition, they began formally training young people who felt the call to be missionaries. An evening "Go-Ye Institute" was opened in the Tabernacle Chapel. Andrew lectured on basic Bible principles, and Jennie taught inspirational lessons on prayer, Christian living, and witnessing. Visiting missionaries gave special lectures. A missionary "cabinet" was formed. Two-by-two prayer teams were organized which followed four basic rules of action:

- Get a prayer partner.
- Meet once a week at a certain time and place.
- Read the Bible before praying.
- Use a map to locate the missionaries' fields as you pray.

Before long, the Go-Ye Fellowship needed a center for its activities, not just a box number or street address, but a real missionary compound where classes and rallies could be held. It had to be informal, attractive, and conducive to their activities. Considering alternatives, Andrew and Jennie chose their own house at 1307 Waterloo Street. The property was not only centrally located, but large enough for a chapel seating about sixty people. The landscaped garden added a charm that couldn't be found elsewhere.

Jennie initiated a biweekly radio program on Los Angeles station KTM focusing on missionary evangelism. Later, stations KMTR and KGER aired the program. Andrew gave a series of doctrinal Bible studies, and Jennie inspirational sermonettes on Christian Living. Evangelists, musicians, and missionaries were often guests on the program. Andrew would sometimes play his harp. Wherever they went now, Jennie carried a portable tape recorder to dictate in spare moments her radio sermons. As a result of these broadcasts, Bible classes sprang up in the outlying cities of Santa Monica, Pasadena, and Glendale, where, utilizing his chalk-talk techniques, Andrew gave Bible lessons and Jennie lectured on missions and Christian living.

For transportation, the Mitchells used the family Model-T touring car, complete with black side curtains to protect from rain. Since Andrew did not drive, Jennie chauffeured them from place to place. But there were difficulties. She paid more attention to her conversation than to her driving. She lurched over curbs, stopped suddenly without cause, ran out of gas in the middle of traffic, thrashed along for a mile before realizing that a tire had gone flat. Once she "bumped" a man walking down the side of the road. One day she turned up the off-ramp of a busy freeway. Andrew, in sudden panic, ordered her out of the driver's seat. "We will not die in this automobile!" he exclaimed. Pride hurt, she surrendered the wheel. Thereafter, she commandeered the cars of friends and acquaintances to take her where she had to go.

In the next three years several more Go-Ye missionaries left Los Angeles for foreign missionary service. Katherine Baerg sailed to Yunnan province in China. Ethel Alair joined John and Ethel Lagar in the Chaco region of Argentina. Rose Linden, who had come to the USA seeking support for her work in North India, rejoined her husband there. Mae Watson returned to Egypt. Forrest and Mary Esther Forbes, after a first term in Southwest China, left for the remote Alpine section of Burma.

Letters with foreign stamps began arriving at 1307 Waterloo Street, bearing reports, prayer requests, and stories of missionary adventure, which greatly encouraged the Go-Ye people. From Alpine Burma, Forrest Forbes described their contact with the vanishing race of Mongolian pygmies who had been enslaved by Tibetan invaders. From Sumatra, Hubert Mitchell wrote:

> "We are at the breaking point in the work now...namely the raising up of eight Kubu native teachers to reach the remainder of this

> jungle race. When I started working among them less than one year ago...no society had ever dealt with them...Now these men know the Gospel and can tell it to others intelligently, and they can pray. Some of them can read the *oalos* language and can write it. From the 250 who have believed, these eight are ready to take the Gospel into the deep jungles to hundreds of others....These boys are not clothed in fine raiment. If they could be placed in a show window on Broadway, you would soon have a crowd. Their native costume is just a loin cloth....They have an odor that is very obnoxious, but one soon gets used to it. Five days ago we baptized ten Chinese, four Malay Mohammedans. It was a glorious sight. The Chinese are bringing in their friends. It looks like a real move from heaven among this virile race. The Chinese are a great people...."

Hubert added a personal note on his family:

> "Helen is a real soldier. She speaks Malay quite well and has meetings with the women two or three times a week. Little David and Paul keep her sewing and watching them—they are so full of mischief. They both sing together, and what a noise! David can start and carry a tune a short ways; Paul just hollers. David confuses English and Malay. They are a great pair. How we thank God for them!"

From China, Katherine Baerg wrote:

> "As I look about and see these people who are working only to live, and living only to die, having no hope beyond the grave, their only aim to have many children and teach them to smoke opium, I cannot help but realize my insufficiency to help them. But the transforming power of the true and living God is able to make new creatures out of them...."

Jennie broadcast the letters over the radio and read them to the Bible classes and the rallies at Waterloo Street. They were windows onto peoples, cultures, and areas of the world that few would ever see. They kept new applicants knocking at the Go-Ye door, and funds coming in to support the missionaries already in the field.

As the Go-Ye Fellowship grew, Jennie's main task was inspiring and encouraging others, both around her and abroad. Her letters to missionaries were sermonettes, bolstering their strength and courage. "We have a 'vertical' relationship with Heaven," she wrote. "It is established by our redemption and the new birth in His likeness. We keep it strong by prayer and reading the Word. Our 'horizontal' relationship is with those whom we meet. We

All day meeting on compound. Victory vase top center made with stones Andrew gathered from around the world. 1957.

cannot allow divisions to develop. Rather we should quickly repent, confess, and forgive." Realizing how easily people fall astray, she advised, "It is a good thing to do some good act every day; to witness to someone every day and to pray everyday, and many times a day."

A favorite theme was "Stagger Not," after St. Paul's words in Romans 4:20: "He [Abraham] staggered not at the promises of God through unbelief." "...Courage, brother," she wrote, "do not think that you are a victim of circumstances, and that there is no way out. Get down the Old Book. Read again the sure and grand promises....It is time to believe God rather than circumstances, things, men, or devils....stagger not." The Go-Ye missionaries looked forward to her letters. Paul Fleming, who later founded the New Tribes Mission, wrote from British Malaysia that her admonitions lifted him from "down in the cellar to the top of the mountain."

To bolster a sense of community, Jennie and Andrew devised a newsletter, the first Go-Ye Digest, a thirty-six page, pocket-sized booklet, which appeared in October, 1936. With illustrations by Andrew, an inspirational sermon by Jennie, and letters from missionaries in China, Argentina, Sumatra, and India, it was an instant success.

Jennie's answer to problems was unorthodox. She resisted fear or discouragement, which she regarded as the tactics of Satan. Like Joshua, she relied heavily upon "sanctified shouting." When it looked as if a missionary was going down in defeat, she shouted her favorite slogan, like David challenging Goliath: "The Devil is a liar!" She took literally the Scripture; "Resist the devil, and he will flee from you!" Often the family heard her shout: "Satan, release that sick missionary!" or "Satan, take your hands off that situation!" Likewise, she shouted praise to the Lord for His answers and aid.

She used "shouting papers," little slips of yellow paper spread around the Mitchell house proclaiming a particular need or problem – "$5,000 Lord!" or "Victory over the devil in Burma!" She tacked these to a door or window, taped them above the kitchen sink or beside the bathroom mirror, pinned them in the fold of a curtain. To the children who watched this, God apparently did notice these slips, because positive results invariably followed. Jennie's "shouting slips" seemed to loosen the help from Heaven.

Although the country was in the throes of the Great Depression, the lack of money was no barrier, especially when thousands of unevangelized people still remained to be harvested in God's ripe fields. Had not the Lord told her, "With God, nothing shall be impossible?" In 1938, to generate support, she toured the Open Bible Standard Churches in Iowa and Nebraska, telling the story of the Go-Ye Fellowship, a testimony of "faith in action." At the convention in Iowa, she so stirred the delegates, that newsletters described her as leaving a "Golden trail of blessing." She arranged with the Open Bible Standard Churches that they would henceforth co-operate informally with the missionary effort of the Go-Ye.

In the fall of 1939, as Germany was invading Poland, the Go-Ye Fellowship was preparing a contingent of missionaries for the Orient. The group included several Mitchell children and their families. Hubert and his wife, Helen Pomeroy, with their three children were returning to Sumatra for a second term; David and Helen Morken (previously Helen Mitchell) and their two children, were on their first assignment to the same village in Sumatra as the Hubert Mitchells; and Jean Mitchell ("Snooks") was going for the first time to work with Carl and Rose Linden, both Go-Ye missionaries, in Landour, Mussoorie, India. As the SS Hikawa Maru steamed out of San Francisco Bay, Jennie admitted, through tears, it was difficult to see ten leave at once. "It leaves a big hole in the family," she said. However, arriving back at 1307 Waterloo, she announced, "It's time to celebrate! This is the time we have looked forward to and worked for – our own children going out into the Harvest. Let's dance in honor of this great event."

Eighteen-year-old Marietta strummed the piano. As the girl pressed the keys, she felt the holiness of the occasion and did not watch her parents. But out of the corner of her eye she saw them pass by in a kind of waltz, in solemn, joyous celebration. From that time on they danced in their home for every significant occasion, every wedding, and the birth of each new grandchild and great grandchild.

In Sumatra, both the Morkens and Mitchells were under the joint sponsorship of the Christian and Missionary Alliance, the Go-Ye, and the Open Bible Standard Churches. Both families were burning with enthusiasm to reach the remote tribes of Indonesia. In September 1940, after a year in the Sumatra jungle, Hubert's wife, Helen, gave birth to their fourth child, little Jean Marie. Three days later, however, the mother fell ill and died. The two families, huddling together in the wilderness far from home, were devastated. In shock and deep sorrow, Hubert, alone with three small children and a baby, buried his wife in a jungle grave, covered with a cement slab for protection. His sister, Helen, David's wife, was now in charge of the six children. The men took turns staying with her, while the other ventured into the jungle to contact the Kubu tribes. Jean, cabled in India, came to help. A wet-nurse was found for the new baby. In the United States, the Mitchells wept – and kept a flow of letters to Sumatra.

In December, 1941, war engulfed the entire South Pacific. Malaysia fell swiftly to the advancing Japanese army. The invasion of the Dutch East Indies followed soon after. In Sumatra, all non-Asians, including the Mitchell families and other Open Bible missionaries, were advised to leave as quickly as possible or face capture and internment in Japanese concentration camps. Within days, however, customary communications and transportation broke down and orderly retreat gave way to panic among the population. It became "everyone for himself." The Dutch Government Controller personally hiked ten kilometers to Djambi to urge the missionaries to leave.

Helen Morken was adamant against leaving. "Here only a year and we have to go?"

"I know the language," Hubert pointed out. "I could stay, hide, run, live in the jungles – but if I die, it will leave four children orphans."

The Dutch Officials argued that if the missionaries stayed, it would only jeopardize their own position. "It will be doubly hard for us," they said.

A vote was taken and it was decided they should evacuate. To complicate things, baby Jean Marie was still being wet-nursed by an Indonesian woman, who would have to be left behind. In addition, several of the other children had whooping cough! Hastily packing essentials, the families distributed their household belongings to the local villagers. As the families fled, the Dutch official cabled the Go-Ye Fellowship and Open Bible Mission leaders in America for emergency evacuation funds. Unfortunately, money could not be sent, since banks had been closed and international assets frozen.

In Los Angeles, Jennie and the Go-Ye staff, along with other missionary leaders, immediately initiated sessions of fasting and prayer. The last KPM Dutch Mail Service ship was waiting at the dock as the missionaries arrived in the port city of Telukbetung. There were fifteen in the party, including the Ralph Isbill and Hart Armstrong families. Although travel funds had not yet arrived, the American Consul guaranteed them, thus allowing the Americans to board the ship. Unfortunately, as was learned later, several missionary colleagues of the Mitchell-Morken family in Sumatra did not escape, but were captured and imprisoned by the Japanese, including Dr. Robert A. Jaffray, who died before liberation in 1945.

Their ship, following an evasive route across the Indian Ocean and South Atlantic, arrived in New York after three perilous months at sea. As they passed the Statue of Liberty, a fellow passenger handed the ladies new hats. Weeping, they sang, "God Bless America."

In Los Angeles, the telephone rang at 1307 Waterloo.

"Helen? Is this really Helen?" cried Jennie. "And David? And Hubert? Are all the children there?" Jubilant receptions awaited the missionary families in both Des Moines and Los Angeles.

Although there was joy, it was sad to see Hubert and the children stepping off the train without their mother. Hubert held the new baby, Jean Marie, in his arms. To Jennie, history was repeating itself. Hubert's family looked just like the Andrew Mitchell family after the death of Sadie years before—joyless, disconsolate, morose. Grieving, Hubert established a house for the family in Los Angeles. He began ministering with Youth for Christ and in the downtown Los Angeles Christian Service Men's Center.

All the Mitchell family's prayers now focused upon Jean Mitchell, who still remained abroad. After a short time in Sumatra following the death of Hubert's wife, she had returned to the language institute in Landour where she resumed studying Hindi. From there, after the war began, she went to Karwi in mid-India to work with a Norwegian Mission.

With Jean was a missionary named Rachel Edwardsen. Rachel's support from Norway had been cut off since the German occupation of her country. Jean had been sharing her salary with her, as well as letters she received from Los Angeles. As the months passed, Jean's letters contained more and more information about the Norwegian girl. "She's tired of having to face the public here," Jean wrote. "She's taken to wearing dark glasses in the village so that the men can't see her eyes. Their sensual looks bother her. Sometimes they ask us, 'Where's your husband?' She replies that we are virgins, not prostitutes, as they suppose (*kamari,* not *randi*). Poor thing, she wants a husband. She's awfully tired and lonely, and she hasn't had a furlough from her duties here in eight years."

Hubert, sensitive to his sister and her friend's predicament, sent a cable which read in part, "Sing a lot, Jean...Don't let the Devil get you down."

In fact, Rachel Edwardsen had for a long time been praying for someone to love. "Lord, in the whole world isn't there a man?" She would add a postscript to the prayer, "Give me a man who loves your Word and who prays." When Hubert's cablegram to Jean arrived, her heart leapt: "There he is!"

In Los Angeles, Jennie, a teasing twinkle in her eye, suggested to Hubert, "Why don't you write to that Norwegian girl that Jean's been talking about. She sounds awfully nice."

"All right," said Hubert. He wrote a letter to Rachel, followed by another and then another. Her replies were more than cordial, they were warm and enthusiastic.

One day, toward the end of 1943, Andrew suggested, "Since Rachel hasn't had a vacation for so long, why don't we invite her here?"

"A splendid idea!" exclaimed Jennie.

The next day Andrew sent a cable to Jean: "WE SUGGEST URGING RACHEL EDWARDSEN TO COME TO USA."

Shortly after this, Hubert wrote proposing marriage. "I cannot understand it," he said, "God has planted in me a deep love for you."

Rachel responded by cable, quoting I Peter 1:8: "Whom having not seen we love...I'm coming with love, Rachel." Privately, she prayed: "Lord, get me there before his children get too old."

In 1944, travel was difficult, but sea passage was finally booked. In early April, Rachel arrived in New York, looking quite worn-out and down-at-the-heels. She was met by friends of the Mitchells, who put her on the train to California.

Hubert, meanwhile, announced the marriage to his children, "You're going to have a new mommy," he told them. "Daddy loved her before he saw her."

The Go-Ye Fellowship gave Rachel a heroine's welcome. To them, she was a warrior returning from battle, possessing great merit and honor. A standing-room-only crowd packed Pastor Louis Turnbull's Bethel Temple in Los Angeles to cheer the announcement of her wedding to Hubert.

On April 21, the couple was married in the Church of the Open Door in Los Angeles, Dr. Charles Fuller performing the ceremony. The church overflowed with friends and well-wishers. The entire evangelical community of Los Angeles had turned out to celebrate with them.

As the ceremony began, some caged birds on the platform began singing. Jennie suddenly recalled her meadowlark preacher from the Nebraska prairie forty years before. Tears welled in her eyes. How happy and full her life had become! Not only was her family growing strong in the Lord, but the Go-Ye was thriving. Soon the war would be over, and the society which had started from a Sunday School class and a penny on the Bible ten years ago would again take up the true fight, continuing as the physical and spiritual quartermaster to many of God's soldiers around the world. Many battles remained yet to be won.

Chapter 8

CARIBBEAN CHALLENGE

Mid-summer 1944. The wide-winged Pan-American Clipper floated gracefully on its pontoons at the Miami Airport sea dock preparing for the flight to the Caribbean. Andrew and Jennie, waiting to board, were making their first trip abroad, a visit to missionary friends serving in the island nations of Cuba, Haiti, Puerto Rico, and the Dominican Republic. The Go-Ye Fellowship had a number of missionary contacts in the Caribbean, some known personally to the Mitchells and some having contacted them after hearing their radio broadcasts. The Mitchells' purpose was not only to visit friends, but to survey the area for sending future Go-Ye missionaries. Although now in their sixties, they felt young and were eager to visit any country where loving Christian families would shelter them.

Jennie's firstborn daughter, Marietta, age twenty-two, having completed her junior year at Wheaton College in Illinois, was going along as secretary and general aide. As a teenager, she had been dubious about the correctness of trying to "convert" people of other cultures, holding a rather negative opinion of some of the missionaries she had met while growing up at home on Waterloo Street. She had secretly labeled them "inferior." Now, as a college girl, she had her own career plans. Although excited and eager to travel, she was careful to distinguish her role during the trip. When a college friend asked if she were planning to bc a missionary, she hastily denied it, "It's not hereditary, you know."

The trio travelled light. Baggage included one autoharp in a green flannel bag, a mouth harp, a few song sheets, a number of small plaster Gospel plaques, a reel-to-reel recorder for taping radio sermons, several Bibles, a French dictionary, several rolls of white newsprint for illustrated drawings, five or six boxes of colored chalk, a few changes of summer clothing, and a swim suit for "the aide."

Accustomed to the arid, Mediterranean climate of Southern California, Andrew and Jennie found the warm, rainy, tropical Caribbean, inviting. They flew first to Havana, and then island-hopped in a small eight-seater, twin-engine plane to Haiti, Santa Domingo, and Puerto Rico. The plane flew low over the jungles and white beaches, giving the passengers striking views of the island paradise.

Island transportation was novel and exciting. Small banana boats, plying back and forth over the crystal waters, carried passengers and freight between islands. Overland, camions (open-sided buses) bumped along over gravel and pitted tarmac roads. Besides human passengers, they carried pigs, chickens, goats, and boxes of produce. Although heavily loaded, they forded shallow rivers and streams, and labored into and out of valleys, their engines growling as if to explode. Squeezed tightly in narrow seats, Andrew and Jennie revelled in the sights, sounds, and smells of the new culture.

"Everyone is so lovely and dark. It makes their white teeth just beautiful," Jennie observed.

"Yes, they are beautiful people," Andrew agreed.

Riding the bus carried special responsibilities. From time to time they joined the brigade of hands passing the little tins of baby urine from the back or inside seats to be dumped out a window.

Autos, trucks, wagons, and ox-drawn carts passed them on the narrow roads. Occasionally they came to a cluster of tin-roofed houses stretched along the side of the road. Chickens scrambled to avoid the bus, which neither slowed for them, nor stopped when it ran over one. They passed herds of goats and pigs herded by small children. Although the islands were uniformly lush and green, the trees and brush now and then parted to reveal a large pineapple, sugarcane, or sisal hemp plantation.

While Jennie and Andrew may have felt some strangeness, they found the Spanish and French-Creole cultures exciting. The newness only heightened their inquisitiveness to know more about the people and their customs. In the markets they were everywhere – sipping *cafe con leche* in the little coffee shops, sightseeing old forts, and sampling exotic fruits: breadfruit, plantain, papaya, mango. They mingled with the people, promoting as much verbal exchange as possible. Through interpreters, they explained who they were and their mission. This sometimes led to improvisation. Once, when an interpreter had trouble translating "fellowship," Jennie explained, "Tell them it means 'Many fellows in the same ship.'"

From the first, Marietta saw that Jennie and Andrew did not fit her stereotype of missionaries. For one thing, they exhibited a sincere appreciation for the people they met. Not put off by a person's poverty, dress, or physical uncleanliness, they maintained a spirit of goodwill and compassion, seeking to discover, by a kind of x-ray vision which penetrated beneath external appearance, a person's true worth. Hidden beneath an arrogance of unbelief was a heart longing for rescue and truth. They refrained from a "we-you" mentality, never once referring to "the natives," but regarding the people as similar to themselves and therefore, their natural neighbors. Their

"[Andrew and Jennie] mingled with the people, promoting as much verbal exchange as possible. Through interpreters, they explained who they were and their mission."

point of view was always, "We are all one stock, one kind," and "Everyone is made in the likeness of God and bears His Image."

In Haiti, the Mitchells visited the Island of Tortuga, which, in the 18th century, had been a stronghold for pirates. Sitting awkwardly during the long afternoon in the little banana cargo boat, Jennie developed a severe cramp in her thigh. By the time they reached the dock, the pain was so intense she cried in agony. As the rest of the party scrambled up the ladder onto the pier, Jennie lay embarrassed on the floor of the boat, unable to move. The onlookers stared down at her, some curious, a few with sympathy. Presently, a broad-shouldered Haitian man, his black skin shiny with sweat, waded out to the boat, lifted Jennie in his arms, and splashed his way back to the pier. Marietta blushed as the Haitian children crowded up to see Jennie's white legs. Without losing her composure, Jennie graciously thanked the man and, with both hands massaging her muscle-knotted leg, began laughing and talking with the people, making a joke about helpless Americans.

Contacting the local missionary, Jennie and Andrew arranged to hold services every night in either a town hall or a local house. Jennie usually preceded Andrew. Her talks were informal. Speaking through an interpreter, she told a story, an anecdote, or related an incident from her life or from the Bible. Stamping her foot or shaking her finger at the crowd for emphasis, she seemed like everyone's gently chiding mother. Her relaxed wit and earthy good humor evoked laughter from the audience. Sometimes she would get off on a tangent – "rabbit chasing," she called it, afterwards feeling chagrin at not having kept to the subject. Finished, she would introduce Andrew and, with a wave to the audience, take her seat.

Andrew's "chalk talks" were enormously popular. He quickly sketched large, colorful pictures, which at the end of his illustrated sermon he offered to the audience—an invitation that usually invoked a scramble.

One warm evening at the close of the service, the Mitchells distributed their "Bless card," a glossy cardboard card, slightly smaller than a calling card, bearing in Spanish the inscription from Romans 12:14, "Bless them which persecute you; bless, and curse not." The word "BLESS" was printed over a sketched background of scrolls. On the opposite side the instructions read, "Carry this card on your person. Let it be a reminder that being in Christ, we have this heavenly privilege with its accompanying wisdom and power." The people, many of whom had never before seen a verse of Scripture—*the Word of God*—much less possessed one which they could read whenever they wanted, accepted these tokens with reverence.

In the background, the travelers sensed "other powers" that were not sympathetic or even neutral toward the evangelists' efforts. The first was voodoo, the region's folk cult of magical and quasi-religious practices and beliefs. Brought to Haiti from Dahomey in French West Africa by slaves in the 18th century, voodoo was practiced in various forms throughout the Caribbean. It was particularly strong in Haiti.

The cult involved belief in a supreme deity known as *Bon Dieu*, as well as a larger group of lesser deities, the *loa*, some of which were considered African gods. Ceremonies involved dancing to drums, animal sacrifice, the chanting of prayers, feasting, the casting of spells and magic, and, most significantly, spirit possession. During the ceremony, people invited the loa to inhabit their bodies. Lapsing into a trance, the individual assumed the manners and characteristics of the particular loa spirit which had taken possession. It might cause the person to dance, sing, converse with onlookers, pronounce blessings or curses, or to babble and cavort in a strange and bizarre manner. To Jennie and Andrew, such practices only perpetuated darkness in the souls who surrendered to them.

The second resistance the Mitchells encountered was the Roman Catholic Church, which openly disapproved of the Protestant missionaries who had come to preach the Gospel of Christ. In the cathedrals the priests urged the population to shun the evangelists. From the evangelicals' point of view, the Catholic Church, while it pretended to represent Christ, and perhaps did at one time, had, over the centuries, erected in this region such a legalistic institution, draped round with ritual, law, and dogmatic interpretations of the Gospel, that the true "good news" of Christ had been twisted and smothered, and was no longer healing the humanity it was intended to transform.

Salvation was obtained not through genuine rebirth in Christ, in which

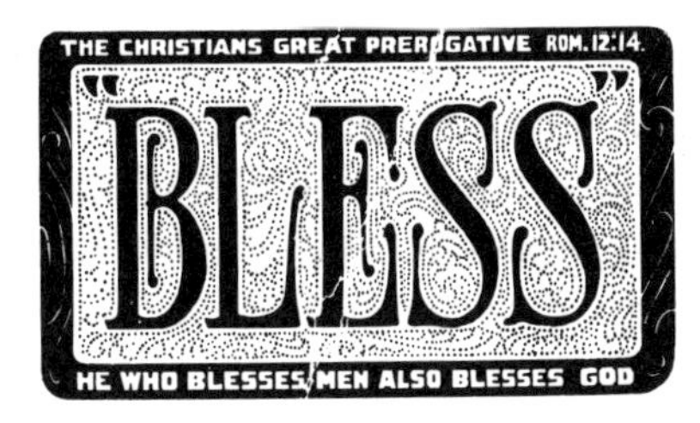

To Bless—as far as is possible—every situation and occasion of which we are a part is the prerogative of the Christian. Bless and curse not, is the command.
CARRY THIS CARD ON YOUR PERSON-
Let it be a constant reminder that being in Christ, we have this heavenly privilege with its accompanying wisdom and power.
For Card, send to- The A.E. Mitchell Pub. Co. 1307 Waterloo St. Los Angeles, 26

This "Bless" card was written by A. E. Mitchell.

the heart is changed and the individual launched in a new direction toward God, but through perfunctory church membership, involving primarily "works"—penance, confession, mechanical praying—and "sacraments" which conferred God's grace. As the resident missionaries assessed it, the people, despite their church affiliation, remained neck-deep in sin, their lives a perpetual round of sinning, followed by confession. The chains of sin that shackled their souls remained unbroken. As a businessman one day explained to Andrew: "I prefer to hire people converted by the evangelists, because they don't drink, they don't lie, they don't steal. They're honest, upright, and they work hard."

Ironically, here was a vast segment of humanity, worshipping icons of Christ, Mary, and the Apostles, praying to and venerating a multitude of Christian "saints," attending Latin masses they did not understand, reverently respecting Church custom and dogma—but who had never actually heard the Word of Christ! As Jennie and Andrew continued to preach the Gospel in shabby halls and open-air meetings, they could not mistake the hunger for God among those who came to hear them.

Their policy, of course, was not to attack the local religions or customs, but simply to present the True Gospel, which by itself would draw hungry hearts. One night in Haiti, however, in a fit of inspired drama, Andrew rushed to the door of the little church where they were speaking, and, pointing out into the darkness, shouted, "What have these great steepled cathedrals and these drums and evil dances done to give you hope and a happy heart? After dancing and screaming all night in voodoo worship, what good does it do to attend mass the next morning? What has the old way done to give you a true hope beyond death?" This sudden enthusiasm for the joy of the new birth in Christ, brought the black Haitian audience to its feet shouting "Hallelujah!"

Although at every meeting people came forward to receive Christ, it was difficult to gauge how deeply the message penetrated. From time to time, the Mitchells were given small indications. Wilfred and Grace Gulick, whom the Mitchells were visiting, had been in Haiti for over ten years. Besides erecting a church, they had established a dispensary and an obstetrics clinic, which was heavily used by the local population. One day a woman came to the clinic where Andrew was visiting and announced that, after hearing him preach, she had, in tribute, named her new baby after him.

While with the Gulicks, the Mitchells one morning found two small children, a seven-year-old boy and his five-year-old sister at the door of the mission. They had slept all night on the cold stone floor of the front porch. Orphans, they had come seeking help from Jennie and Andrew, who immediately took them into the home, fed them, and gave them clean clothes. The children were, in fact, only two of many thousands of homeless and ragged children. Jennie, responding immediately in the only way she knew, cabled the Go-Ye office in Los Angeles and raised one thousand dollars to help. Within two months, eleven large boxes containing children's clothes arrived from California – khaki shirts for the boys and dresses for the girls. To each was pinned a colorful little card reading, "Hallelujah." It was an inadequate solution, she knew, to the tide of human need surging everywhere around her.

The visit to the West Indies lasted four months. Arriving in Los Angeles in October, the Mitchells were surprised to find stacks of letters requesting increased missionary activity in other parts of the world. Enthusiastic from their Caribbean experience, they threw themselves into the work. They wrote letters, gave radio programs, interviewed missionaries, and planned the Go-Ye's future missionary strategy. Jennie's days began at 5 a.m. when she rose for prayer and early morning walks in the backyard. Often they ended at midnight or later, long after the others had retired.

In late January, 1945, she contracted pneumonia. It began with what appeared to be a feverish cold. "Oh, I'll be just fine," she said, waving away Andrew's concern. The fever persisted, and within a week she was too weak to get out of bed. Deep, uncontrolled attacks of coughing left her trembling. "She must go to the hospital," the doctor told Andrew.

Pneumonia was a killer, and Andrew knew that she might well die. Her age was a complication. He wired the family: "MAMA IN HOSPITAL WITH PNEUMONIA. YOUR PRAYERS FOR HER LIFE URGENTLY NEEDED."

Andrew stayed with Jennie as much as the hospital rules allowed, praying at her bedside. To his dismay, her illness grew worse. The fever continued rising, and she became delirious, losing awareness even of Andrew. She grew too weak to cough. Her lungs filled with fluid. Andrew trembled to hear her labored breathing. At home, letters and cables from friends and family began piling up on the dining-room table.

The last week in February, a family living on a snow-covered farm just out of Des Moines received the one-cent card post-marked Los Angeles, bearing a short note scrawled with a blunt lead pencil: "I am still in the hospital very weak, but I'm going to get well. All your prayers have pulled me back. I could have touched the Pearly Gates. – Jennie." Although Jennie left the hospital in early March, she did not completely regain her old strength till summer.

Throughout 1945 and 1946 the Go-Ye Fellowship was a bee-hive of activity. Carol Jackson was sent off as the first Go-Ye missionary to Brazil. Hubert and Rachel Mitchell, following the birth of their first child, Anne Karine, left for India. Jean also returned for a second term to India. In Puerto Rico, the Rose family established the Puerto Rico Gospel Press to print Gospel tracts and Christian literature. In Los Angeles, the Go-Ye Digest, combined with another newsletter to become the Go-Ye Challenge.

For nearly twenty years now, Andrew, through his A.E. Mitchell Art Company, had been carving and manufacturing aluminum Scripture wall plaques. Sold in bookstores all over the United States, they had become a popular and treasured item for thousands of people. In 1947, he turned the manufacturing and distribution of these plaques over to the Zondervan Publishing Company, focusing his attention on a new line of plaques in foreign languages. These would be mass-produced, using inexpensive rubber molds distributed by missionaries in foreign countries. He reasoned: "If plaster can be used in such places as India for making idols, why not replace idols with the Word of God?" With the help of missionaries serving in various lands, he began carving mottoes in Spanish, Hindi, Marathi, Chinese, Aztec, Otomi, and Tarascan. In June, 1947, when Jennie and Andrew left for Mexico at the invitation of the Melvin Todds, serving in south central Mexico, their suitcases were bulging with rubber molds carved in Spanish.

In Mexico, the new plaques were an instant success. The Mexican Indians were fascinated with the process of pouring plaster of Paris into a rubber mold and pulling out perfect replicas of Scripture which they could then hang in their houses. One day when the Mitchells' car broke down near Mt. Popocatepetl, Andrew climbed with several Indian men to a mission up on the side of the mountain. At the home of an Indian convert, Andrew cleared a space in the center of the dirt floor, placed a rubber mold on a box, and began preparing a batch of plaster. Before pouring the plaster, he preached on the love of God, a love of such intensity that Jesus loved even enemies. When the plaster had hardened, he pulled out a perfect plaque bearing the inscription "God is Love" in the Indian dialect. Tremendously impressed, the Indians passed the motto admiringly from hand to hand. Before leaving, Andrew decorated it with water colors and hung it on the wall of the small house. He left the mold with a volunteer who promised to make more for whoever wanted them.

As in the Caribbean, the people in Mexico were hungry to hear, read, and possess Scripture. In another town, an elderly woman, seeing a plaque for the first time, said to her son, "Take down the images and hang this up."

In Mexico, the Mitchells also visited Jennie's sister Nellie. Since the death of her husband, George Murdock, in 1941, Nellie had taken an active involvement in the Go-Ye Fellowship. After her early experience as a missionary in the Philippines in 1905, she had been looking for another opportunity to serve. For thirty-five years she had focused upon the necessary demands of keeping a home, raising a family, and helping to manage a small upholstery business. Her husband now gone, and her two younger daughters, Josephine and Genevieve, grown and married, she had returned to previous priorities. At 72, hair silver-white, she was working at the Summer Institute of Linguistics in Mexico City, helping the Wycliffe Translators.

Named after John Wycliffe, the fourteenth century Englishman who had translated the Bible from Latin for his countrymen, and who had advocated a return to the Bible as the chief authority of Christian faith, the Wycliffe group was working among Indian tribes in Mexico, translating the Scriptures into native languages. It was slow and painstaking work. Frequently, before even a line could be translated, the group, through research taking months and sometimes years, had to compile dictionaries, structure new phonetic alphabets, and decipher the grammar of unwritten tribal languages. The importance of their work to missionaries throughout the world could not be over-emphasized.

The Mitchells met Cameron Townsend and Dr. Kenneth Pike, both Wycliffe translators, along with a number of their co-workers. The group was delighted with Andrew's plaques carved in Indian languages. They urged him to leave several molds for them to use. In return, Townsend kindly asked one of his men to take the Mitchells on an 800-mile auto trip throughout Mexico. This unexpected gesture of goodwill gave Andrew and Jennie glimpses of peoples and places they would not otherwise have seen. The trip lasted eight weeks. They hiked mountain trails and clambered through cactus and thorn bush. It was hard on Jennie, but comparatively easy for Andrew, who at age seventy, was still nimble.

Chapter 9

PULSE OF THE ORIENT

In 1945, in a general letter to the family, Jennie said of her daughter Jean: "I've come to the conclusion that she needs, most of all, a good husband, a true lover. Now where is he? Have any of you seen him around?"

Jean was returning to India for a second term, Marietta was beginning studies at the Biblical Seminary and New York University, and Esther was just completing her undergraduate education at Wheaton College in Illinois. As their letters revealed, life was pressing each to make a choice for marriage. Like every mother, Jennie wanted her girls to give their hearts to the right men.

Marriage was not a trivial decision. The girls must not be swept off their feet by a romantic infatuation that provided no true basis for marriage. Their husbands had to be loving, honest, and sensible, with courage to face the trials of life. Above all, they must hold the same spiritual views. While choosing a spouse involved judgment and good sense, the most important ingredient was faith that God would provide guidance. Jennie counseled Esther, whose frequent letters described the men she was meeting at Wheaton: "Remember, God has the right husband for you. He is to be a prince among men and going the same direction you are going."

Esther, the youngest, was the first to announce her engagement. Murray Russell, class president at Wheaton, proposed during her senior year. Helen, Esther's oldest sister, made the announcement at a garden banquet of the Go-Ye's Youth Missionary Fellowship in Hollywood. From the moment they met Murray, Jennie and Andrew were completely satisfied. A tall, personable good-natured young man, Murray was the son of missionary parents in Ethiopia. A year later, the two were married in Hollywood, with Andrew officiating. At the close of the ceremony, the couple knelt and, praying aloud, consecrated themselves to a life's work as missionaries in Ethiopia.

Since their return from Mexico, Jennie had also been receiving romantic bits of news from Jean in India:

> "A real Norwegian Viking from Tonsberg, the oldest city in Norway, a famous whaling port, is coming to join our Norwegian missionary staff here in Karwi....

Andrew with daughters Helen, Marietta, and Jean at the wedding of daughter Esther to Murray Russell, 1946.

> "I was so excited at meeting my old Indian friends that I hardly noticed the new Norwegian missionary gazing quietly at me....
>
> "The other night we walked home from a village meeting. The heavy rain had turned the roads to mud and all I had on my feet were white, American-made open sandals. Before I understood what was happening, Kaare was handing me a big overcoat, a funny looking hat, and a pair of huge rubber boots....
>
> "Often at night we sit in Indian villages preaching to the people. Kaare sits with his mandolin, playing and singing, his back against the mud wall of an Indian house and a warm, full moon lighting his face....
>
> "We finally met again in Landour at the Institute to study the language....We spend long, golden days hiking over the paths, singing, praying, and studying God's Word together. God also is walking with us, quietly making His will known to us...."

After weeks of anticipation and prayer, Jennie wrote to her older children, "I wanted to let you all know about Kaare Wilhelmsen and Jean, but I felt I must wait until Jean was absolutely sure. None of us could have planned anything so beautiful for her. I have a feeling that Mother Sadie knows and is glad." She added that the wedding was planned for early the next year, February, 1949, and that she and Andrew were going to Calcutta, India, to attend.

In the same letter, Jennie announced the budding of another romance in New York. "There is a young man in the seminary in New York who was born of missionary parents in India and is returning there. He and Marietta are enjoying a splendid friendship. We met him and like him. His name is Joseph Smith and he is something on the order of Murray, a very godly Brethren." Joe, in fact, was the son of Henry Light Smith who had established the Brethren in Christ Mission at Bihar, India, in 1913. His grandfather, Samuel R. Smith, had been a General Secretary in the Brethren in Christ Church and had founded Messiah College at Grantham, Pennsylvania in 1909.

During Christmas, while Jennie and Andrew were preparing for their first trip to the Orient, news arrived from New York that Marietta and Joe had decided to get married. The wedding was also planned for early February. On February 9, one week before Jennie and Andrew were to leave for Jean's wedding in India, Andrew officiated, together with Rev. Harry Buckwalter, Joe's stepfather, at the marriage of Marietta and Joe in Pasadena. Marietta, who had planned to go with her parents to India, postponed that trip for a short honeymoon up the California coast. "Give my wedding veil to Jean," she told Jennie. "...with all my love for her and Kaare."

It was a typical Go-Ye send-off, attended by about one hundred people. What had formerly been held at dockside was this time held in a public departure lounge at the Los Angeles International Airport. The usual speeches, singing, and prayers evoked curiosity and some amusement from other travellers in the busy lounge.

At the check-in counter, the airline clerk found Jennie and Andrew's luggage to be overweight. One suitcase had to be left behind. Whose would it be? "Mine," said Jennie. Andrew's sister, Eva, quickly emptied Jennie's large hat box. Selecting a plumed hat, which she placed on Jennie's head, she quickly repacked the hat box with the clothing Jennie would most need for her round-the-world trip. She did not forget the wedding gown which Jennie was carrying from Esther, nor the veil and headpiece from Marietta.

Hubert met his parents at the airport in Calcutta. In February, Calcutta, situated on the Hooghly River, thirty-five miles from the border of East Pakistan (now Bangladesh), sixty miles inland from the Bay of Bengal, was not quite as unbearably hot as it would be later in the summer. Still, it was hot and muggy, and the Mitchells had not walked a hundred yards before perspiration dampened their clothes.

Hubert was the International Director of Youth for Christ in Calcutta. He had arranged for Jean and Kaare's wedding to be held in the historic William Carey Baptist Church located in the old Bazaar area, a church which had for years been the center of much glowing missionary activity.

Jennie and Andrew arrived in the midst of frenzied last-minute preparations. Dull, gray candles, borrowed from the Catholic church, were being coated white with Jean's shoe polish. The cake was on order: three tiers high, each separated from the other by silver pillars, and set on a stand as high as the bride herself. Since Jennie's formal dress had been left behind at the airport in Los Angeles, a new one was ordered from an Indian tailor. The man took measurements and, copying a design from a catalog, delivered a new dress for Jennie in two days. Cost: $8.00.

The church was filled with friends of many nationalities, Indian, Chinese, Armenian, American, and English. Jean's sister-in-law, Rachel, delayed by the cars, rickshaws, trams, and immense old bulls jamming the streets, got to the wedding just in time to pin up her hair. She was dismayed to find that she had not brought hairpins. Jennie came to the rescue, "Oh, I put a lot of extra ones in my hair this morning...." and she began pulling them out. At last the organ sounded the wedding march. Mitchell nephews and nieces lighted candles and scattered flowers along the aisle. At the altar, Andrew gave a brief talk on the meaning of marriage, followed by Hubert, who spoke to the bride and groom of their duties to each other, their work, their God, their coming joys and sorrows. Reverend Corlett then led the two in pledging their vows. At the end, Andrew and Jennie stepped forward and, placing their hands on the heads of the newlyweds, blessed them. Jean had always wondered what the children of Old Testament days felt when their parents blessed them. Now she knew! A reception followed in a nearby room of the church. The next day, the family, elbowing a path through the Calcutta crowds, brought them to the railroad station, sending them off for a short honeymoon at the seaside.

Jennie and Andrew had long wanted to see Calcutta. Capital of the Indian Province of West Bengal, one of the richest provinces of India, Calcutta was a major industrial and shipping center. The world's foremost processor of jute, it employed more than a quarter of a million people in this activity alone. In addition, its factories produced machinery, electrical goods, textiles, and chemicals. Its harbor was one of the busiest in the world, with nearly twenty miles of wharves lining both banks of the Hooghly River.

Calcutta was a city of stark contrasts. While a central core existed on the European model, built in the early days of British rule, with wide streets, spacious parks, churches, hospitals, banks, theatres, and fashionable residential areas, the greater surrounding area, totaling some forty square miles, consisted of a vast and unimaginably horrible network of slums—*bustees*.

For fifty years, Calcutta's reputation had been growing as the most squalid, impoverished, disease-ridden city on earth, in which hundreds died daily of starvation, cholera, typhoid, leprosy, not to mention religious and civil violence. While a wealthy minority lived comfortably in modern, even lavish, apartments and homes, the majority of Calcutta's inhabitants lived in the most squalid conditions imaginable—makeshift lean-tos of cardboard, corrugated tin, remnants of packing cases, mud bricks—unventilated and without electricity, running water, or any sanitary facility. A vast number of people had no shelter whatsoever, except what rags could be pulled over their heads. They lived, ate, slept, and died on the street, washing in gutters, begging alms, and competing with dogs for scraps.

Beggars in Calcutta were legion. At every corner, one was accosted by people begging alms. A filthy, wretched tide of humanity, they flooded about one, men hobbling on crutches, disfigured children, women holding out emaciated babies, persons with swollen limbs and features wasted by disease, all with hands outstretched, supplicating in mournful tones for the least contribution of money or food. At the perimeter lay the totally crippled, those without arms or legs, calling over the crowd for one's attention.

The violence hovering over Calcutta was unmistakable. One felt that at any moment a mob, out of frustration, might coalesce to ransack and destroy. Fights erupted continually in the streets, in shops, on trams, in buses. Policemen, halting and directing traffic, contradicting the will of ill-tempered drivers and pedestrians, were accompanied by armed guards. Buses and cabs, which sometimes struck pedestrians on the crowded streets, were equipped with a wire mesh to protect the driver from mob retaliation.

The violence was not surprising. Calcutta was packed to a suffocating density of nearly one hundred thousand people per square mile. All neighborly respect, tolerance, or compassion, which even a modicum of physical space and privacy might have promoted, had been trampled away by the relentless crush of an impoverished humanity. The appalling poverty, which had long since destroyed all hope of betterment in the majority of people, had engendered a seething undercurrent of anger that erupted at the slightest provocation. The population consisted of antagonistic groups whose religious, racial, economic, or social characteristics made them feared or hated by their neighbors. The poor hated the wealthy; the wealthy feared the poor; the Muslims hated the Hindus, and the Hindus the Muslims; the Communists hated the industrialists; and the multifarious castes of the Indian social system provided ample excuse for anyone to despise almost anyone else.

Andrew and Jennie in India with Bishop Athanasius of the Mar Thoma Syrian Christian Church.

In August, 1947, India had attained its independence from England. The creation of Pakistan as a separate Muslim state had resulted in deep civil unrest throughout India. The slaughter between Muslims and Hindus, as the two populations departed to their respective political and geographic areas, had left nearly 4,000 dead in Calcutta alone. Two years later, the violence was continuing. On the very day the Mitchells arrived, a terrorist mob attacked six people in the street and burned them alive.

The missionaries working in Calcutta were not insulated from the city's violence. Hubert had been threatened frequently, and once, while preaching to a crowd gathered in an open space near the Old Carey Church, had been mobbed. His outdoor meetings were usually broadcast with loud speakers from within the church yard, sometimes to as many as five hundred people who gathered to listen and watch. One afternoon, as several Christian converts testified to a large gathering, a group of about twenty-five men marched through the gate and up to the platform demanding to speak with Hubert Mitchell. "You are openly opposing our religion," they told him in threatening tones. "You must stop it at once."

The charge, of course, held truth. Since the Hindus worshipped a pantheon of gods and idols, numbering, by conservative count, over three hundred million, the message of the Christian Scripture, with its strong admonition to worship only the one True God, cut deeply. The atmosphere grew tense as the leader continued to read from the Scripture quoted by a recent convert: "...sorcerers and idolaters and all liars shall have their part in the lake which burneth with fire and brimstone...."

Hearing this, the crowd, which had been following the interchange closely, sided with the band of troublemakers. Screaming and yelling, they rushed upon the missionaries. They threw down Hubert's accordion, smashed the public address equipment, shoved the speakers off the platform, and beat up the Hindu converts. Although a policeman did arrive, the angry crowd threatened him away. In the end, protected by some unwritten code, perhaps from the days of British rule, that white foreigners should not be harmed, Hubert escaped physical injury, although the incident tested his courage.

At first, Andrew and Jennie spoke only at teas and dinners among church people. Not satisfied with this, and despite Hubert's harrowing experiences, they began speaking in the outdoor meetings. It felt good. "Just like Bible days as I stood there speaking to the multitude," Jennie exulted.

One afternoon, during an outdoor meeting, a new convert warned the missionaries that a Hindu group was planning to stone the evangelists. Standing at the center of the gathering crowd, the evangelists, despite the warning, continued with the meeting. Again, the service involved several new Indian converts, who took turns speaking to the crowd. Presently, a Hindu "holy man" appeared at the edge of the circle of onlookers. Barefoot and barechested, wearing only a loin cloth, with beads looped about his neck, a walking stick in one hand, his long black hair glistening with oil, face painted with grease, and dark skin powdered white with ashes, he stopped opposite each of the Indian speakers and glared fiercely into each man's face as he spoke. The effect was powerful. One convert, intimidated by this wild apparition of magic and superstition, choked off his words and shrank back. The restive crowd, ever alert to the slightest conflict, immediately focused upon this interesting and potentially violent development.

Jennie, realizing that an evil influence was seeking to penetrate and destroy the meeting, immediately moved to counter it. Stepping towards the man, she focused her gaze upon him. As he moved around the circle, she followed opposite, staring into his eyes. Her manner was not antagonistic, but calm and determined, projecting an inner power that no one could mistake. Purposely, she placed herself between the man and the new converts. Inwardly, she was trembling; the urgent prayer in her heart was so deep it lacked even voice.

Abruptly, with a scowl, the man turned and disappeared into the crowd, swallowed up again in the cauldron of humanity that was India. With his departure, the mood of violence quickly dissipated, and the meeting continued to its peaceful and uplifting conclusion. Jennie later remarked, "More than anything, it proved that the weapons of our warfare are spiritual and not physical."

For decades, western missionaries had encountered bizarre and incredible religious practices. Holy men, hoping to gain religious "merit" and salvation, inflicted upon themselves the most bizarre and repulsive forms of abuse. They would lie down upon thorny cactus or beds of nails, pierce their tongues with spikes, sit or stand with arms continuously extended above their heads, or with a leg over an opposite shoulder—until, over the years, the muscles withered and the joints calcified. Some vowed never to lie down. Still others buried themselves in the ground with only their heads showing. Remaining thus, they were practically eaten alive by worms.

Against such centuries-old beliefs and practices, Andrew and Jennie prayed and preached. In letters home, she told the Go-Ye, "The greatest job for India is PRAYER. You will pray, won't you, that Jesus will keep our hearts flooded with His love and that we may give out the Word in power and also with great warmth!"

Jennie's heart went out to the multitudes of beggars that approached them from every direction, some with hands cut off, some blind, others with limbs terribly swollen, children purposely maimed at birth to increase their earnings as beggars, all ragged and terribly dirty. She wrote to the Go-Ye: "....We feel absolutely no strangeness in India. My heart does exceedingly yearn over this city. It is as if these were our people and we had always lived here....I cannot bear to act like a stone wall as the beggars come asking for

Plaque used in India with Hindi words meaning "Victory in Jesus."

alms....How I thank the dear Lord Jesus that the dirt does not bother me the least little bit. The eyes of the people...always attract my attention."

Realizing that any physical solution to this magnitude of human suffering was beyond her, Jennie turned instead to spiritual remedies. Her "shouting papers" of earlier years became in Calcutta, "Hallelujah Papers." Collecting several thousand annas, an Indian coin worth about two cents in American money, Jennie inserted a coin in a small Scripture card which read, in Hindi, "Bolo, Hallelujah," a simple praise to God. On the streets she encouraged those receiving them to repeat the words of praise to God in Hindi. Her faith was that somehow, in some way, God would magnify her gift.

Casting about for a way to broadcast the Christian message, Jennie conceived a project to place a neon sign high on top of the William Carey Church proclaiming, "Jesus Saves," which could be seen at night over all the Bazaar area. At meetings and fund-raisers, Jennie used a special offering plate to collect the money for this...a highly polished, black, pointed-toe dress shoe once belonging to the Evangelist, Billy Sunday. From 1900 to 1930, Billy Sunday had been one of America's most popular evangelists. A converted baseball player, he had brought his athletic energy to the tent revival platform. He was noted for his vigorous preaching against sin, religious hypocrisy, and "booze." Tens of thousands of penitents had marched down his "sawdust trail" to the altar. "Ma Sunday" had given Jennie the shoe, saying that Billy would have been glad to know that his shoe continued to help in spreading the Gospel around the world.

Leaving Calcutta, Andrew and Jennie travelled to Ceylon, Bombay, and Lucknow, eventually ending up in Banda, United Province, for a visit with the Wilhelmsens. The couple's little house, which had cow-dung and lime plaster floors, and double-wide front doors opening onto the street, was located in a very primitive and filthy area, bounded by a drain ditch on one side and the city dump on the other. The area was predominantly Hindu, with some Muslims. From the roof of the house could be seen at least twenty mosques and Hindu temples. The couple's living room was their meeting place for Gospel services, and was often filled with curious listeners.

Jennie accompanied Jean to visit Muslim women, secluded, as custom required, in *purdahs*, away from the sight of non-family men and other strangers. It was in these private services that Jennie opened her heart. Her tears, smiles, and tender voice spoke just as clearly to the women as the interpreter's words.

The Wilhelmsens' preaching of the Gospel had begun to make an impact in the town, and was causing some unrest. The missionaries were confronted in the streets, taunted, and sometimes threatened with stones. Undismayed by this violence, Andrew and Jennie one day took off their shoes and waded across the very mucky and sewage-filled ditch next to the house, heading into a thick cluster of villagers' shacks, their hands filled with "Hallelujah" cards. Though she watched them anxiously, Jean was unwilling to discourage their effort to reach the people. Several hours later, they returned the same way, in exuberant spirits, carrying fruit, vegetables, and coconuts. "Heathen India just opened its heart to a couple of old messengers of God's Word from America," Jennie exclaimed. From that time on, the cards were passed out wherever they went. Jean's most vivid memory was of Jennie passing out Hallelujah cards, each holding in a slot a one-anna piece.

During the ten-day festival of Muharram, held to celebrate the start of the Muslim New Year, the visitors were treated to a spectacle so fantastic it surpassed anything they had seen so far – "fire-walking." For eight days, young male candidates trained by fasting, dancing, and marching around their cultic standards to the rhythmic beating of drums. On the eighth day, about two hundred pits were dug throughout the city, filled with wood, and set afire. In the late evening, when the fires were burning red hot, the fanatical Muslim devotees, some of them children, began leaping barefooted into the flames. Most scampered, jumped, or hopped quickly through the coals, but one old priest waded into the fire and began throwing the live coals over his head as if bathing in water. The heat was so intense that onlookers had to stay well back to avoid singeing their clothing. Although none of the fire-walkers wore any protective garments, afterward their skin showed no trace of burns or injury.

From the fire pits, the fire-walkers danced through the streets to the river where they made offerings. Following this, they fell on their faces as though dead. After a few moments they awakened as if from a trance, returning to the everyday world where they joked, talked, and smoked with the onlookers, as if nothing out of the ordinary had happened.

Many educated Muslims looked on this spectacle with disgust, while the Hindus, with an eye for profit, opened stalls selling sweets and toys. Standing in the bright glow of the fires, which appeared like so many furnaces of hell, Andrew and Jennie watched dumbfounded, unable to say or do anything. Presently, in a fit of agitation, Andrew, peeling off his coat, proclaimed loudly, "If they can do this in Satan's power, then I must not sit on the sidelines watching."

In a letter to the family, Jean described her father: "I believe that Daddy would have jumped into the fire in the Name of the Lord, had we not restrained him."

As the summer came upon India, the heat and humidity became intolerable. Jennie and Andrew travelled with Jean and Kaare to Landour, in the cooler foothills of the Himalayas in Northern India where Kaare was beginning his second year of Hindi study. In Landour, Jennie felt the need to assemble the family in spirit, if not in the flesh. She took a roll call by letter. The Mitchell children were spread to the far corners of the world. By Christmas, 1949, communist forces under Mao Tse-tung had taken China. David and Helen Morken and their six children, along with other missionaries, were under house arrest at the China Inland Mission Compound in Shanghai, awaiting expulsion; Joe and Marietta were preparing for their first missionary assignment to India under the Brethren in Christ Church; Murray and Esther Russell had volunteered for Ethiopia, where Murray's parents had pioneered in the early part of the century; Bryant and Lola Mitchell were at the Open Bible College in Des Moines, Iowa, training young missionary couples for work abroad. Using a carboned air letter, Jennie wrote to each: "My Dear Children, please put a great deal in between these lines of love and understanding extended to you all....If you love me, be careful of one another. Life is so short, death is so certain. We need each other so desperately."

Andrew and Jennie did not experience much culture shock. Both moved easily in alien countries, seldom threatened or frightened, and always quite at home. Andrew climbed briskly on the steep mountain trails, walking stick in hand, wearing a grey felt hat, coat and tie, and clean white shirt. His autoharp was always ready. He maintained the same natural, unassuming self-dignity whether walking in sand, mud, over rocks, or even through excrement. Jennie, with affable good-nature, tackled the steepest mountain path wearing her usual adornments, neck beads, artificial shoulder corsage, and even, sometimes, a fancy plumed hat.

Like Marietta in the Caribbean, Jean also was struck by the godly spirit of love with which her parents regarded the family of man. However dirty or dingy a person might appear, the two always looked for what was beautiful. The lowly, cowherding Indian peasant women might, in their poverty, be drab, but Jennie and Andrew saw only their childlike innocence, their bright eyes and smiles, their white teeth, the colorful jewelry they wore on ear, nose, arms, and ankles.

Marietta Mitchell Smith with Wanjiku, a Kikuyu lawyer from Kenya, whom she led to Christ while in India.

As for their own children, Jennie and Andrew continued to make each feel special, building up self-esteem, giving a sense of unique mission and purpose before God. They had travelled to these remote areas of the earth to encourage them, to renew them with a sense of triumph and victory.

Their love was reinforced at times with thoughtful and practical action. Hearing that Leoda, the sister of their new son-in-law, Joseph Smith, was arriving in Bihar in North India as a first-time missionary with her husband Allen Buckwalter, Jennie and Andrew travelled by train halfway across India to the Brethren in Christ Mission to prepare the house for them. "Surprise!

Surprise! Welcome to Bihar!" shouted Jennie as she embraced the young couple. "We just wanted to check out where you would be locating." In fact, Jennie's "checkouts" were her method of assessing the spiritual or matrimonial health of new members of the ever-expanding Mitchell family. Fortunately, her inquiries were neither nosey nor offensive, but always in a spirit that was both generous and uplifting.

Bidding farewell to India, Andrew and Jennie travelled to Borneo before returning to America. With missionary Bob Williams, they journeyed by river launch up the broad Kapuas River to visit Go-Ye missionaries serving in Dyak villages. The river stretched from the western seaport of Pontianak some five hundred miles inland through dense tropical rain forest. It was the first real "jungle" that Jennie and Andrew had seen— crocodiles, exotic birds, orangutans. Grass-roofed huts, built upon stilts, crowded close upon the river's edge. Jennie was one of the first Western woman that many had ever seen. Sometimes they crowded close upon her, cautiously reaching out to touch her hand, arms, or hair.

Uprisings were not uncommon, and they travelled with faith in God's protection. However, the slight misfortune they experienced came not from the wilderness, but from centers of power far away. One evening, they heard by radio that the Indonesian money, for which they had exchanged their American dollars, had been devalued by an overwhelming fifty percent. In less than an hour, half of their meager travel funds were gone. In a letter to the Go-Ye, they commented: "What continued lessons we have of the transitory status the things of this life possess! How easily our confidence and trust wrap around these things instead of around Him who liveth and abideth forever."

Andrew undertook to create new mottoes in the Indonesian language. Using terms from the local vocabularies, he carved molds proclaiming, "Jesus never Fails!" and "God is Able!" As elsewhere, they met with astounding success. Exulting, he wrote to the Go-Ye, "These Scripture mottoes are replacing the charms and idols of former days. Age-old roots of superstition and bondage are being pulled up and withered by the light of the Gospel."

The wild jungles of Borneo had lessons to teach. Seeing the giant Topang trees smothered by a tangle of parasitic vines, Jennie was moved to write:

> "Never had we seen such a tangle of vine and tree. So covered with parasites were these great giants of the forest that it was difficult to decide which was the original trunk.
>
> "These creepers simply wriggle their way up the trees exactly like a serpent. It is impossible to pull them off without tearing the bark because thousands of tiny claws have embedded themselves in the tree.

"These parasites sap the very life out of the tree, and here and there you see the remains – great, gaunt skeletons standing against the blue sky, every leaf gone; all smaller branches gone, and the creepers now gone also. The tree is dead, wrecked....a monument to the work of destroyers....the smaller has killed the mightier.

"Yes, there are men, noble men, godly men made in the image of the Creator for His glory, but who are also smothered, defeated, wrecked, arms hanging helpless.

"How? Satan, the tormentor, the oppressor and depressor, has used every device to sap the strength....This archenemy knows the weak spot in every life, and it is there he puts in his tentacles – oppressions, imaginations, disappointments, physical weaknesses, moral weaknesses, discouragements – to sap the life, both physical and spiritual.

"I know another stately tree, the Cedar of Lebanon, that, instead of nourishing parasites, kills them. The life within is so strong and robust that, instead of feeding the parasites, it chokes them off.

"HE THAT IS WITHIN YOU IS GREATER THAN HE THAT IS IN THE WORLD." (I John 4:4b)

"Satan is not almighty. He was defeated at Calvary. All believers are given power over him. Like the Cedars of Lebanon, believers may dismiss all parasites of every description.

"RESIST THE DEVIL, AND HE WILL FLEE FROM YOU." (James 4:7)

During this visit to the Dyak tribes in the jungles along the tributaries of the Kapuas River, the Mitchells witnessed both miracles and tragedy. In one village, they met a chief who had been recently converted, after a girl in his tribe was miraculously cleansed of leprosy. The visiting missionaries could not mistake his devotion to the Lord that had been revealed.

However, while Jennie and Andrew were visiting John and Frances Toliver, missionaries at a small Dyak village, the Tolivers' two-year-old boy, David, fell unnoticed into the murky river. A frantic search for the child by tribesmen scouring the river in canoes yielded nothing. Finally, the parents acknowledged the terrible conclusion that a crocodile must have taken the child to a watery grave. Their grief and despair were terrible to witness. The Mitchells' hearts melted in compassion. The tragedy struck doubly hard because the couple was alone in a foreign land, among strange peoples, far from family and friends.

Having glimpsed missionaries pioneering for God in the Orient, the Mitchells were determined more than ever to press forward to fulfill the challenge of world evangelism for the Go-Ye Fellowship.

Chapter 10

FRONT LINE JAPAN

During Christmas, 1950, an official envelope printed in goldenrod and black arrived at 1307 Waterloo, mixed among the many Christmas letters. Robert Cook, President of Youth for Christ International, was inviting Andrew to Japan to help prepare for the Youth for Christ Congress to be held in Tokyo in 1953. The work would involve street evangelizing and organizing Japanese youth. Andrew need not stay two years, but whatever time he could spend would be appreciated. He would be working closely with David Morken, Director of Youth for Christ in Tokyo, Phil Rounds of the Open Bible Missions in Japan, and Sam Wolgemuth, Overseas Director of Youth for Christ in the United States.

For Andrew, it was an opportunity to minister in street evangelism with his son-in-law, David Morken. Following their expulsion from China, where they had been under house arrest by the Communists for a year and a half, the Morkens had joined Youth for Christ in Japan. Neither Jennie nor Andrew had seen them for over two years.

In Japan Andrew could preach against the tide of Communism which was then flooding over the Orient. In an article in the Hollywood *Citizen-News*, entitled "GOING TO JAPAN, MINISTER, 74, WARS ON REDS," Andrew said, "I have no illusions about the nature of my work. I consider the Japanese people a bulwark against the spread of Communism in the Far East. I shall do everything in my power to help them turn their backs on the master of the Kremlin, and look to the Almighty for their survival. The only way to conquer Communism is to offer these misguided individuals something better – the Word of God."

In March, 1951, the Morkens greeted Andrew at the Tokyo airport. It was a joyous reunion, and the only regret was that Jennie had not come too. "I see you brought everything," said Helen, eyeing her father's 50-year-old autoharp, and his battered aluminum suitcase filled with his artist's supplies of chalk, rubber motto molds, Bible, and writing materials.

Tokyo was a sprawling city of nearly five million people. Although the war had devastated large residential and commercial areas of Tokyo, the city was now largely rebuilt. Outside the central commercial district, suburbs of one and two-storied houses, densely packed along narrow twisting lanes, stretched for miles. A dusty brown haze of industrial smoke was already beginning to blanket the city. Despite pockets of poverty, Tokyo exhibited a vitality and prosperity that surprised foreign visitors. Shops were filled with merchandise, and street traffic was busy. The dread and weariness of the war years was gone.

The American army which had occupied Japan under General MacArthur, now comprised the bulk of a UN force fighting the Communists in Korea. Japan was the staging area for that war. American servicemen could be seen on the streets of every major city in the country.

During the long summer evenings, Andrew joined David and the Youth for Christ teams on the busy Tokyo streets, preaching the Gospel message. David's rich voice attracted large crowds—a colorful mix of businessmen, laborers, Japanese women in kimonos, curious children, and American servicemen. Andrew, his quick hand flashing over art paper attached to an easel, illustrated David's subject. Each stroke of color brought the topic nearer to life. With David at the microphone and Andrew sketching, the crowds both heard and saw the Bible story.

As the Y.F.C. meetings in Tokyo progressed, it became clear that if the Congress were to be large and truly representative, they would have to reach out beyond Tokyo to other Japanese cities and villages. It was decided that Gospel teams would fan out through Japan holding Bible and prayer services in homes and co-operating Christian churches. Andrew immediately thought of Jennie, who could be the other half of his team. David and Helen enthusiastically agreed. As her letters indicated, she was lonely traveling to and from radio broadcasts and meetings without Andrew. It was settled. Andrew sent a telegram, and within a week they were welcoming Jennie to Japan.

"Isn't this jolly!" she exclaimed, embracing Andrew and her children, excited and enthusiastic at preaching the Gospel to a new people.

One of their first activities was officiating at the opening of the new Open Bible Mission in Sumida, pastored by Jacob Collins. It was one of several churches started by this group in Japan, and nothing was more inspiring to Jennie and Andrew than a new church.

The Mitchells' itinerary extended south from Tokyo to Kyoto, Ayabe, Hiroshima, and Nagasaki and Sasebo on the Island of Kyushu. Their group included three interpreters, two young men and a woman. Jennie had brought along her list of notables, prominent Christian men and women she had met around the world, Baptist, Lutheran, Mennonite, Presbyterian, and Pentecostal. The Christian evangelistic community was small, and its members well known to each other despite their varying denominations. The mention of a name or two frequently opened doors and hearts.

Outside Tokyo, the Mitchells discovered a Japan quite different from the sprawling capital city: a strikingly beautiful island nation of misty mountains, inland seas and bays, thatched villages, rice fields, and scenic ocean vistas. The Japanese farmers, villagers, and fishermen lived a frugal existence, simple and close to nature. A delicate, clean, almost fastidious people, they had a deep aesthetic appreciation of nature.

The indigenous religion of Japan was Shintoism, a 1500 year old animistic cult that worshipped indwelling spirits or divinities, called *kami*. A kami could be any animate or inanimate object that invoked feelings of awe or reverence – a bird, a fish, a rock, a mountain, a forest, or a river. They could be good or bad, gods or demons. In addition, Shintoism provided a creation myth that not only explained the origins of Japan, but, before the War, had helped legitimize the government, particularly the Emperor's claim to divinity.

After the war, in answer to MacArthur's call for "Bibles to Japan," Christian missionaries had flooded into the country, establishing churches in many cities. Wherever they went now, the Mitchells were greeted by a missionary or Japanese Christian pastor who arranged their lodging and organized their speaking engagements.

Andrew and Jennie's first service was in Ayabe, the headquarters for the Omoto sect of Shintoism, whose members believed they were the true foundation of all religions. The giant Shinto shrine in Ayabe could hold nearly 5,000 worshippers. Holding the fort for the Lord in Ayabe was Pastor Taku Harada, a Bible Baptist trained in New York. At 60, he had been twenty years in Ayabe. A dedicated and enthusiastic man, Pastor Harada had arranged the Mitchells' lodging and meals, and scheduled several speaking engagements. At the station he bowed low in welcome to them.

The first meeting at the church went well. As the servicc progressed, it was apparent that the audience was moved by the sincerity and dedication of this elderly couple who had journeyed thousands of miles to speak to them. When Andrew invited the listeners to make a decision for Christ, about twenty-five people came forward out of the fifty or sixty present. Pastor Harada was overjoyed.

One afternoon, several days after their arrival in Ayabe, Jennie left the house alone to walk around the city. However, without an interpreter, meeting people was difficult. Finally she met an attractive Japanese girl who spoke English. "Would you help me?" Jennie asked. "I want to meet people in your town, only I can't say a thing in Japanese. Would you talk for me to the people?" The girl was delighted and eagerly agreed to accompany her the next day. "Bless your heart, child," Jennie said. "Then please come in the morning and we'll go out."

Early the next morning the girl came to the house where the Mitchells were staying. With raincoats and umbrellas, the two started out in the light rain. They had not gone far when they encountered a woman in a narrow alley.

Dressed in a checkered kimono, the woman hurried along in short mincing steps, her wooden shoes clattering on the stones. She walked with her head down and seemed pre-occupied. In one hand she carried a small package, in the other a paper umbrella. As she neared, Jennie stopped and smiled. Blocked in the narrow lane, the woman stopped and eyed the strangely attired, white-haired Westerner.

The interpreter greeted the woman in Japanese, hastily explaining who Jennie was and where she was from. Smiling uncertainly, the woman listened and bowed politely, eyes downcast.

Jennie said, "Tell her that I am so happy to visit her beautiful town and to meet her." Again, the woman smiled and bowed politely.

"Tell her that I am actually here for someone else, who cannot come in person, but who wants very much to meet her and to know her." Again the girl translated. The woman glanced curiously at Jennie.

"Tell her," said Jennie, "that His name is Jesus and that He is the Son of God, and that He has sent me to offer His love and forgiveness to her."

The girl showed surprise at this, almost embarrassment, but nevertheless made the translation.

The woman murmured and appeared disconcerted. They thought she did not understand, so the girl repeated the words. For a moment, the woman stood silent, regarding them with uncertain eyes. Presently, her bland, polite smile of inattention vanished. Her mouth dropped and her face wrinkled into a tight, painful expression. Huge tears filled her eyes. Dropping her package and umbrella, she put her hand to her mouth, and before Jennie or the girl could do anything, collapsed back against the wall of a house.

"Good Heavens!" cried Jennie, rushing forward, but not before the woman sagged to her knees on the pavement, wailing and crying pitifully. The two knelt beside her. After some minutes she finally answered their anxious queries, speaking haltingly, her face turned down and away.

As she listened, the young girl muttered several low exclamations of surprise, casting astonished looks at Jennie. When at last she turned to translate, her expression showed awe and disbelief. She did not speak directly, but scrambled back to kneel on the hard wet paving stones, head bowed low to the ground.

"What on earth...?" said Jennie. "Raise up, child....What did she say?"

"She say..." her voice dropped almost to a whisper, so that Jennie had to lean forward on hands and knees to catch the words, "...this morning she on way to kill self...because not happy."

And then Jennie was crying, too, sitting on the wet street and embracing with both arms the little woman in the checkered kimono. The two might have been sisters, had not the one been Caucasian and the other Oriental. Tears mixing with rain on her cheeks, Jennie told her of the love of God and prayed that she would commit her life, not to death, but to the Lord.

The Mitchells remained in Ayabe one week. When they left, Pastor Harada was so much encouraged that he clung to them at the station, unwilling to let them go, and wept as he followed their train down the track.

In many towns, the Mitchells held three or four meetings a day—home prayer meetings, open-air meetings, meetings in the market, and at schools. They sought every opportunity to fulfill Christ's admonition: "Preach the Gospel to every creature." In Yokosuka, a naval base near Yokohama, the team held an open-air meeting attended by American sailors and Japanese workmen. While Jennie talked, Andrew drew on paper tacked to an old wooden door. After the meeting, the team wandered in the streets near the base, a seedy district of bars, brothels, and shops filled with black-market goods, catering to U.S. Naval personnel.

The Mitchells had heard that this city alone had over 10,000 registered prostitutes, and they believed it. Women, their faces smeared brightly with makeup and their clothes revealing as much as they concealed, loitered in doorways and leaned from windows. They called to the passersby, mostly sailors. During the extreme poverty following the war, many families sent their daughters out to earn money for food. Servicemen called them "bread and butter girls." Tears came to Jennie's eyes as she saw the lost innocence behind their alluring smiles. Some, no older than 13 or 14, might have been her own daughters. From their side, the women regarded the Mitchells curiously, some with amusement. One or two glanced solicitously at Andrew. Presently, the Mitchells came upon a line of men waiting outside a brothel.

"You pray for me," said Jennie. "I'm going to talk with those boys."

While the other team members watched, Jennie and Andrew approached the line of men, most of whom were smoking, some of whom were drunk. While Andrew stood by, Jennie talked with the men.

"I'm Mrs. Mitchell," she said. "When I saw you standing here, I felt strongly that I should speak a word to you for Jesus. I know that you're lonely, being away from home. Perhaps you're afraid. But, don't you think this is beneath you? Remember your wives and mothers waiting for you at home. They wouldn't like to see you here. I'm sure if they were here, you wouldn't be doing this. Believe me when I say that God has something better for you than this....Turn away from this."

The men were respectful. After all, she might have been their own mother. However, they remained passively in line, ignoring her as best they could. Only one young man stepped out of the line and walked away, ignoring two companions who called after him. Others slipped through the door as their turn came. Before disappearing into the lurid glow inside, several cast wry glances back at those who stood listening to Jennie. For about fifteen minutes, she continued talking, moving from one man to another down the line, usually holding their hand or arm while she spoke. Finally, she quit and, taking Andrew by the arm, walked away.

"It's hard, so hard," she said. "They are alone and afraid, and the temptation is so great."

Perhaps the most difficult visits were those to Hiroshima and Nagasaki. In both cities, the horror of the atomic bomb attack was still much in evidence. How does one preach to people who have experienced such devastation? In Nagasaki, Andrew chose for his subject the message, "Look and Live." As the Israelites crossing the desert had been saved from death by looking upon the brazen serpent held up by Moses, the Japanese people must look to the uplifted Christ for salvation. In the small Presbyterian chapel, about twenty-five people stood, confessed their sin, and prayed for salvation.

Going to and from meetings, the Mitchells often got wet from the rain, their clothing remaining damp for the rest of the day. In addition, the all-night train rides, sitting upright in a chair car, did not allow them much rest. Arriving one rainy night at the door of a Christian home at which they had been told to expect lodging, they found the house empty and locked. A Japanese neighbor kindly took Jennie in while Andrew went with the police to find someone to give them shelter. An Episcopalian missionary finally located a family who was willing to put them up. By the time he returned for Jennie, Andrew was wet to the skin and shivering with cold. The next evening people came for a prayer and Bible study service, which lasted until midnight. Andrew spent the night coughing and blowing his nose.

Finding the summer heat more difficult to bear than the winter cold, the Japanese had built their houses open to the outdoors on all sides. The walls, consisting of thin partitions made of wood and rice paper, slid aside on wooden grooves to admit cooling breezes. The floors were made of smooth, shiny, straw matting upon which the family took its meals and slept. Shoes were removed at the door. Despite winter temperatures which brought snow in most parts of the country, heating was not provided except for an occasional charcoal brazier. His circulation not what it had been in earlier years, Andrew had trouble keeping warm on the cold floors in the unheated rooms.

The small "Bless cards" and mottoes which the Mitchells had used so effectively in the Caribbean were likewise distributed. In every town Jennie attempted to organize a "Bless club," a group – usually women – who sought to bless others by giving testimony, praying, witnessing, preaching the Gospel, or by performing some kind action.

Even while they were busy touring Japan, the Mitchells managed to keep their "other bases" covered. Jennie carried along her German *Uher* tape recorder with which she prepared radio tapes to send to the United States. "What a heavy thing this is to carry about!" she exclaimed to Andrew. "Remind me to get a lighter one the next time we go somewhere."

In Shimonoseki, a town on the Sea of Japan just across from Korea, the Mitchells were invited to preach in a Korean church. Etifisan, one of their interpreters, a Korean who had been educated in Japan and spoke both languages fluently, arranged the visit. The small church was packed to overflowing, the women in their long flowing skirts and canoe-shaped shoes, the stalwart Korean men standing sternly straight and respectful.

Andrew gave the Bible lesson. At the end, sensing a heightened spiritual air permeating the congregation, he whispered to Jennie, "I do not believe this meeting ought to stop now." Jennie agreed. To the congregation Andrew announced, "If there is anyone here who has any trouble, let him or her come to the front and we will pray with them."

At first the people were silent. The Mitchells waited. Presently, the Korean pastor's wife stepped forward with a woman, saying, "This woman is troubled with evil spirits. In ignorance, she has worshipped the devil and is now in his power. She has walked about forty miles to get here."

Although Jesus had given His disciples the power and authority to cast out demons, it was a power contingent upon spiritual courage and faith. When the disciples had complained they were not able to rid a man of unclean spirits, Jesus had told them the act required fasting and prayer. The Mitchells had never before attempted to cast out demons. They knew only that Satan held no power over anyone, unless that person surrendered to him, which this woman had apparently done. Jennie's heart went out to her. Taking her by the hand, Jennie boldly declared, "Today, this woman shall be delivered."

To her astonishment, the woman, who was smaller than Jennie, with dark hair twisted high on her head, wrenched her hand away. Snarling hatefully, she cursed and retreated across the room, glaring at Jennie with red and baleful eyes. The Mitchells exchanged glances. The sudden commotion electrified the congregation, several people jumping to their feet to get a better view.

"In countless ways the devil seeks to rob people of life, entangling them until all self-control is lost," Jennie said to the church. "But we have a God greater than all of this, who wants this precious woman free." Turning to the woman, Jennie said, "Satan, if you are in this body, demonstrate yourself now!" As if knocked from her feet, the woman fell to the floor and began writhing about. Twisting onto her back, she slithered across the front of the church like a serpent, as if controlled by an unseen presence. The next instant she was on her feet and running for the door.

"No!" shouted Jennie. "Lock the door!"

Several stout Korean men rushed for the door, slamming and locking it shut.

"Dear lady, hear me," Jennie said, addressing the woman, this behavior is Satan's, not yours. You must renounce it before our prayers will be answered."

For answer, the woman ran at Jennie and would have struck her had not several men grabbed her. She screamed, frothed at the mouth, and spat at the Mitchells.

Neither Andrew or Jennie knew precisely what to do. Certainly, they had no time for fasting. They had only prayer, singing, and the reading of Scripture. An intuition told them they must proceed methodically. First, the environment had to be purified by uplifting each heart toward God through hymns and music. Second, their faith had to be empowered through the reading of Scripture. Each had to be reminded of the authority Jesus had given them. Finally, the congregation must express unity and coherence, addressing God in prayer together.

Immediately, Andrew began leading the congregation in singing hymns, followed by reading of the Scriptures. The first verse testified to the reality of devilish powers:

> "Be sober, be vigilant; because your adversary the devil, as a roaring lion, walketh about, seeking whom he may devour: whom resist steadfast in the faith...." (I Peter 5:8-9)

This was followed by Christ's empowerment of his disciples:

> "...Heal the sick, cleanse the lepers, raise the dead, cast out devils: freely ye have received, freely give." (Matthew 10:8)

For believers, Christ had given the following prescription:

> "Wherefore take unto you the whole armor of God, that ye may be able to withstand in the evil day...the helmet of salvation, and the sword of the Spirit, which is the word of God: Praying always with all prayer and supplication in the Spirit, and watching thereunto with all perseverance and supplication for all saints." (Ephesians 6:11-18)

For Jesus had promised:

> "...Verily, verily I say unto you, Whatsoever ye shall ask the Father in my name, He will give it you." (John 16:23)

Finally came the Scripture that validated it, the living, eternal reality of Christ:

> "Jesus Christ the same yesterday, and today, and forever." (Hebrews 13:8)

For two-and-a-half hours, the congregation, led by Jennie and Andrew, labored in song, prayer, and the reading of the Scriptures. Gradually, the woman stopped thrashing about and agreed to sit in a chair. Encouraged, Jennie said, "Perhaps she wants a drink of water." However, when the pastor's wife brought a cup, the woman slapped it violently away.

"We have done what we can," Andrew sighed, "perhaps we should leave her alone."

"Not yet," said Jennie. "She must make the effort to renounce it herself, and so far she hasn't done that."

"Yes, but what...?"

"She must speak the name of Jesus – at least that."

"Good idea!" Andrew said.

Etifisan translated. For the first time, the woman became genuinely attentive and obedient. The congregation strained forward, watching in weary but eager silence.

"Jesus," the woman said softly in English. "Jesus," she repeated more loudly. "..*Jesus*!"

The woman grew calm. Her body, which had been held rigid and tense for hours, twitching and convulsing, relaxed and slumped forward. Her face, so long clouded with a dark, hateful malevolence, cleared. Her eyes grew peaceful. Glancing around, she appeared almost to awaken.

Applause, shouts, and exclamations of wonder came from the congregation.

"Hallelujah" and "Amen," sighed Andrew and Jennie.

The woman was given nourishment and remained for the evening services. Later, approaching Andrew, she said through an interpreter, "I'm so sorry I acted the way I did. I heard all you said, but I had no control over myself."

The Korean pastor said to the Mitchells, "All of us have learned a power in prayer that we had not known before."

For her parting word to the people, Jennie related the story of the woman who, in her faith, had pressed through the crowd to touch Christ's garment to be healed. "Faith is our tie with God," she said.

The next morning at six, the pastor gathered his family for a prayer meeting, together with Jennie and Andrew and a number of the congregation. As she knelt among the people, Jennie was startled to feel several ladies touching her dress ever so gently. Turning to them, she said, "Can you feel Him? Jesus is here among us, even as we pray."

Much later, the Mitchells heard that a church had been established in the woman's town, and that she was telling everybody of the power in the name of Jesus.

After three months, the Mitchells returned to Tokyo. They had visited over 50 cities, met over a hundred Christian pastors and missionaries, and preached to thousands of people. It had been a whirlwind journey which had severely tested their physical endurance. At ages 75 (Andrew) and 67 (Jennie), they sometimes had trouble keeping up with the younger Y.F.C. leaders. However, they had come through it, tired, but otherwise in good health.

The overwhelming majority of their encounters had been positive. Only here and there had they met resistance. In some places, rowdies had disturbed meetings with shouts, taunts, or the shaking of fists. All of this was to be expected. Given an assignment for the Lord, the Mitchells did not count the cost or risk.

During their absence from home, three sets of children had departed to foreign assignments: Jean and Kaare Wilhelmsen to Trinidad, Marietta and Joe Smith to India, and Murray and Esther Russell to Ethiopia. Before returning to Los Angeles, Andrew and Jennie planned to visit Go-Ye missionaries in Hong Kong, Taiwan, and Borneo. To this agenda they included short stopovers in India and Ethiopia. It was September. They hoped to arrive in Ethiopia in time to celebrate Christmas with their children.

Chapter 11

AFRICAN CRUCIBLE

Jennie's youngest daughter, Esther Russell, stood at her kitchen table in Gore, in the province of Ilibabur in western Ethiopia, near the Sudanese border, kneading dough. She had gotten up early to make bread before Jennie and Andrew rose for breakfast. They had arrived ten days before on their way home from Japan. Murray had met them in Addis Ababa, where they spent a short time with his parents before driving on to Gore to celebrate Christmas with her and the children. Esther had hugged and clung to Jennie. She had never been happier to see anyone. Impulsively, she resolved at the first opportunity to tell her everything.

It was almost too much for her. Too much! Thinking back now, she could not imagine what she had expected of missionary life! She thought she knew, because all her family were either missionaries themselves or involved in training and sending them. Murray himself was the son of a missionary. Yes, she was in it up to her neck all right.

But the reality was different than she ever imagined it would be during those months as the wife of a student at the Theological Seminary in Pittsburgh. Had she really thought hers was to be a life of spreading the Word to a noble but fallen people, eager to pursue God if only shown the Way?

Murray had told her about the culture, history, and people of Ethiopia. A rugged country, Ethiopia had both 15,000 foot mountains and deserts below sea level. It was the source of the Blue Nile. Its recorded history stretched back 3,000 years. The Hebrews of Solomon's day called the land "Cush," meaning "swarthy faced." Emperor Haile Selassie called himself the "King of Kings" and claimed direct descent from Solomon and the Queen of Sheba. Ethiopia's Coptic Church was among the oldest churches in Christendom, illustrating worship as it may have been in Christ's time. The country had never been conquered or colonized, except for a brief occupation by the Italians during World War II.

Up to the moment they had landed, Esther had trembled with excitement and anticipation. From the air, the countryside, after the seasonal rains, appeared like a picture postcard, clean and fresh, white houses dotting green, rolling hills, with stands of eucalyptus trees swaying softly in the wind. The horse and ox-carts, and the laborers carrying bundles on their heads, added quaintness. But then, when they finally stepped among the village people, it all became different, very different.

Murray's parents met them in Addis Ababa, the capital city. Fred Russell was well-known to Ethiopian government officials, having lived in Ethiopia since 1921, serving as an agricultural missionary. His first assignment was to demonstrate the use of farm equipment bought by the government. Later, he became the first English tutor to the Crown Prince. Murray had been born and raised in Ethiopia. He took pride in showing Esther and his two little children, Alice and John, around the capital city.

Situated high in the mountains, Addis Ababa – "New Flower" – was a city of nearly a half-million people. Like other third world cities straining to enter the twentieth century, it was a city of contrasts, at once modern and ancient, rural and cosmopolitan, wealthy and impoverished. Esther was struck with the primitive conditions. She saw a sprawling encampment of low, crudely built, tin-roofed mud houses, interlaced by narrow, twisting, muddy alleys and lanes. A few, wide, asphalt streets built during the Italian occupation followed the irregular contour of the hills, providing corridors of commerce along which European-style buildings had been constructed. Occasionally, one saw a grand house behind a high wall topped with broken glass to keep out thieves, but surrounded on all sides by wretched huts and hovels. While a few people appeared prosperous, most were dirty, ragged, and impoverished. Beggars lived on the street in boxes. The air smelled of burning garbage. Esther thought: If this is the capital city, what must our mission town be like?

Two weeks later they drove by Land Rover to Gore in the western part of the country, their first assignment for the United Presbyterian Mission. The trip took three days. The primitive villages they passed through had no hotels, and two nights they camped on the road, staying one night with other missionaries. The deeper into the countryside they drove, the more Esther appreciated the insulating luxury of their Land Rover. She clutched little Alice and John about her.

With a population of 2,000, Gore was the largest town in the province of Ilibabur. Located in the mountains, it was situated on a high hill surrounded by thick rain forest. Except for several buildings in the European fashion, which had been constructed by the Italians, every house was one-story and built of mud mixed with straw, over a frame of sticks and poles, whitewashed on the outside. The main street, off of which angled alleys and footpaths, was unpaved. There were no sidewalks. Housefronts opened onto the mud of the street. The street's singular feature was a deep gully gouged by the recent rains – in some places as deep as a man – that wove back and forth like a miniature canyon. Their vehicle, groaning in and out of the gully, drew everyone's attention. From every dark doorway, yellow eyes watched with an intense curiosity, almost suspicion.

Their house turned out to be an old Italian compound. Although the buildings were crumbling and musty, with high ceilings and cold cement floors, Esther was relieved. At least it did not have clay floors. Although the windows had no glass, they were screened and closed with wooden shutters. There was no electricity and only one indoor water faucet. The toilet was a box commode over a bucket. Cooking, lighting, and refrigeration were accomplished using crude kerosene appliances. A wide veranda surrounded the house, providing a good play area for the children. Unfortunately, the compound was situated just below the cattle market, and during the rains the filth from this area washed like a thick, black river through the yard.

Ruth Beatty, a nurse with the United Presbyterian Mission, greeted them. A kind, energetic woman, she had been in Gore for five years. Esther sighed with relief to see another white face. In fact, a number of East Indians and Europeans – Italians and Greeks – lived in Gore, having settled there after the war. The Indians taught in the school, and the Europeans operated the mercantile, a garage, and a restaurant-bar.

The twenty or so schoolboys who lived in the hostel behind the house, also welcomed them. They seemed friendly enough, willing to do whatever one might ask. Unlike many of the townspeople, they seemed to be "on our side." The small church and clinic, which the Russells were to pastor and administer, stood across the path from their house.

Esther's first trips into the marketplace were unpleasant. She took two of the older boys from the hostel with her to interpret. As they walked through the dusty street, a crowd of children followed along, all very dirty and ragged, some naked. They ran at her side, shouting and touching her clothes. "Ferenjee! Ferenjee!" (Foreigner! Foreigner!) they cried incessantly. Eventually, one of the students harshly ordered them away, and they retreated to a little distance, where they continued to follow in a crowd. From the doorways, the adults watched with seeming amusement.

Worst of all were the flies. At home in Pittsburgh, a single house fly buzzing in the kitchen had been cause for persistent stalking with a swatter. Here flies were as plentiful as dirt. Stepping outdoors one was engulfed – huge, black, filthy flies swarming everywhere, tangling in one's hair, crawling over one's face and neck, besieging one's nostrils, eyes, and mouth. Most Ethiopians carried horsehair fly-whisks which they continually and languidly swung before their faces to keep the flies away. Babies and young children, too young to defend themselves, sat in the road, arms at their sides, apparently oblivious to the flies on their faces, rimming their eyes. As the dry season continued, the plague of flies got worse, till by spring just before the rainy season, they became intolerable. Indeed, May was known as the "Month of Flies." Esther shuddered to think of it.

The "merkato," or market place, was located at the far end of the town in a broad, sloping field that led down toward the forest. In this crowded, dusty area, farmers and merchants sold their produce and other articles, displayed upon blankets or mats spread upon the ground. Here one could buy all manner of food and goods. People came from all over to buy, sell, and barter.

Food was plentiful, but uninviting. The vegetables, fruit, raw grain, and nuts appeared dirty and stale. Who had handled it and for how long? At a meat stall, a cow had been slaughtered. The meat hung from hooks or lay upon the single plank which served as a counter. The meat was so covered with flies it was difficult to determine the worth of the cut. Near the stall, dogs lapped at the pools of blood, watchful for any scrap of gristle or bone that might be dropped. Wistfully, Esther recalled the clean Pittsburgh markets with their racks of canned goods, fresh bread, bottled milk, packaged butter and cheese, inspected meats, and clean, fresh produce.

When she stopped to buy something, a crowd invariably gathered. They watched everything about her – her lips moving, her eyes, the tilt of her head. Their dark, black skin showed white with a powder of dust. Some sought to touch her. Older women sometimes pinched her arms, commenting to themselves, until admonished by the student interpreter. Frequently the crowd laughed at something said, and the interpreters appeared embarrassed. Though difficult, Esther did her best to ignore this.

At home, sanitation, especially in the preparation of food, was her first priority. Bacteria savagely hostile to Westerners abounded. The Russells in Addis had warned them to eat only those fruits which had to be pealed, such as bananas and oranges, to always boil and filter their drinking water, to rinse raw vegetables in a mild Clorox solution, and to cook all meats well done to destroy maggots and bacteria.

Esther had been appalled at the sanitary habits of their new cook, a young, quiet, sullen-looking girl named Twabitch. The first day, the girl had gone to the toilet and then returned to resume slicing bread without first washing her hands. It took many explanations and demonstrations to make the girl understand that, before doing anything in the kitchen, she must always wash her hands with soap. Esther's greatest fear was that one of the family – young Alice and John – would be taken with some disease. Although the girl was the "cook," Esther continued to supervise the food, leaving her only peripheral tasks – peeling vegetables, washing, and cleaning up. Esther felt the girl resented this.

As for hired help, one could not assume that any of the people knew anything about tasks Westerners took for granted. One morning she glanced out the window to see the newly-hired gardener pounding on their outside faucet with a large rock, trying to force out the water. Esther ran out the door shouting, "No! No!" She demonstrated several times how to turn the spigot on and off. Although he smiled and bobbed his head in understanding, she watched afterwards from the house to make sure.

Two days before Jennie and Andrew arrived, the hostel boys had gone on strike when they found worms in their morning cereal. A few of the boys made nasty remarks in Amharic, which Esther could not understand, but which she suspected were disrespectful. Murray took the row much better than she. He had, after all, grown up here.

Besides being unclean, the environment was dangerous. Some of the rivers in the area were filled with crocodiles. Lakes and other standing ground water were, in many parts of the country, infested with schistosomes, a parasitic worm that caused severe blood loss and tissue damage to persons drinking or bathing with it.

Travelling between towns could be a precarious venture. The roads were hazardous and often impassable. The week before, Murray had gotten stuck in a mudhole and Esther had been called to pull him out with their second vehicle.

Nothing seemed safe. Recently, hawks had swooped down under the protective cover of their chicken coop and carried away the last three baby chicks. Then a maddened dog wandered into the compound. Fortunately, the gardener managed to kill it with a hoe before it bit anyone. It horrified Esther to think that Alice and John might have tried to pet it. "Never, never touch a dog!" she admonished them afterwards.

Dogs were not well regarded in Ethiopia, perhaps because so many were diseased. Many Ethiopians carried heavy sticks, not to walk with, but to strike away any dogs that approached. Ethiopians could not understand the Western penchant for keeping dogs as pets *in the house*, and feeding them good food.

At night, the compound was locked and guarded, first from the great number of thieves, and second against hyenas which roamed the streets after dark. Lying in bed, Esther trembled as she listened to them screaming just beyond the compound walls.

Esther wondered if she would succeed as a missionary. At times, she was tempted to pack her bags, collect her children, and fly home.

To complicate matters, she was now two months pregnant! Although she hadn't yet begun to show, she could not mistake the deep, subtle stirrings of new life within her. What might have been a source for rejoicing in another place, now filled her with dread. She could not bear the thought of bringing a child into these circumstances.

Their official responsibilities were:

1. Study Amharic and pass the language exams required by the United Presbyterian Mission. This was important because if they could not speak the language, they would not accomplish much with the people. 2. Pastor the church and conduct regular Bible classes and prayer groups. 3. Administer the hostel and have some "spiritual impact" upon the students. 4. Hold regular meetings for women – e.g., a sewing class. 5. Maintain good relations with the local government and businessmen in the town. 6. Post regular prayer letters to the constituency in the USA. 7. Maintain the mission compound.

The second evening after Jennie and Andrew's arrival, the kerosene refrigerator caught fire and Andrew snatched Esther's best lace tablecloth from the dining room table to put it out. "Not that, Daddy, not that!" Esther had screamed, but her objection came too late, for Andrew was already smothering the flames with the precious cloth. Esther had laughed and then cried, all somewhat hysterically. "I'll send another cloth when we get back," Jennie promised, attempting to console her daughter.

Today, as Esther kneaded the soft bread dough, she thought the time had come to talk frankly with her mother. She was just about to set the bread to rise when she heard a commotion in the yard. Walking to the door, she saw the gardener, who also served as the compound "sebanya," or guard, talking loudly with "Mrs. Green," the beggar lady, so named by Esther because of the same filthy shred of green dress she wore, gathered with a safety pin on her left shoulder. The woman came to the compound once or twice a week to receive handouts. With matted hair, diseased bare feet, face and hands crusted with filth, she did not exactly elicit welcomes from Esther. When she did not acknowledge Esther's initial overtures, Esther concluded she must be mentally deranged. By her fourth visit, Esther had stopped going out to her. Nevertheless, the woman kept coming. This morning, Esther returned to the kitchen and continued kneading the bread.

Presently, Jennie came into the kitchen. "Who is that woman in the yard?" she asked.

"A beggar," Esther replied. "She comes all the time. Just ignore her and she'll go away."

"Oh," said Jennie, and went back out.

A few minutes later Esther heard the screen door open and close. She got to the front door just in time to see Jennie, accompanied by one of the student interpreters, approaching Mrs. Green. In the most natural fashion, Jennie put her arm around the woman's shoulders, as if hugging a neighbor back home. "My dear sister," Jennie said, "I have news for you. Jesus loves you." While the woman, who was covered head to foot with vermin, scratched herself, Jennie explained the Gospel message. They stood a long time, one old lady talking to another. Finally, Jennie placed something in the woman's hand, a coin or possibly a piece of candy. Bowing repeatedly, the woman limped down the path and out the gate, the gift clutched in her hand.

Hurrying back to the kitchen, Esther began kneading the bread vigorously, her heart suddenly churning in anger and guilt. Hot tears of shame splashed down into the dough and the fine sprinkle of flour on the table. Clumsily, she attempted to wipe her eyes with the back of her hand, but the more she fumbled at her face, the more she cried. She could not ignore the quiet, inner voice that spoke to her: *Esther, you also have given to Mrs. Green, but what were your motives...to get rid of her quickly, unable to see her diseased feet dripping on your veranda where your small children play. Or perhaps you wanted others to see your virtue in giving something to a beggar? Esther, today Mrs. Green has been touched by My love. You also must be filled with My Holy love.*

Esther noticed that Jennie and Andrew, although guests, wasted no time in spreading the Gospel. In his spare moments Andrew designed and carved new mottoes, using translations in Amharic script provided by the students. Jennie found a quiet room with lockable doors and made radio transcriptions for broadcasts in the USA. In addition, the two took any opportunity to witness for Christ. Discovering the public market, they set up a booth where they poured plaster mottoes and preached the Gospel from the texts on the mottoes, two students interpreting. Their activity attracted a large crowd. The police, standing at the perimeter, their rifles slung over their shoulders, watched but said nothing to the white-haired foreigners, although a few days later, missionary Murray was told that this should not happen again.

They also assisted in the little church the Russells pastored. They gave evening sermons and weekly Bible study classes. Jennie was startled to discover that none of the Ethiopian women could read. Asking Murray about this, she was amazed to learn that the government intended literacy for men only, because women were not supposed to have the ability to learn!

"What a ridiculous notion!" exclaimed Jennie. "Murray, you must teach them!"

"I'm trying," he replied. Indeed, he had already begun teaching a dozen Ethiopian women how to read, meeting with them at the church for two hours every afternoon. The Ethiopian men of the church scoffed at this crazy idea, but Murray continued, bolstered by Jennie's encouragement. Esther wondered if Jennie realized how brave these women were to go against the traditions of their culture. On a Sunday morning a few weeks later, an Ethiopian woman stood up in church and slowly but bravely read Scriptures to the amazed congregation.

One morning, a distraught villager came running to the missionary compound crying out that a young woman had just hanged herself. Jennie and Esther hurried to the home. While stepping over the high mud doorsill, Jennie scraped her leg. She forgot the injury in the excitement of calling for the nurse and comforting the relatives. The next day, her leg was red and swollen. For several days she stayed in bed with her leg elevated. However, she continued in good humor, blessing those who came to visit her, and testifying to the goodness of the Lord even in emergencies. Esther admonished her, "Mother, out here you've got to watch out!"

"You're right, of course," replied Jennie. "But like David, I have two 'following angels' called 'Goodness and Mercy,' who I'm sure would not let anything serious happen while I am out on the Lord's work."

One afternoon Esther and Jennie walked into the town to buy food. As they trudged through the dusty street, several government teachers, who had evidently heard of the old white-haired foreign lady, approached them, seemingly eager to strike up a conversation. As Esther watched, Jennie put herself forward in a way that she, Esther, had never been able to. Jennie's disarming smile and clumsy attempt to greet them in Amharic provoked smiles and laughter and seemed to draw them all closer. She spoke so casually and warmly that Esther thought she must have met them before somewhere. They invited her to visit their school the next day and speak to the students. Jennie laughed and accepted with delight, while Esther swallowed hard, never having been thus invited.

The school was a filthy, windowless barn that had once held goats, cows, and chickens. Now, one hundred and thirty-five young students sat on rough benches. A few grown men were also taking the opportunity to study for the first time in their lives. While Esther approached the situation warily, Jennie brimmed with enthusiasm. She had brought along her old black bag containing Andrew's fold-up easel, a flannelgraph board, and a number of pictures. Esther gasped, however, when Jennie also pulled out of the bag the beautiful satin brocade Chinese coat, the reversible one that Esther had once hinted she would like to have. She hadn't seen it in years. What in the world was it doing in the bag? This filthy barn was certainly no place for such a valuable heirloom!

With the help of a teacher who interpreted, Jennie began her favorite story, the parable of the prodigal son. The smelly barn became quiet. As she came to the climax, when the wayward son, who had fallen to working as a

Ethiopian pastor prays over church offerings.

swineherd, decides to return to his father and seek forgiveness, Jennie did what Esther had seen her do so often: she switched to human actors to tell the story. "Now," Jennie asked, "who would like to be the prodigal son?" Immediately, a tall, older boy in ragged shorts raised his hand. "All right, that's fine, come right up here," Jennie motioned to him. The class giggled and squirmed in excitement as the boy rose from his seat and stepped forward. His dark skin glistened a dusty grey from the dirt. His hair was matted and his feet swollen with infected jiggers.

"Now," Jennie continued with the story, "when the father saw the boy coming down the road, he called to his servants, 'It's my boy! Go and get the best robe and put it on him!'"

Esther gasped audibly as Jennie shook out the beautiful oriental robe and asked the boy, "Now which side do you want out, the pink side or the black side?"

The boy chose the pink side. As Esther watched in dismay, Jennie wrapped the lovely, clean robe around him. Hot with indignation, Esther stepped forward and exclaimed under her breath, "Mother, you just don't do things that way here!"

Startled, Jennie looked into her daughter's face. She paused only an instant before replying, "Oh, it's all right, dear," and then continued with the story as if Esther simply had been reminding her of the story.

The next instant, Esther heard the Still Small Voice remonstrating: *Esther, you have seen a demonstration of Holy love and you are offended....You are more concerned with a piece of cloth than with the value of human souls....These people will never forget the truth of this Bible story.*

The next Sunday, Esther and Jennie went for a picnic outside of town. It was a beautiful clear day, the blue Ethiopian sky filled with wispy laces of cloud. Esther could not appreciate any of it. Finally the frustration she felt at being a missionary wife, mother, and teacher in "this terrible place," erupted in a torrent of dark words. While Jennie listened silently, Esther vented her feelings, ending with, "Mother, don't you think we should leave?"

After a pause, Jennie took Esther's hand and said gently, "Esther, you need a change of heart. That's all. Just a change of heart."

"Oh, Mother....you don't understand!" Esther cried, turning away, tears filling her eyes. Presently, the Still Small Voice spoke again: *More than anyone else, your mother understands. She understands perfectly well the selfishness in nearly every corner of your heart. She loves you too deeply to be untrue when you have cried for help.*

"All right," Esther confessed, "but how do I do that? I want to teach and help people. I want to live here and contribute. I want to love and serve God. I do...."

"I know you do, Dearest, I know," said Jennie. "But love comes from God. We must look to Him. Besides that, a woman has to work at life. Life doesn't come ready made. We are free to choose and direct our lives, and sometimes it isn't easy. Life is not a haphazard series of strokes thrown on a canvas. It is crafted by one's self."

For the remainder of their stay, Jennie said no more to her daughter, never scolded, never pointed to fault. Instead, Esther could feel Jennie surrounding her with love.

The United Presbyterian Mission's language examinations were held every month. Andrew and Jennie offered to watch the children so that Esther and Murray could study. Andrew taught them songs on his autoharp and Jennie played games. The children blindfolded Grandma and led her around the house. Then Grandma would change roles and lead them around the house, amid much giggling and gaiety.

Esther was almost in despair at ever mastering the Amharic language. While she knew sufficient grammar and vocabulary, she lacked conversational fluency, choosing to rely upon student interpreters. One morning Jennie said, "Esther, let's go for a walk to the market." Esther did not suspect anything, until, in the middle of the donkey market, Jennie greeted a man with a big smile, "Ashuma, I have something I want to show you." Fumbling in her bag, Jennie produced a small paper book. It was a wordless book, colored pages telling the Gospel story.

Immediately, Esther realized that Jennie intended to have her interpret to the barefoot villager. At first, Esther flushed and fumbled, her mind grasping for words. Gradually, she found herself speaking simple Amharic. To her astonishment, the man was following her words – he understood! For the first time, Esther was talking and looking into the face of an Ethiopian, who genuinely wanted to hear what she had to say. He was not just an anonymous peasant, but a human being she might like to know. For the first time, her fear dissolved and joy came into her heart. Jennie engineered several such encounters.

Murray took Jennie and Andrew to a number of churches in the surrounding towns and villages. Some were impoverished, with scarcely enough money to keep going and certainly not enough to provide for charity. To these congregations, Andrew preached stewardship as a mainspring of the Gospel program – the taking care of what God had entrusted to us. God had revealed Himself and provided the means of our salvation, and now it was humankind's duty to promote it in the world. The maintenance of the church was paramount. The Scriptures were replete with admonitions to liberality:

> Give and it shall be given unto you....(Luke 6:38)
>
> He which soweth sparingly shall reap also sparingly; and he which soweth bountifully shall reap also bountifully. Every man according as he purposeth in his heart, so let him give; not grudgingly, or of necessity: for God loveth a cheerful giver. (II Corinthians 9:6, 7)

On one occasion, Andrew, having just received for his birthday seventy-five dollars, a dollar for each year of his life, laid the money out and challenged the congregation to cover it with their own. One by one, each bill was covered. To everyone's pleasure, more money kept coming.

Another time, Jennie preached the story of Elijah the Tishbite who asked the poor widow with not enough meal and oil to feed even herself or her child, to "bake me a little cake first." As the widow gave to Elijah, so did the Lord give to her. Following the story, Jennie brought out her "Billy Sunday Shoe" and took a missionary offering for the neon sign atop the William Carey Church in Calcutta. The congregation, which up to this time had not given enough even to support its own church, collected one hundred eighty dollars for India.

One morning Esther overheard Jennie praying through her partially open bedroom door. Jennie sat on the edge of her bed, head bowed. Though Esther felt she shouldn't, she listened:

"...Sometimes I think I shall die of loneliness, Lord. I often lack self-assurance, too. In speaking, I flit from one thought to another; I'm just not theologically organized like Father. I need help in this...

"...Help me to take dominion, Lord, not casual, but a firm position. This is a real challenge. I'll need more spiritual exercise—prayer, fasting, study of the Word, and worship. But dominion is what I want. Help me to achieve it...

"...Above all, help us all to drive down our stakes and strengthen our cords, so that we don't change our mind with every wind that blows, but hold steady to what we have begun. I am absolutely assured that You are leading every one of us. Let our roots go down deep and be anchored in You."

Two weeks before they left, Jennie came to Esther and said, "I know you've been worried about this pregnancy. Don't be. God will take care of everything. You'll see. What we need to do is celebrate! I think we should have a party! A baby shower!"

Before Esther could protest, Jennie excitedly set about making plans for the party. The rest of the morning she was out inviting the Ethiopian neighbors, and all the Greek and East Indian women she had met. A pretty baby basket was decorated in blue silk. Twabitch prepared sweet cakes and candies to serve the guests. The younger children twisted crepe paper for the "umbrella" that the "shower" was going to "rain" over. Before long, Esther, who had, in fact, been complaining about her condition, caught Jennie's zest. "I love to see you smile," Jennie said.

Ten women came to the shower, all dressed in colorful clothes. A number brought food. Two Indian friends made special cakes. Jennie led the group in prayer, blessing the coming child. The group sang songs, ate, and warmly congratulated Esther.

Jennie and Andrew left amid many tears. Watching her parents board the plane, Esther recounted the lessons her mother had taught her. Jennie had gently proven by example that she, Esther, could serve and serve well. Neither could know that Esther and Murray would remain in Africa another twenty-five years, serving gladly and with effective ministry.

Six months later, when their child was born, a girl, Esther and Murray named her Jennifer, after Jennie.

Chapter 12

MOVING MOUNTAINS

In late 1954, Jean and Kaare Wilhelmsen invited the Mitchells to Trinidad, the richest and smallest island in the British West Indies. At the same time, Carol Jackson, Go-Ye missionary in Brazil, asked them to visit her in South America.

The previous year, Jean and Kaare had left their station in India, not intending to return. In Los Angeles, they heard through the Go-Ye Fellowship of a need for missionaries in Trinidad. The country seemed ideally suited to them – a tropical climate and a large population of East Indian emigrants, primarily Hindu (both Kaare and Jean were fluent in Hindi). They immediately applied for and were granted the opportunity to open a new mission field under the joint sponsorship of the Go-Ye and the Open Bible Standard Missions.

Trinidad was a great challenge. As Jean's letters described it:

> "Giants of huge proportions hold these people captive....Carnival, the biggest event of the year, has just finished....They dance and drink in the streets for two days and seem to delight in all that is vile and vulgar....Open-air meetings are our main contact. A Christian friend who hauls sand and gravel in his truck loans it to us for meetings at night....We load it with a folding organ, movie projector, floodlights, and a group of young Christians....Three to four hundred people turn out to see what it is all about."

The situation was reminiscent of the biblical city of Samaria described in Acts 8 where people had practiced idolatry and black magic, but were nevertheless eager to receive the Word of God. But the Wilhelmsens needed help. The mission in Trinidad was growing rapidly, and experienced people were needed to minister all over the island. As well, a Bible Institute was being formed to train island leaders. Would Jennie and Andrew come?

The opportunity seemed tailored to the Mitchells' abilities and experience.

"After all," said Jennie, thrilled, "in Trinidad, we can speak in English instead of using interpreters!"

"Yes, and we can help prepare new leaders," said Andrew, relishing the thought of discussing doctrine, of leading in-depth Bible studies.

"The climate is warm," added Jennie, recalling the cold, damp weather of Japan.

"And we've had experience ministering to both East Indians and Africans, who are the people of Trinidad...."

"And it's on the way to Brazil where Carol has invited us. We could spend nine months or a year in Trinidad and then go on to Brazil...."

This autoharp accompanied Andrew on all of his journeys.

"Well, what are we waiting for? Let's go!"

Go-Ye Fellowship funds were limited. To raise money, the Mitchells scheduled a speaking trip through northern California, Oregon, and Washington. Jennie's sister, Nellie, who had just turned eighty, drove, while Jennie and Andrew, both in their seventies, conserved their energy for the meetings. In forty days, the aged trio spoke to eighty different groups.

Jennie meets pastor's wife, Ruth Stewart. Photo courtesy of Mann Flint.

Everyone was eager to support their new work in Trinidad and Brazil. People who had settled back into the easy chair of middle age were stirred to action at the sight of these gray-haired grandparents arriving in town in an old Packard, trailing blue smoke, singing, laughing, determined to serve the Lord with all they had.

Their forthright, practical message startled the congregations: "Too often," Jennie said, "we lack deep-rooted certainty of our relationship with God. This makes us limp in the presence of contrary forces. The world, the flesh, and the devil sweep over us like a blast on a field of wheat. We don't recognize the fact that God has placed us in a reigning position, that Jesus paid for us with His life, delivering us from the power of darkness, the bondage of sin. Our feet are thus set upon a rock. It is our victory to hurl these mighty facts into the very face of the accuser. We are to use our God-given authority against all evil. How shall we do it? First, saturate ourselves in the Word of God; second, seek constant communion with God; and third, *be always in action for God*—which is what we have come here to talk with you about."

By fall of 1955, the three had returned home safely ("no accidents—our accompanying angels were with us all the way..."), and were packing for South America. They flew first to Puerto Rico and then on to the Windward Islands. The sight of the Caribbean brought back memories of Haiti ten years before. This time they saw British Antigua, French Martinique, the spice islands of Grenada and Tobago, landing finally at the large international airport at Port of Spain, Trinidad. They were met by Jean and Kaare and a number of Trinidadians.

Named by early Spanish explorers in honor of the Holy Trinity, Trinidad was the point of departure for all shipping down the east coast of South America. Famous for its asphalt pits, the island was rich in oil deposits and was a major industrial center for oil drilling and refining. The population was a mixture of blacks from Africa and East Indians from India, with a sprinkling of Europeans.

English was the official language, but many people spoke Spanish and Hindi. Although most people were Roman Catholic, many Hindu temples and some Muslim mosques could be found on the island. Anglican and Presbyterian missionaries had established a number of Protestant churches which the evangelists found to be cold, staid, and often not well-attended.

The student body of the Open Bible Institute in Trinidad consisted of twenty-one young men, seven of whom were from Hindu homes. In nearly every case, the Hindu students had broken with their families to attend the Institute. Some lived in rooms provided by sympathetic Christian families. One fellow lived out of his car. After a long day's work in the cane fields, the men, grimy with sweat, washed at village faucets before walking or cycling to school. Classes were held three nights a week. On two nights, the students went in teams to the villages to preach. Thus far, five Sunday Schools had developed in the villages visited by these teams.

The Trinidadians were a fun-loving people, given to hilarity and celebration. Their idea of Christian worship was a strange, polluted mixture of voodoo, magic, and emotional dissipation. Together with the Wilhelmsens and other missionaries, Jennie and Andrew sought to return the dignity and solemnity of worship. They taught the people the old songs and hymns, and attempted to provide a sober and biblical foundation upon which a true spirituality could be built.

The Mitchells went along with the Wilhelmsens to evangelize in the villages. It reminded Jennie and Andrew of the street meetings in India and Haiti, where the Gospel light had to be forcibly taken into unregenerate darkness. Jean described a typical foray: "Last night we returned home late from a village preaching tour where some three hundred people stood for two hours in the open air to hear the Word of God. The area is so dark with sin that we are greatly relieved when we return safely. The open door of a bar is our platform. Because there is no electricity, we attach our rented loud speakers to our car battery. The last time, we packed three cars full of new believers to go with us. There are so many drunken men in the crowd that it takes all of us to keep things quiet."

At the small church in San Fernando, Jennie helped lead a prayer group which Jean had started, calling it the "Mountain Movers." The group met every Thursday morning from eight until noon, usually having fasted the day before. Often no more than a dozen to twenty faithful "prayer warriors" attended. Bible reading, testimonies, and prayer constituted the entire program. Jennie was particularly interested in the group because she had been attempting to "move mountains" by prayer all her adult life. For the first few weeks, only a few small hills were actually moved – until one morning a real mountain was carried into the meeting. His name was Theophilus Joseph.

A painting contractor by trade, Theophilus had, while painting large oil storage tanks, suffered a stroke that had left his left leg paralyzed. Because of the disability, his painting contract was cancelled. Theophilus continued going to his Methodist Church, but he walked with the aid of crutches, dragging his useless leg. Hearing of the people in the San Fernando Church who prayed for the sick, he went to the Mountain Movers Prayer Meeting and was prayed for, but without visible result. He attended a second time, but again without change. He began to think that he was beyond human or divine help when he decided to return one last time. If nothing happened this time, he wouldn't go again. Walking was so difficult that his wife had to lift his foot over the threshold to get him into the prayer room.

Missionary Don Bryan was in charge of the meeting that day. A man of discernment and faith, Bryan recognized that here was a "mountain" that had to be moved – or the group was not what it claimed to be. Indeed, God seemed to be testing their efforts by returning the man to them. As the group prayed, Don reached up and touched Theophilus on the forehead, commanding him in the name of Jesus to run and jump.

As Theophilus described it later, at Bryan's touch he felt a current of energy surge through his body, beginning at his toes and rising through to the top of his head. "Is this the power of God?" he thought. Presently, his leg felt different. Gone was the heavy numbness. For the first time in months he could wiggle his toes. Tentatively, he moved his foot. To his astonishment he could turn it straight and even lift it. Standing, he took one step, then another, stopping to twist his ankle and flex his knee. Finally, he stood entirely on the crippled leg to test its strength. It held! He did a little hop, skip, and a jump. "I can walk!" he shouted, "I can walk!"

He returned to the oil depot to see his former employer, who at first did not believe the story. Theophilus demonstrated his agility by climbing a twelve-foot ladder – whereupon his contract was reopened and he completed the painting job. In gratitude to the Mountain Movers, he painted the Church and Bible School buildings. He testified in many places throughout the island.

The result was increased attendance at the Mountain Movers prayer meetings. People began coming from all over the island – in taxis and buses, on bicycles, and on foot – to attend the weekly meetings. Before long, hundreds were praying together. As the crowds grew, so did the feeling that a Holy Presence was also in attendance.

More than ever before, Jennie saw the power that prayer could have when united in a concentrated effort by a group of people. Their combined intercession opened a massive channel for Heaven's power and grace to flood upon the world. How it brought people together! For the first time, Blacks, Anglos, and East Indians, among whom frictions and bad feeling were traditional, now stood as one, bonded by the one true unifying power of Christ. Yes, the Mountain Movers was truly an example of "putting the Bible into action."

After remaining in Trinidad about a year, the Mitchells flew on to Brazil to visit Carol Jackson and to "spy out" the prospects for beginning another Go-Ye mission there.

They arrived in Sao Paulo, Brazil, in October, 1956, after a long day of flying in a DC-3 over the seemingly endless Amazon Jungle. What a vast country, Brazil, as large as the United States, plus another Texas to boot! It was a beautiful spring day in the Southern Hemisphere, and Sao Paulo, with a skyline longer than New York's and a population almost as great as London, gleamed like a diamond.

With the help of Carol Jackson, the Mitchells surveyed south eastern Brazil below Rio de Janeiro, visiting Campinas, Sorocaba, Curitiba, Puerto Alegre, and several smaller villages and towns. What they found surpassed their expectations. First of all, the country was densely populated. A missionary, living in a central location, could easily reach a large number of people. Second, the roads were passable, and generally reliable transportation existed. Third, although other missionaries – Baptist, Presbyterian, Methodist, Pentecostal, and Congregationalist – were already established, they were not numerous. There was room for more.

Most importantly, they saw a need for the vibrant evangelical message. The people – a mixture of Blacks, native Indians, and Europeans – were poor, sometimes wretchedly so. The poverty was a breeding ground for all manner of vice and evil – prostitution, gambling, drinking, and thievery. As they talked with the people, Jennie and Andrew concluded that Brazil was, indeed, a place where the light of the Gospel must be brought to shine!

Trinidad and Brazil had excited them. Arriving back in Los Angeles, the Mitchells first act was to inform the Go-Ye they had decided to return to Brazil as missionaries themselves, and to serve there as long as their strength held out. Somewhere within, a gate had opened, flooding them with energy and determination to do God's work. Jennie's sister, Nellie, who had been managing the foreign art Scripture molds and plaque business of the Go-Ye Fellowship in their absence, caught the excitement. "I'm going, too," she announced. She had just turned eighty-one.

"Hallelujah!" cried Jennie. "We'll all go!"

They decided that Nellie would go first, along with Zenna Lee Pinkerton and Gail Galusha. Jennie and Andrew would follow as soon as the Go-Ye Fellowship could get permanent mission status in Brazil. Unfortunately, a month before her departure, Nellie became critically ill with fainting spells and seizures. Fearing the worst, Jennie and Andrew summoned her family to what looked like a deathbed farewell. Jennie sent a cable to the Open Bible Church in San Fernando, Trinidad – the Mountain Movers – requesting prayer for Nellie. On a Sunday morning, the entire congregation in San Fernando united in prayer to save Nellie's life. The next day, back in Los Angeles, the crisis suddenly passed and Nellie, within a few days, returned to health. In September, she left with the group for Brazil under the sponsorship of the Go-Ye, stopping in Trinidad to testify to the congregation which had offered their prayers for her life.

Before heading off to Brazil, where by now the Go-Ye had obtained permanent mission status and was registered as the *Go-Ye Fellowship do Brazil*, Jennie was keen to do one other thing. Ever alert to the uses of birthdays and anniversaries, she began planning a special event for Andrew's 80th birthday coming up in early March, 1957. Studying the schedules of their children ministering in foreign countries, she saw that all had furloughs around Easter of that year. What an ideal time for a Mitchell family reunion! The opportunity to have everyone together – all the sons, daughters, and grandchildren – might not happen again in her or Andrew's lifetime. Some of the grandchildren were now at the threshold of their own marriages. How quickly life was passing!

Jennie scheduled six days during Easter for the meeting. Invitations went by airmail to Ethiopia, Hong Kong, Trinidad, India, Chicago, and Des Moines. They rented a mountain lodge near Big Bear Lake in the San Bernardino Mountains outside Los Angeles. Pastor J. Vernon McGee of the Church of the Open Door, and Dr. L. T. Talbot of BIOLA invited the Mitchells to have a Sunday afternoon family meeting in the Church of the Open Door. Jennie conceived that the reunion should not be just a time of family fellowship, but should serve as an example of what a family before God could be.

She prayed that everyone would come. In a letter to the family, she wrote, "We are holding the reunion very tenderly before the Lord. I do not want there to be one fly in the ointment. We are laughing at impossibilities and shouting victory all over the place."

Ten days before Easter, the family began arriving. Murray and Esther Russell came from Ethiopia with four children (one child, Priscilla, had been buried there); Kaare and Jean Wilhelmsen arrived from Trinidad with their two boys; David and Helen Morken flew in from Hong Kong with six children; from India, Joe and Marietta Smith arrived with three children; Hubert and Rachel brought their six children from Chicago; Bryant and Lola Lee Mitchell drove from Des Moines with one of their two daughters. Altogether, thirty-nine members of the family were present.

Preparations for the reunion were stepped up. An agenda was prepared which included:

THE MITCHELL FAMILY RENUNION

PURPOSE: To review the past, appreciate the present, plan the future.

To introduce the offspring to each other; renew family ties; build and help each other.

FAMILY THEME: "Exalting Christ together."

ACTIVITIES:

1. Family album: Each family shows family pictures and slides to bring everyone up to date.

2. Talents Up Front: Everyone does something to entertain – readings, poetry, music.

3. Childrens' Story Hour: Storytellers, get ready to spellbind the children!

4. Fun for the Young: Games and play activities, both indoors and out.

5. "My Happiest Recollections": Memories from the "older children."

6. Chalk Talk: Father's benediction to us in chalk.

7. Family Bible Study: Precious moments around the Bible, family style.

8. Harmonizing in Prayer: Agreeing together over common needs.

9. "Adventures with God": Testimonies of personal struggles and triumphs.

10. Grandchildren in Review: A display of handcraft, skills, talents, etc.

The following addendum was anonymously distributed, some suspect by several of the teenage grandchildren.

GROUND RULES:

1. Worrying is prohibited. $5 fine if caught.

2. No hard words allowed. Those guilty will be sent back home where they can do it all the time.

3. Bad language prohibited, especially such expressions as "Hurry up," "I don't have time," "They are my in-laws," etc.

4. Don't tease the Grandparents. Don't jostle them. They are frail and easily broken.

5. English is the official language. Don't confuse us with your foreign language. The only exception is when parents may want to use something stronger for discipline.

The reunion celebrated two birthdays, Andrew's 80th, one month past, and Jennie's 72nd, five weeks ahead. For fun, Andrew and Jennie sat up in the lodge's darkened balcony with fishing rods. Casting down lines to their children and grandchildren below, they hoisted up one birthday gift after another, amid much whooping and hollering.

Andrew gave the Bible lessons. His children marvelled at the freshness of his presentation. They had heard him before, of course, early in their lives, at countless lessons around the breakfast table. Now, they listened with a new awareness, as adults and as parents and nurturers of others, who had "been through the wars."

"That was the most attentive audience I've ever had!" Andrew told Jennie later.

Bryant, the eldest Mitchell child, became official portraitist, taking photographs of all the children. He prepared written tributes to Andrew and Jennie:

To Mother Jennie:

"We celebrate our Mother because she loves the family into which

> she married. Never did she force affection or obedience from her children, but won them to herself carefully and surely until they chose to call her 'mama'....By God's provision, she is a true complement to her husband. She is always staunch in her support of his convictions....Her heart has always stretched to include us all, and her tears have been for six....She takes personal hurt, lets it hurt, and doesn't fight back. On the other hand, she's a fighter, but her warfare is always against the proper enemy....Who else calls the devil a liar as she makes the breakfast muffins?"

To Andrew:

> "What wonderful ingredients you mixed for our childhood! ...Happy story hours, songs, simple food, rope festooned pepper trees, tons of rocks, jokes and surprises, sunshine and fresh air, play and toil.
>
> "Through some fatherly magic, you made each feel that he or she was your especially beloved, though, to an outsider you appeared as impartial as an umpire. With stubborn boys, your justice crackled like lightning; with sick girls your understanding was almost feminine. You never crushed the spirit or dampened the ardor of aspiring youth....
>
> "We are thankful for your guidance through the years of youthful decision. We were not conscious of too much control. May we have the sense and fortitude to do as well by our children. Your love and respect for the Word of God have endeared its pages to our hearts. You have been a teacher of righteousness, your lessons underscored with Christlike actions.
>
> "Your children will never have a large estate over which to quibble. Instead, you have prepared a heavenly estate. You were a good investment counsellor.
>
> "The years have not diminished the stature of your life. Your mind is quick, your back straight, your spirit gay, and your reputation untarnished.
>
> "Words are a but poor tribute. Rather, we pledge to you the tribute of our lives, given fully for the cause of Christ."

On Easter afternoon, the family gathered at the Church of the Open Door, 6th and Hope Streets, in Los Angeles, where the center platform was banked with white Easter lilies. An estimated eighteen hundred people, many from the Go-Ye Bible classes and radio listeners, watched as the family sang to the accompaniment of Hubert's piano accordion. Andrew and Jennie hoped that this public witness of six families in the service of the Lord might encourage parents to invest in prayer and Christian nurture for their own children.

At the close of the day, the family reunited once more in a final circle on the grassy level at the rear of the garden at 1307 Waterloo Street. This time, many friends joined in. An adult holding the hand of a child, all pulled along by the motion of the revolving circle, they sang, "Yes, I'll go wherever Thou dost lead." It was an emotional event, and tears filled many eyes.

From this final gathering, the family members were flung out again to the far reaches of the world. All now knew that they belonged to each other. Forever after, they would be affected by each other's concerns—births, marriages, educations, successes, failures, and deaths. All of life was a mutual sharing. Most of all, they saw that a Christian family was God's norm. And it worked! *It worked*! As such, it was a foretaste of what God had planned for them for all eternity. Jennie and Andrew had always said so....

Chapter 13

MISSIONARY GRANDPARENTS IN BRAZIL

Andrew sat in the mission house in Venda Nova, Brazil, soaking a sore foot and carving a plaque. His habit was not to waste the least bit of time. Life was short and so much work for the Lord remained to do. The week before, he had sent off to his son Bryant in Des Moines eight oil paintings of Brazil, its people and the countryside. Bryant would sell them to raise money for the Go-Ye missionary effort. Already, supporters in the United States had bought a dozen or more of his paintings. His knife, held in hands that looked younger than the rest of him, cut the soft casting plaster quickly and expertly. Around his stool, the white dust covered the floor. Outside, the air was beautifully clear. Through the front window he could see the Catholic school on the opposite hill, as well as the radio towers which at night served as beacons for planes landing in Belo Horizonte five miles away.

About twenty-two inches long and ten inches wide, the new plaque depicted a parchment scroll with curled edges. A flower stem extended down the left side, ending in two roses, one a bud, the other blooming. The inscription read, "By this shall all men know that ye are my disciples, if ye have love one to another" (John 13:34-5).

This plaque was the last of three Andrew was preparing for his son, Hubert Mitchell, to take back to the United States. Hubert was coming at the end of the month to attend the World Baptist Conference in Rio de Janeiro. He would take the plaques to Los Angeles where the Mitchell Art Company would have matchplates made and finished plaques cast in aluminum. Andrew would receive rubber molds of them in perhaps four months, from which Nellie could then begin pouring plaster replicas for distribution in Brazil. Hubert not only saved postage but ensured that the molds arrived safely in the U.S.

Andrew and Jennie had been in Brazil almost two years, having come in September, 1958. His mottoes and plaques were extremely popular. His "School of the Cross" lessons had been translated into Portuguese and were being distributed throughout Brazil. Jennie was giving weekly radio broadcasts in nearby Belo Horizonte. They had established contacts with missionaries all over the country. Most importantly, despite age, health troubles, language barriers, and some persecution from the Catholic church, they had succeeded in reaching the people and were establishing a solid base. There were four now in Venda Nova: Jennie and Andrew, Carol Jackson, and Jennie's sister Nellie.

Carol Jackson, a veteran Go-Ye missionary in Puerto Alegre in southern Brazil for the last nineteen years, served as their interpreter. Single, about forty years old, she was an invaluable helper. A shy, modest woman, she exhibited a quiet courage that did not shrink from even the most threatening situations. Her patience, wisdom, and winning smile had opened the way for them many times. She spoke Portuguese fluently, played the accordion, and preached effectively, using a flannelgraph. In Venda Nova, she organized and taught the local children.

Nellie Murdock decorating plaques.

Nellie Murdock, Jennie's sister, had preceded them to Brazil by a year and a half, living with another missionary in a small town about twenty-five miles from Venda Nova. Nellie supervised the manufacture and distribution of Andrew's plaster plaques and mottoes. The business was thriving. Every week, hundreds of plaster mottoes in Portuguese went out by truck and air to various parts of Brazil. When they travelled to other towns, they always took along two or three suitcases of mottos to sell or give away. Nellie decorated the plaques just the way the Brazilians liked them – vibrant with color. It was her heart's desire to scatter them all over the country. In their travels, they often found that the plaques had preceded them.

Venda Nova was a small town about three hundred miles north of Rio de Janeiro. It was located outside of Belo Horizonte ("Beautiful Horizon"), a city of about five hundred thousand people and the capital of Minas Gerais. They had chosen this suburb of Belo Horizonte for several reasons. First, it was a center of rail, bus, and plane transportation, and within a day of the major cities of Rio de Janeiro, Sao Paulo, and Brasilia, the new capital. Second, it had a temperate climate. In August, the weather was delightfully cool and bracing, counted as one of the healthiest climates in Brazil.

Belo Horizonte also had printers to produce Andrew's "School of the Cross" lessons. Thus far, he had completed nearly fifty lessons of a first book entitled, "What is the Cross?" which had been translated into Portuguese, printed, and were being distributed in bookstores and by missionaries. He was now working on the second book of the series, entitled "The Lamb of God." He planned five books altogether.

Aside from his carvings, these lessons were the cornerstone of his ministry in Brazil. They gave the newly converted Brazilian a grasp of the Bible's central message. Although crosses were as common as trees in Brazil, few people understood their spiritual significance.

The Mitchells' house in Venda Nova, which they shared with Nellie and Carol Jackson, was a roomy, comfortable three-bedroom bungalow, with white stuccoed walls and a red tile roof. At the rear, in what formerly was a concrete pig pen, the landlord had built a workshop where Nellie, together with two young Brazilian boys, now manufactured mottoes. Although small, it was a tidy, cheerful place with several work tables. The Mitchells used the large front room of the house for neighborhood meetings.

The Brazilian people were friendly and easygoing, and one seldom witnessed any misbehavior. The population was a mixture of indigenous Indians, Europeans, and Blacks, the Blacks having been imported a century before as slaves by the Europeans. For a hundred years, the groups had been mixing, and, as far as Andrew could tell, little or no color discrimination existed. Although lighter skin was preferred, one was not looked down upon for having dark skin. Andrew found it remarkable that such harmony existed between such a mixture of races.

The Mitchells' ministry in Brazil consisted of what they did best—play the harp, distribute Gospel mottoes, instruct from Andrew's "School of the Cross" study lessons, and preach the Gospel, using Andrew's chalk drawings. It wasn't much, but they reasoned: "The disciples had none of these things.

We have them, plus what the disciples did have – the message of God's Word and a compassion for souls which are lost."

Since other missionaries were willing to take the Word to the middle and upper classes, the Mitchells followed Christ's injunction to "Preach the gospel to the poor" (Luke 4:18). They had started in the poorest neighborhoods. With Carol acting as interpreter, they visited the houses in the immediate vicinity, Andrew carrying his harp and chalk, Jennie her "Alleluia" (Hallelujah) plaques. They introduced themselves, spoke a few words about Christ or the meaning of a plaque, sang a song or two to the accompaniment of Andrew's harp, prayed with the family, and passed on to the next house. They always invited each neighbor to visit their own home. At parting, Jennie left a plaque, and Andrew a sketch. In the first week they received forty-five visitors to their house, poor Brazilians curious to see who these grandparents were. Before long they began hearing the children of the neighborhood lustily singing the "Hallelujah" song.

They extended their activities into the hillside districts, which were steep and useless for good houses, but where poor Brazilians lived in pitiful shanties of sticks and tin, no bigger than closets. On every side stood tired mothers besieged by swarms of children tugging at their skirts. With one child still in arms, the women were often pregnant with yet another. The fathers were usually nowhere to be found. Wherever the Mitchells went, the dark eyes of the poor spoke to them, "Does this new religion have anything to offer us? We do not have enough clothes to cover our nakedness or to keep warm on the cold, rainy days. Is there any hope for us?"

Within a month, Jennie and Nellie had organized a women's meeting held every Saturday to help the women with practical concerns, and, of course, to present the Lord. On Tuesday afternoons Jennie held a "mother's" meeting, at which she stressed the essential points of motherhood. "A good mother is the first and best teacher a child can have," she told the women. "A Christian mother is the child's first example of love, which is the best illustration to the child of God's love. A good mother keeps secrets and promises, and never says to a child, 'You are too much bother.'" Jennie's good-natured, loving manner, as she hugged them, laughing and talking as if she had known them all their lives, immediately dispelled their suspicions. Their affection for her was immediate. Most tried to follow whatever suggestions she gave.

Seeing so many children in ragged clothing, she and Carol requested shipments of children's pants and dresses from the U.S. Cash donations were used to purchase material in Brazil, which the women made into clothing using sewing machines acquired for this purpose.

Jennie did not leave the house without her bag filled with tracts and "Alleluia" plaques. She seized every opportunity to testify, on crowded trains, buses, and streets, to the old, the young, the rich, the poor, the educated, the illiterate. She attempted to sow "beside all waters." There was an urgency about her: *Don't wait. Use every minute. Souls are passing you may never see again. Use all the Portuguese you have. Go to that tired mother with the crying baby. Comfort her and give her the good news. Give your tract to that businessman. Ask that young student to listen to you read a chapter of John in Portuguese. Ask for his help in the pronunciation. Slip a tract into that man's hand as he is leaving the train. And that lady has a pocket just the right size to hold a tract and plaque.*

It was often hard to judge the impact of their activity. In many cases they were planting seeds they would never harvest. One day on a bus, Jennie spied a woman sitting with her little boy in a seat ahead. The woman appeared ineffably sad – an expression of one abused, lonely, and without hope. Touching the mother on the shoulder, she handed her a plaque enclosed in a neat little box. The woman could not read the motto, and so the man next to her explained what it was. When Jennie said, "Presente," the woman's dead face came to life. Jennie indicated the hook embedded on the back of the plaster and said, "Casa" (house). The woman smiled and said something in Portuguese which Jennie did not understand. As she and her son stepped off the bus, she turned and smiled at Jennie – a warm, sincerely grateful expression. As with so many, Jennie never saw her again. Such encounters were repeated countless times.

In some cases, however, the Mitchells witnessed the results of their efforts. One morning Jennie and Carol started out to do street witnessing. On the way out the door, Jennie said, "I'm going to use my Portuguese to greet the first person we meet." A few steps down the street they encountered a man walking alone. Jennie promptly introduced herself and presented a Hallelujah plaque. He was courteous and grateful, and responded, "I know English. Let me go along and help you."

His name was Abilio and he introduced them to people all over town, eventually taking them to the cotton factory where they were allowed to minister. From that day on, Abilio often dropped by the mission house, where he enjoyed talking with Andrew, who sometimes asked him to interpret. Although a Catholic and a personal friend of the priest, Abilio was also a worldly man who enjoyed dancing, drinking, attending the theater, and picking up women in bars. He was mature and intelligent. Andrew enjoyed discussing spiritual questions with him. In Abilio, Andrew sensed a deep spiritual longing. One day Andrew asked, "Abilio, what are you going to do with your life?"

Abilio shrugged. "I do not know, Senhor Mitchell."

"Choose the highest, Abilio," Andrew said boldly, "and give all that you have to it."

Abilio considered this for a while, and then said, "Yes, I agree, but how does one find the highest?"

"One cannot find it," said Andrew. "One must trust God to reveal it."

Abilio smiled somewhat skeptically. "Yes, but how and when will God do that?" he asked.

"Unexpectedly," said Andrew.

Shortly afterwards, at the close of an evening service, Andrew gave an invitation to his listeners to surrender to Christ. About twenty people were in attendance, including Abilio. To please Andrew, Abilio raised his hand with the others, although in his heart he scoffed at the idea. However, *God saw that hand.*

Months went by. The Mitchells, watching Abilio, kept praying for his conversion. Abilio kept right on with his drinking, theater going, dancing, and girls. One night at a dance hall with a woman he was thinking of asking to come home with him, a clear voice, as he later described it, spoke to him in his mind, *This is not for you*. It startled him. Immediately he withdrew from the dance floor and sat on the side.

The next afternoon after work he went to the local bar for his usual drink with friends. But as he raised his glass, the voice spoke again, *This is not for you*. Immediately he set the glass down and started out the door. A friend called to him, "Abilio! Where are you going? Come on, let's go out with the girls and have a good time!" Abilio paused. For the first time in his life, he turned and said, "No, I cannot go."

Later that evening, thinking he must do something, he started for the cinema, but as he was about to enter the building, he heard the voice a third time, *This is not for you, Abilio*.

Deeply troubled, he came to Andrew and said. "What is happening to me, Senhor Andrew?"

"A very great thing, Abilio," Andrew said. "God is speaking to you, sending His Holy Spirit to guide your life. Trust Him."

Returning to his room, Abilio knelt down and, in stumbling, uncertain words, many borrowed from the missionaries, he asked to know God, to be on the side of God. "...In Jesus' name I ask this," he said.

A few days later, during a coffee break with business acquaintances, a powerful feeling urged him to describe his situation to them. "I can't believe it," he said, "I am a changed man. And do you know what it is? I have accepted Christ as my Savior. Truly accepted Him, I mean, in my heart. I could not have thought possible the change I have experienced."

The men were surprised at this confession, but they nevertheless smiled and listened politely. Obtaining materials from the Mitchells, Abilio began a vigorous house-to-house ministry. After work, he knocked on doors up and down the streets, giving out tracts and encouraging people to attend the mission services. He sought Andrew's aid in a systematic study of Scripture, which he now devoured at an astonishing rate. A few months later he found a suitable building and started a church. An enthusiastic and convincing speaker, he drew many people. Soon after this he accepted an offer to preach five times a week on a local Gospel radio program. Always, Abilio told his friends that the Mitchells had never given up on him and that he was "Senhor Mitchell's missionary."

In small towns away from Venda Nova the Mitchells activities followed the same pattern. Before service, they organized a meeting on the public square, which was usually filled with young men and women and families promenading. With loudspeakers aimed in all directions, and Andrew playing his harp and singing, they usually attracted a large crowd.

The street meetings were a prelude to an evening meeting in a local church or hall, to which the crowd was invited. They were always careful to tell why a white-haired trio had come so far from home, an intriguing fact to many of their listeners. They distributed the first lesson of Andrew's "School of the Cross" free to any who wanted it. As well, Jennie handed out Alleluia plaques. At the end of the service, Andrew's chalk drawings went to the person who correctly answered a question on Scripture, such as, "Where is the name Satan first mentioned in the Bible?" or "What is the name of the brother of Moses?" Such questions greatly stirred the people's interest.

As in Haiti, the Catholic Church resisted the efforts of the evangelists. Despite a deep spiritual longing, the people were full of fear, and the least threat by the priests was enough to keep them away.

Nothing disturbed Andrew more than watching painted statues of Mary being carried through the streets during festivals and holidays, led by a priest commanding the people to prostrate themselves as it passed. "Mariolatry," Andrew called it. He never tired of telling his audiences that Jesus, not Mary, had been crucified for their sins. Some of his plaques struck at this issue. One read, "There is one God and one Mediator between God and men, the man Christ Jesus." (I Timothy 2:5)

Travel about Brazil was difficult and sometimes impossible. On a one-hundred-fifty mile trip to a town where the Mitchells had been asked to fill in for an advertised evangelistic team which could not go, they encountered one adversity after another. The bus left Belo Horizonte at 5:30 a.m. It was to be an eleven-hour trip on three different buses....

...Andrew, Jennie, Nellie, and Carol carry four heavy suitcases, bags, bundles, and loudspeaker on board....no seat for Andrew....he soon finds that a pickpocket has stolen purse from his hip pocket....thank God, he still has valuable papers and some money....they change buses....heavy rain begins....bus slips from side to side on dirt road....all men are asked to get out and push bus from ditch....road caves in, all passengers out again....men push....road grader blocks road.... men turn bus around and they return to previous town....sleep the night in bus....rain....

New bus arrives 7 a.m.....One mile out of town bus slides into cave-in....Andrew orders his three ladies out to walk back to town....two men hired to carry luggage, but his briefcase with sweaters and lesson notes missing....Nellie at age eighty-five too tired to trudge in mud and rain....Andrew and Carol walk ahead to get taxi....they find a cattle train at station with one passenger car....hurry to get on board....step so high that older ladies cannot get on....men at station hoist and push them aboard....car crowded, no seats....Andrew offers one-hundred cruzeiros for a seat for Nellie....no response....Carol smiles, passes out colored tracts with passages from John in Portuguese....passengers bow heads and read....two men rise and offer seats to the elderly ladies....they reach home at last and wire church: "Will try again when able...."

Shortly after their arrival in Brazil, Andrew had gone with a Worldwide Evangelization Crusade missionary named Frank Reed to the primitive country about one-hundred-fifty miles northwest of Belo Horizonte, to evangelize among the charcoal burners, people earning a precarious living in one of the least respected occupations in Brazil.

The country was littered with ramshackle houses, set in low trees and bush amid rolling hills that stretched for hundreds of miles into the interior. On the roads people carried bundles on their heads and rode donkeys or small horses. The soil was sticky and very red, and the once white houses were now a dirty pink.

The charcoal burners existed at the low end of the Brazilian social order. Green wood, stacked in huge furnaces, was dehydrated in kilns under great heat over a period of days. After the furnace had cooled for three days, the wood, now charcoal, was removed and sold. Filling and emptying the furnaces was hard, filthy work. A man working at this occupation could expect to earn only about one dollar a day. No one ministered to these poor people. The priests came only when paid.

Andrew and Frank lodged the night with a man named Giraldo, whom Frank had recently led to Christ. His dark face was wide and flat, and looked as if it had once received a good punch from a fist. He and his wife and five children lived in a single-room mud hut, approximately nine feet square, with a floor of unleveled earth. The house had room for only a very large bed in one corner where the family slept. Two small oil lamps provided light.

The family was delighted and obviously honored to have the missionaries stay with them. For dinner they served rice and beans on tin plates. Sitting on the bed, Andrew, who had a delicate stomach, ate some sweet bread and warm milk which he had brought along. That night he slept in a corner with his clothes on, shivering with cold. Although the day had been beautiful and warm, the night was raw and cold. He wondered how he would endure. The next day he bought some cheap blankets in the town store and thereafter slept more comfortably.

In the morning they visited houses in the vicinity, Giraldo leading them about. They visited perhaps a half-dozen houses before noon. At each house they played the harp, sang, prayed, and preached the Word.

One visit was at the house of a "spiritualist." Many of the people, while nominally Catholic, gave their true allegiance to a practice part voodoo, part Christian, involving seances, and worship before shrines of Christian statues thought to possess extraordinary powers. Here, a number of people gathered to hear them, including an old man covered with wrinkles and dirt who appeared to be nearing the end of his life. Andrew could see that he believed in what they said and wanted to be baptized. Drawing a picture of a caterpillar, cocoon, and butterfly, Andrew told the story of Calvary, emphasizing the transformation open to everyone through Christ. At their invitation to accept Christ, the old man responded eagerly. Andrew felt a strong love for him. "Tell him," he said to Frank, "that I will see him on the other side."

For the next week, they drove in Frank's truck to as many huts in the area as they could find, returning at night to the small town to preach. Frank was particularly anxious to find a man who for six years had been hiding from the law for killing a man. He supposedly lived somewhere near the river, with a canoe ready for escape in case the police found him. After driving several miles on a narrow, twisting road, they came to a place where the road broke into small trails. They met a boy who led them up a trail to a charcoal furnace where a soot-covered man was removing charcoal. After some talk, the man was persuaded to lead them to a wretched hut near the river. They did not see any canoe. As they approached, the fugitive they were seeking emerged from the hut. A shy, diffident man about fifty years old, he appeared passive and kind. They talked for some time, Frank assuring him that if he trusted in the Lord, he would be guided in what to do. Finally, the man accepted what they said. In a heart-wrenching scene, he dropped to his knees and, tears streaming down his face, said in Portuguese, "Yes, I want to know God! Please, Lord Jesus, forgive my sin!"

On the way out, the charcoal man who had led them to the fugitive gave Andrew a beautiful crystal. This was not unusual, for the area was littered with rock crystals. He appeared very crestfallen that they were leaving, and Andrew surmised that he, too, wanted salvation, and so, sitting down on a fallen tree, they repeated the story and invited him also. He too accepted, and so they left two happy men instead of one.

Only God knew what eventual result their brief visit to the charcoal burners would have. Nevertheless, Andrew had gathered more hope from these neglected souls in one week than after months of preaching to the more worldly and sophisticated in Belo Horizonte. Upon leaving for Venda Nova, Andrew told Giraldo and his family that, next time, Jennie would come also. And in fact, Jennie and Andrew made several trips to this area together.

Months later they heard that fishermen had betrayed the fugitive to the police, who arrested him and brought him to trial. However, when all the evidence was presented, he was acquitted and so was now back with his family.

The threats to life were ever present in Brazil, and the Mitchells did not have to leave Venda Nova to encounter them. One morning on their way to the bus with Carol, they passed a small herd of cattle being driven through the town on their way to slaughter. A Brahma bull suddenly broke away from the herd. Dodging a horseman, the animal headed straight for Jennie and Carol. As the bull charged, the two just managed to climb to safety over a barbed wire fence. Andrew ran after them, expecting to find either or both of them injured. He found Jennie bemoaning a pair of nylons. Lifting her skirt she displayed where the barbs had slashed her leg. A Brazilian neighbor, who had witnessed the near tragedy, came running with iodine. Doctoring her leg, Jennie gave the woman a hug, and they started again for the bus.

Physical injury was not the only threat to the Mitchells' well-being. Minor ailments and allergies kept them wheezing, scratching, and shivering with fever and cold. Nellie was perhaps the most threatened. Since leaving Los Angeles, her life had become very unpredictable. She was susceptible to strokes and blackouts which left her unconscious anywhere from a few minutes to several hours. Upon awakening she would not remember anything, but would get up quickly, go down to the plaque room, and continue working as though nothing had happened. Several times they walked in to find her flat on the floor. Jennie discovered that the word "Hallelujah", when shouted loudly in her ear, seemed to bring her back to life. Thus, when Carol or Andrew heard Jennie shouting "Hallelujah, Nellie, Hallelujah," they knew that Nellie was lying unconscious somewhere.

Jennie's great torment were insect bites which raised large blisters on her legs and arms and were inclined to fester. Although she suffered from pains in her back, her health was sound enough for her to watch out for the other two.

Andrew suffered a variety of ailments, including arthritis, cataracts, asthma, and lameness. Sometimes they walked so much that, for days after, Andrew's feet were so sore he could not stand up. His ankles being weak, the slightest misstep would wrench his foot. On journeys into the countryside he never passed an opportunity to remove his shoes and soak his feet in a convenient river or stream. Eventually, he took to walking with a cane.

Andrew's congestion and hay fever were aggravated by humid weather and the dust of the road. He would choke and gasp for breath. For a while, both he and Jennie thought it might be the beginning of the end, and they resented the "enemy" cutting them off before the work was done.

Both Jennie and Andrew had developed cataracts, and were told by an oculist they would have to endure diminishing eyesight until the cataracts were "ripe," at which time they could be removed. Andrew wrote: "God has been good, giving me eighty-four years. I have no complaint."

By far the most aggravating of Andrew's disabilities was his lack of teeth. Upon their arrival in Brazil, Andrew had had all but two of his teeth pulled. The remaining two lasted only another year and then they also were removed. Unfortunately, his new false teeth were agonizingly uncomfortable, despite repeated fittings. He tried to whittle them into shape, but was afraid of carving them so thin he might swallow them altogether. When not eating, speaking, or in company, he carried his teeth in his pocket to rest his jaw.

During one ten-hour bus trip to Sao Paulo, he put the bothersome lower plate in his coat pocket and leaned back wearily in the seat for a nap. Presently, a tired-looking woman sitting behind them reached over the seat with Andrew's teeth in her hand. The bumpy road had jarred them onto the floor. Laughing with embarrassment, Andrew accepted them gratefully. Jennie, ever on the alert, promptly presented a Hallelujah plaque to the woman and proceded to expound the Gospel.

One day, shortly after Jean and her husband, Kaare Wilhelmsen, had arrived from Trinidad for a visit, Andrew's teeth disappeared from the low stand in his bedroom. A search high and low failed to turn them up. Presently, Jean noticed their dog digging in the garden...probably to hide a bone. She decided to investigate. When she got to the spot, she saw something white gleaming in the dirt: Andrew's teeth. With a shout of triumph she ran into the house, washed off the garden dirt, and sterilized the teeth with Clorox. Although the dog had chewed some deep dents, all the teeth were still there. As the family gathered around, Andrew slipped them into his mouth. Behold! They fit better than before! The dog had chewed them into a comfortable fit. Jennie laughed and cried, "Daddy, the Lord still loves us, always helping in unexpected ways."

The most severe trial for the Mitchells was one that plagued missionaries the world over – petty thievery and burglary. As Christian missionaries, they expected to overcome evil with good. This was what they preached and hoped to practice. However, it was difficult.

For some time, the Mitchells had been missing money. The small children of the neighborhood were, they knew, responsible for some of this thievery. Andrew could not blame them. Children, unless instructed otherwise, will naturally take whatever they fancy. However, older children and adults knew better.

Just across the street lived a large family, all of whose children were boys. They were smiling, friendly, and accommodating. Large amounts of money began disappearing from the Mitchell house when they first began employing different members of this family. Their jovial manner and friendly greetings, however, disarmed the Mitchells, till one day a large amount ($60) turned up missing from Jennie's purse. Jennie remembered seeing a dirty foot mark on a chair by the hiding place. Although they had to be careful not to accuse wrongly, they felt sure they knew who the thief was – a boy named Sebastian in the family across the street. They called the parents over for a talk. They seemed honest people, genuinely ashamed that one of their boys might be stealing. During the interview with Carol, the mother broke down in shame. Both she and the father seemed to profess a desire for conversion. They all agreed to wait and watch. Together, they knelt with the Mitchells and prayed.

Several days later, the parents asked for an interview. They confessed that their son Sebastian had indeed been stealing. The father had dealt with him harshly. Tying a rope around the boy's neck, he had forced him to tell where the money was hidden. Although more of the money was left than anyone expected, the parents had to borrow to return the entire amount. Nevertheless, they were grateful that the missionaries had not gone to the police. Despite the return of the money, the Mitchells felt defeated as missionaries. They prayed that they might win out the Bible way. As a gesture of goodwill, Andrew bought a football for the boys. He did not want to be thought of as an enemy.

In June, 1960, Andrew, Jennie, and Nellie boarded the train for the World Baptist Conference in Rio de Janeiro where Baptists from all over the world were expected to gather, including Billy Graham. The Mitchells were looking forward to seeing their son, Hubert, who was arriving from Chicago. The

Congress was an important event for the evangelical movement in Brazil because it brought many people from the interior.

The Mitchells had some anxiety over Hubert's arrival because in recent months two planes had crashed while landing at the airport. The visibility around the airport was sometimes very poor. That night, Hubert's flight was delayed. While they were waiting, however, Billy Graham arrived on another flight. This was an unexpected pleasure for the Mitchells, for they had not seen him since Tokyo, five years before. As he passed through customs, he saw Andrew on the edge of the crowd. Stepping past the reception committee, he came directly over and said to Andrew, "I'm so glad to see you here." He added that he had just left Hubert in Washington, D.C., and he would probably arrive about midnight.

Billy Graham at World Baptist Conference in Brazil, 1960. From the left: Jim Wallis, Walter Kaschell, Andrew Mitchell, Billy Graham, Hubert Mitchell, Clovis Salviano.

The Congress was a time for meeting old friends and making new ones. The Mitchells were invited to speak to several groups at the Congress. On Sunday, July 3, everyone headed for the Great Stadium, where Billy Graham spoke. Many hundreds accepted his call to Christ.

On the last day of the conference, during an informal meeting on the beach, to which Hubert and Andrew were invited, Andrew talked with Billy Graham again. Graham was interested in learning of Hubert's work in Chicago, asking about the possibility of a campaign in that city. Presently, pictures were taken, the photographers placing Andrew on one side of Billy Graham and Hubert on the other. Billy Graham stood six-foot-three. "I look like a pigmy beside him," Andrew thought.

In October, 1960, Carol Jackson left Brazil after twenty years of service. Jennie and Andrew didn't know what they would do without her. However, replacements soon arrived, Zenna Pinkerton and Irene McClane from the United States. The Venda Nova household now included Jennie, Nellie, Zenna, Irene, and Andrew—"four old women and one old man," Andrew said. Add to these Laurena, the Brazilian maid, and Abilio, the interpreter, and they were seven at table.

In January, 1961, the Mitchells, along with Nellie and a Brazilian boy named Reginald, who helped with the plaques, set out for Manaus, two thousand miles northwest of Belo Horizonte on the upper waters of the Amazon River. They hadn't planned on the trip, which had arisen through a Pilgrim Holiness missionary family visiting Venda Nova. Nellie's plaques had so greatly impressed them that, upon arriving at their mission in Manaus, they wrote saying the Mitchells must try to get the plaques and lessons to that region.

Manaus was nearly a thousand miles up the Amazon and could be reached only by boat or plane. They decided to travel by bus to Brasilia and from there by air to Belem on the coast. From Belem, they would fly up the Amazon to Manaus. They managed to secure a particularly cheap flight to Belem.

Brasilia, the new capital of Brazil, was an ultra-modern city constructed in the wilderness of central Brazil. Intended to facilitate development of the Brazilian interior, the city was connected to the country by roads cut through the jungle in every direction. Immense new twenty-story buildings, which Andrew found "thrillingly monotonous," stretched for miles. Sections of the city were so far apart that walking was impossible. At the perimeter, fifteen to twenty miles away, satellite towns had sprung up, populated by thousands of poor Brazilians living in temporary shacks. They were trucked in from the countryside to build Brasilia's streets and buildings.

Spending the first night with a family in one of the satellite towns, the Mitchells left Brasilia before dawn in a pouring rain. Take-off was touch and go, but they made it and were soon bumping along through the clouds. After six hours of flying over jungle, they began seeing rivers, lakes, and bays, and finally the port city of Belem, just south of the Amazon delta. Their stopover in Belem was only forty-five minutes, time enough for dinner furnished by the airline. They had been comfortable and cool in the airplane, but outside it was hot and humid.

They were astounded at the size of the Amazon, the largest river on earth. Ten times the size of the Mississippi, it was navigable for twenty-five hundred miles by ocean steamers, clear into Peru. Like the Nile, it flooded every year, inundating thousands of square miles, forming lakes, lagoons, and channels miles back from both banks – the reason Manaus had no road connection with the outside world.

A city of over one hundred thousand people, a thousand miles from any other civilized place, Manaus sat just below the equator and was known as the capital of "Green Hell," a vast wilderness of trees, vines, and swamp, inhabited only by primitive Indians, wild animals, and reptiles. A century before, wealthy rubber barons had lived here in obscure luxury, building elaborate mansions and theaters for their pleasures, but abusing the local Indians so much they now killed strangers on sight.

Arriving in Manaus, the Mitchells took a taxi to the house of James Denham, the Pilgrim Holiness missionary, who, with his wife, children, and mother, had been fighting for years to get the Word to this remote part of the world. He operated a small bookstore which held only a meager stock of books. Many titles were represented only by faded, empty dust jackets propped on the shelves. Andrew, wishing he could provide him a greater stock of books, gave him all the "School of the Cross" lessons they had brought, promising to send more when they returned to Belo Horizonte. Immediately, Nellie and Reginaldo began teaching Denham how to pour and decorate plaques, and soon the walls of the shop were covered with mottos.

The Mitchells lodged at the Denhams' residence. The third morning, Jennie rushed up to Andrew exclaiming, "Our clothes have gone to the wash, and money too!" Having lost so much to thieves, the Mitchells had pinned their money inside their garments. Losing all their money so far from home would be a catastrophe. Ignoring Jennie's warning not to move too quickly, Andrew grabbed his hat and cane and rushed into the street in time to see the bundle of wash bouncing along on the washer woman's head two blocks away. He kept it in sight for half a mile through the busy traffic, finally catching up at the foot of a muddy hill near the river. A hundred paces behind, Jennie was following with the house maid, who had come along to prevent them from getting lost in the city. Carefully, Jennie climbed down the slippery hill. At the river bank, the woman had already begun washing the clothes. However, she had unpinned all their money and stacked it in a neat pile beside her. Rewarding the woman with a bill for her care and honesty, the Mitchells took a taxi back to the house, where they rested the remainder of the day.

The next day, the Mitchells were invited to visit the New Tribes missionary group, whose camp was downriver from Manaus. Paul Fleming, the founder of New Tribes, had been one of their students when they had worked with Paul Rader thirty years before. Although Fleming had been killed recently in a plane crash, his work was being carried on by others. A Mr. Hare, the director of the camp, ferried them downriver in a launch. It took an hour to reach the camp, where the entire group of about thirty men, women, and children had assembled on the wharf to meet them. Eight or ten houses on high stilts, including a school, had been built at the edge of the river. Behind loomed the jungle, wild and impenetrable. Before them stretched the great, limitless expanse of the Amazon, on which sailed both Indian canoes and ocean steamers. From this headquarters, the New Tribes missionaries went up and down the river contacting Indian tribes, with whom they traded fishing tackle, knives, beads, machetes, and trinkets for fish, nuts, and eggs. They learned just enough of the Indian's language to begin evangelizing.

Many of the natives were suspicious and hostile. Already the group had lost one man who had been shot with arrows, dismembered, and thrown into the river. One tribe had confronted them with drawn bows, demanding all their goods, with no barter. The New Tribers, thinking their last moments had come, stood their ground, unarmed and showing no resistance, until finally the natives had withdrawn.

Their most celebrated missionary was a lone woman named Sophia Muller who lived with the Indians. Moving from tribe to tribe, she gained their confidence, taught them to read and write, and helped them build churches. Through her efforts several churches were now operating in the jungle.

Back in Manaus, the Baptist pastor presented the Mitchells with two paintings of the Amazon, one for Jennie and Andrew, and one for Nellie, in commemoration of their time in Manuas. Denham and the Pastor were eager for the Mitchells to return, and offered to pay all travel expenses.

Just before their departure, someone mentioned that a month before a plane similar to theirs had crashed in the jungle, killing all aboard, including a woman of the New Tribes group and her child. Trying not to think of this send-off story, the Mitchells boarded the plane for Belem. Again, they took off in a torrential rain. The flight was rough. Landing in Belem, they were told the flight to Brasilia was cancelled because the plane had developed engine trouble coming from Manaus. They spent one day in Belem before flying on to Brasilia, finally arriving back in Belo Horizonte "stagger-tired" but gratified at what they had accomplished.

One day, two Canadian missionaries, Cleda Clacknell and Thelma Mackness, showed up in Venda Nova. They told Andrew and Jennie their dream of establishing a Christian Missionary Conference Center on two-hundred-eighteen acres on the Parana River, five hundred miles northwest of Sao Paulo. To be called the Panorama Conference Center, it would be a place where weary missionaries could rest and recharge their emotional batteries, where national pastors could be inspired and trained. There, holy bonfires could be started which might change the history of Brazil. Unfortunately, a month after they left to begin clearing the land, news came that Cleda had died.

Immediately, Jennie stepped in to help. Writing to the Go-Ye Fellowship, she promoted the project at home in letters and tapes. Soon financial support began arriving. Before long, a sixteen room housing facility had been constructed, complete with modern electrical and water systems. The Mitchells made several trips to the location. Eleven acres were eventually landscaped and the remaining acres rented out for crops.

Early in 1962, the Mitchells began arranging their furlough to the United States. They had been in Brazil nearly five years. Andrew was anxious to get back. He missed the northern continent. In the last months, he had begun thinking of his childhood home in Elora, Ontario, Canada, where he had grown up eighty years before. Their house, he remembered, had been right on the Grand River. He used to fish from the back porch and spear logs floating by in the river. The clear water, the rocks, the trees – ah, what a fine place! No place in the world was so beautiful.

During their time in Brazil, Andrew had kept a journal of their adventures. Now, he began recording the events of his life, beginning at the age of five, which was as far back as he could remember. Eighty years was a long time, but he was surprised how many names and faces came back so vividly. In those days, friends had called him "Scat" Mitchell. Who was this "Scat," he wondered. What had been his youthful goals and ambitions? A vague figure moved about in his memory...hard to pin down, that Scat. One thing though, in seeking the Lord, he had prospered – oh, how he had prospered! Like the man in the Psalm:

> *...a tree firmly planted*
> *by streams of water,*
> *Which yields its fruit in its season,*
> *And its leaf does not wither;*
> *And in whatever he does,*
> *he prospers.* (Psalms 1:4-8)

Now, in the evening of his life, Andrew discovered a joy in telling the sweet providences of the Lord.

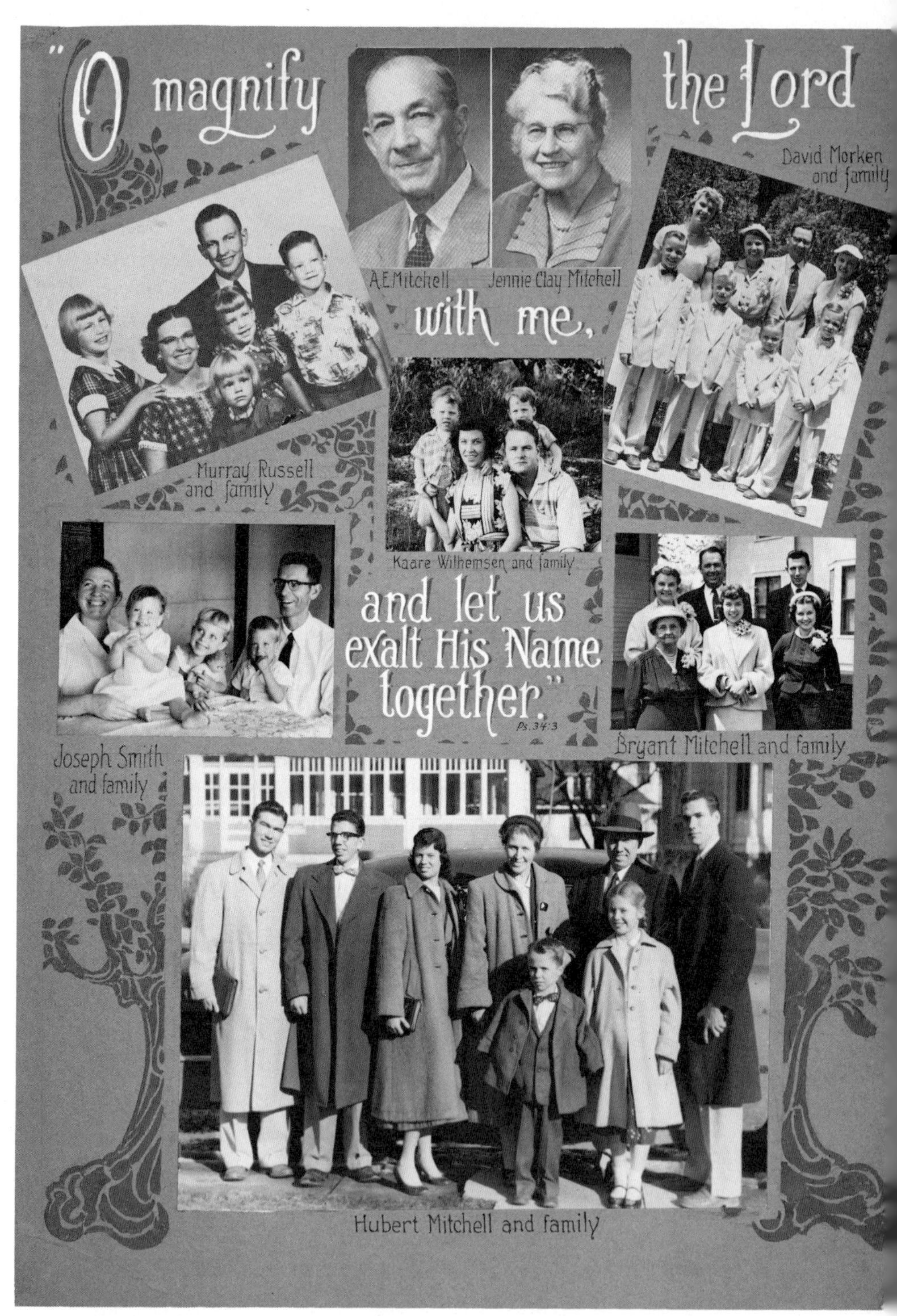

Mitchell family composite, 1955-57.

Chapter 14

PILGRIM AT THE GATE

Andrew and Jennie were welcomed home in May, 1962, after five years of ministry in Brazil. At meetings and conferences they gave enthusiastic reports of the progress made there, particularly of the new Panorama Conference Center which Jennie continued to promote and support. Jennie resumed her weekly radio broadcasts, while Andrew busied himself giving talks in the L.A. area and carving new mottoes. Missionary furloughs routinely lasted for one year, and they intended to remain in the United States at least that long before returning to Brazil. They still possessed a great deal of enthusiasm for the work that remained.

Before leaving Brazil, Andrew had begun to feel the effects of his advancing age. He tired easily and was often cold. In March, 1963, he passed his 86th birthday. Jennie, realizing their future plans were the impetus that gave him strength, began outlining their next missionary trip to Brazil. The necessary immigration permits were obtained. She purchased a new suit for him and a new dress for herself for the "new life" still ahead. However, by mid-1963 it became evident that Andrew would not be returning to Brazil.

A trip to a doctor revealed that he was suffering not just from old age, but from multiple myeloma, a malignancy of the bone marrow. Blood transfusions returned some strength, so that he enjoyed a few trips to the foothills of Sun Valley. Andrew disliked spending time in bed, which he likened to "getting ready for the undertaker." He sat in the front room at 1307 Waterloo, warming in the sunshine that spilled through the east windows. Wrapped in a plum-colored silk bathrobe, with his Bible and ever present notebook at his side, he wrote letters, made sketches for plaques and sculptures, and planned sermons. But his body steadily weakened. Jennie walked with him lest he should fall. In the evenings they sat in the living room alone and softly sang the old hymns they had sung together all over the world.

Despite his failing health, Andrew was still interested in events shaping the destiny of the country. He followed with a great deal of hope the civil rights demonstrations in Alabama and Washington, D.C. For decades he had deplored and regretted the racial situation in America. More than once he had apologized to black pastors and missionaries from Africa and South America for the treatment accorded them in visits to the United States. The

Andrew gives chalk drawing illustrated sermon.

assassination of President Kennedy in November, 1963, stunned him. It was a symptom of the country's deepening spiritual malaise.

In general, Andrew held a dismal view of the current scene. While they had been abroad bringing the Word to impoverished peoples, his own civilization was slipping into spiritual darkness. He had returned from Brazil to find a brave, new, secular world where the spiritual realities he had always known were now seldom acknowledged. His awareness, deepened by images of the Brazilian people – their poverty, their simple faith, their deep spiritual longings – perceived an America abandoned to the pursuit of money, power, fashion, and physical pleasures. Everywhere, Spirit had been replaced by the material, the holy and eternal by the secular and transient.

A humanistic vision asserted that Man, with his reason, was the measure of all things. Could not science reveal all knowledge? Could not enlightened politics reconcile the fractious relations of men, and technology create a utopian world? Troublesome intangibles like envy, hatred, lust, deceit, greed, jealously, pride—the demons that had ever gnawed at men's hearts—were problems for psychology.

Far from possessing an immortal soul, man was but a product of genetics and environment, whose behavior could be shaped and modified at will. The Bible was a book of parables and morality tales. Jesus of Nazareth was not the Son of God—*because God did not exist!* Faith, of course, was pointless. Faith in what? Only logic and reason served a purpose because the world was what one could see and measure.

Andrew had no quarrel with science which revealed the laws of the material world. But science went only so far. Two realms existed: a material realm and a realm of the Spirit. The latter was eternal and transcendent, and could not be measured or substantiated by any human reason or science. Only faith could prove it. The humanists refused faith unless God were proved, but faith alone could prove God.

To Andrew, it was ridiculous to think Man could live solely by the discoverable laws of the material world. Man was a bifurcated being belonging to both realms, a thing of earthly flesh molded in the image of God, who, for his very existence, must discover not only material laws but also the precepts of spirit. "Man shall not live by bread alone," Christ had warned, "but by every word that proceedeth out of the mouth of God" (Matt 4:4). The pride and vanity of the humanist vision, which recognized only material existence, was not only foolish, but dangerous, and could lead mankind to disaster.

Yes, it was disheartening to think what was happening to the country. Unfortunately, there was little Andrew could do about it.

In late February, 1964, Andrew entered the Huntington Hospital in Pasadena. He received a number of blood transfusions which temporarily revived him. In his notebook, he wrote, "I now have the blood of ten other men in my veins. My hands are pink. I look like a gentleman, but I have no strength." At night, Jennie sat with him, praying and quietly singing the old hymns.

Bob Pierce of World Vision visited and introduced Andrew to a newly-elected Cardinal from Rome who was also in the same hospital, convalescing from the amputation of an arm. The Pope had sent the man to Pasadena for treatment by a cancer specialist. The cardinal visited Andrew several times. Invariably, they discussed theological questions centering on the doctrine of redemption through the Cross of Christ. As they talked, Andrew marvelled

Andrew Mitchell

Jennie Clay Mitchell

at how closely they agreed on key issues. "This Catholic believes as I do," he thought, suddenly regretting all the times he had ever thought or spoken ill of Catholic priests in Brazil and elsewhere. The cardinal's visits, he realized, were no accident. "Through this man, God is teaching me one final lesson, which is that *Christ is Lord of all*, Protestant or Catholic. The historical differences are small compared to the great salvation displayed at Calvary. And isn't that what the Go-Ye motto stands for? 'No division in Christ, no unity out of Christ.'"

On his last visit, the Cardinal presented Andrew with a copy of a book he had recently written about the Cross. Andrew reciprocated by giving the Cardinal copies of his Bible studies.

Before Andrew entered the hospital, Jennie had written to the children, "He is putting up a good fight, but he is weak. I feel that you ought to come for a family get-together, just this once more, while Father may be able to enjoy it....We are holding him gently before the throne of mercy, rejoicing in the Scripture, 'Thou wilt keep him in perfect peace whose mind is stayed on Thee, because he trusteth in Thee.'"

On March 1, Andrew's eldest son Bryant arrived from Iowa, where he served as Chairman of the Open Bible Standard Churches. This completed the four children who would come to see Andrew off: Bryant, Hubert, Helen, and Marietta. Only the Wilhelmsens in Singapore and the Russells in Ethiopia were absent. Andrew felt that those on duty in foreign fields should remain like soldiers at their posts. The children took turns sitting with Andrew during the days and nights.

Andrew wanted to live at least until his 87th birthday. On March 10, Jennie brought a large cake with lighted candles to the hospital to celebrate. His family and a number of friends presented him with his old study Bible containing eighty-seven dollar bills, interleaved between the pages. This gift was dedicated to a fund for the publication of his writings.

In the evenings, Bryant tried to engage Andrew's attention by talking of contemporary events. However, Andrew's concern for worldly matters had already passed. He could not speak, and at the mention of these, he promptly wrinkled his nose in distaste. No purely human solutions existed for the real problems men faced, and such talk was out of context now as he faced eternity. His only delight was in the Word of God and the world to come. Only when Bryant read from the scriptures did a peaceful smile flow over his face, as once again he listened to the words that had ever guided his life:

> "Delight thyself also in the Lord;
> and he shall give thee
> the desires of thine heart...." (Psalms 37:4)
>
> "O magnify the Lord with me,
> and let us exalt his name together....
> (Psalm 34:3)
>
> "The Lord is my shepherd;
> I shall not want....
> ...Surely goodness and mercy
> shall follow me
> all the days of my life:
> And I will dwell in the house
> of the Lord forever." (Psalm 23)

Two days later, Andrew slipped into a coma. Once again the family gathered at the bedside. With Bryant and Hubert standing on each side of the bed holding their father's hands, the family joined hands and in prayer committed Andrew to God. On the last night, Bryant lingered, sitting by the bed, from time to time checking his father's pulse. As he held Andrew's hands, he marvelled at how smooth and muscular they were, not aged like the rest of the body.

A black nurse's aide came in to clean Andrew and change the bed linen. As she approached, she remarked on Andrew's hands, which Bryant was softly caressing as he sat by the bed. A sudden impulse prompted him to say, "Yes, his hands tell the story of his life. Look at those strong fingers. They are the capable fingers of a Scotch stone mason. They have laid thousands of stones

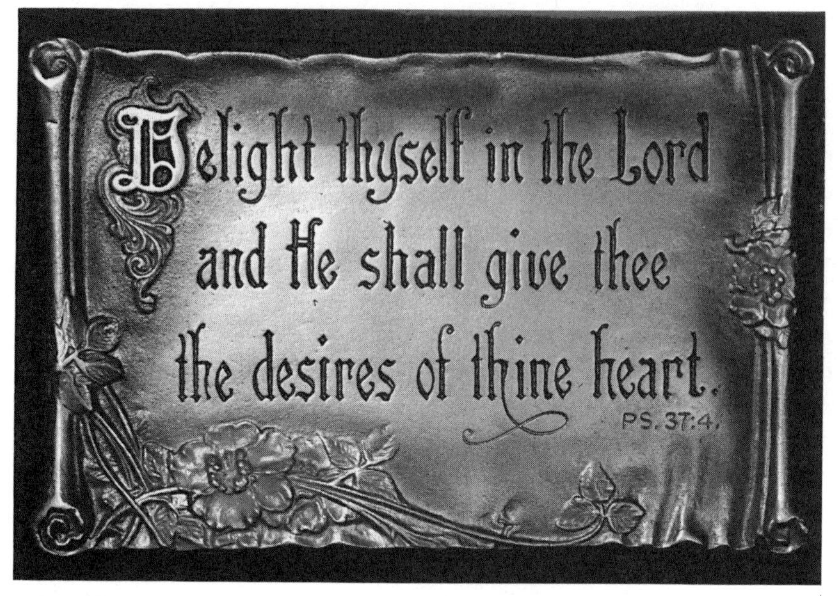

Mitchell aluminum scripture plaque. Courtesy Mitchell Art Company.

in walls on our hillside property. The skin is smooth, worn by mortar and cobblestones.

"He was also a sculptor. Those hands have fashioned clay roses and lilies for photographic art. They have carved plaster into beautiful shapes. He once made a beautiful sculpture of a black men's quartet that sang in our church. He could close his eyes and with his fingertips feel the beautiful texture in stones, weathered wood, and leather. He literally saw with his fingers. He was also a fine pen artist. Those stubby fingers have drawn many commercial designs you may have seen."

The nurse smiled and nodded. Bryant continued: "He was also a musician. Those fingers have played a golden concert harp, a beautiful green, shoulder-high Irish harp, and a sharp steel-string zither. See how the ends of his fingers are as solid as tough rubber. He would literally pounce on the small steel strings and pluck out chords with his thumb and third finger."

The nurse leaned forward and took up Andrew's hand, examining his fingertips closely. "Looks like something happened to this one," she said, indicating a missing joint on one finger.

"As a young man," Bryant said, "Andrew worked in a sewing machine factory. One day, the belt on a high-speed grinder, used to smooth metal parts, caught and twisted a joint off that finger."

A different memory flashed across Bryant's mind, which he did not relate. As a little boy, he had several times been corrected by a sharp slap on the palms of his hands with Andrew's hardwood ruler. Immediately afterwards, Andrew had always grasped his hands and rubbed them, as if to say, "I am sorry, son. I love you." To Bryant, Andrew's hands exemplified both Old Testament law and New Testament grace.

The nurse changed Andrew and left. Later, as the final hour approached, she returned. This time, she held Andrew's hands herself. Massaging them respectfully, she said to Bryant with a warm smile, "Your father was a wonderful man. I'm glad I got to hold his hands." Bryant could not help but think of the hundreds of black men and women in Africa and South America, who had been eternally blessed by the ministries of his father. Andrew had always been one to squeeze spiritual benefit out of every earthly occasion, and now, even at the hour of his death, he had touched someone's heart.

Andrew died just before dawn. Jennie, waiting for the phone call, came immediately and stood at the bed. Later, she cabled the Russells in Ethiopia and the Wilhelmsens in Singapore: "Father with Jesus today. Triumphant departure. Loving you. Mother."

"As the family joined hands, singing the familiar choruses in a final farewell, Jennie suddenly squeezed her daughter Helen Morken's hand and said excitedly, 'Listen to the meadowlarks!'"

At the Greenhills Memorial Park near San Pedro Harbor, the Palos Verdes Hills were green with spring grass. Eucalyptus and pepper trees were dressed in beautiful new leaves. Sparkles of sunlight danced on the ocean.

At the grave, surrounded by her children, Jennie stood straight and strong like a tree in a storm whose branches are whipped by the wind, but whose roots are firm and deep. She had no regrets or sorrowful memories about anything. She had done what she could and was faithful through every testing moment. Unknown to the others, she had written Andrew a farewell letter and placed it, together with a plaque, "Rich Toward God," in the pocket of his burial suit. The letter was also addressed to Sadie, Andrew's first wife, who, 50 years before, had born their first four children. Jennie had instructed that the plaque, "O magnify the Lord with me, and let us exalt His name together," be wired to the inner lid of the casket.

As the family joined hands, singing the familiar choruses in a final farewell, Jennie suddenly squeezed her daughter Helen Morken's hand and said excitedly, "Listen to the meadowlarks! There's a whole chorus of them!" Indeed, Helen heard it, too, the lilting sound of birds coming from every direction. To Jennie, the same God who had whispered His presence to a little four-year-old so many years ago on the empty Nebraska prairie was now speaking to His beloved in her hour of sorrow. From then on, whenever she wanted to visit Andrew's grave, Jennie always said, "Let's go out and hear the meadowlarks!"

Two weeks later, a letter arrived from Jean and Kaare in Hong Kong. Enclosed was a poem written by Jean:

WHO IS THIS PILGRIM?

Who is this pilgrim coming in the Gate....
who stands, no, not tall, but very straight?
Earth's dust still clings to his sandaled feet,
as though loath to give him up.
And round him crowds a host of friends,
all come to welcome him.
In his hand a pallet, wet with paint,
a smudge of colored chalk upon his wondering face;
Slung on his shoulder a dark, green bag,
his harp and Bible tucked inside.
No ordinary pilgrim this; he seems to know the way,
yes, sure and happy; dare I say it — even gay!
For he has learned the way to heaven's gate,
Singing as he comes....

Chapter 15

TYPHOON JENNIE: WORLD CITIZEN

Jennie lived for fourteen years after Andrew's death. During those years, he remained alive in her heart. She continued to celebrate both his birthday and their wedding anniversary. She kept his hat hanging in the kitchen. More than anything, she read and reread his writings, and so renewed the days when they used to read, study, and pray together. He had once said, "I believe that the very first thing we will want to do when we get to heaven will be to go to school." Now, she imagined him sitting with Paul, with the Book open and asking questions, *Just what did you mean when you wrote this verse in the Epistles?* Together they would clear up the difficulty.

Jennie had always been a strong, big-boned woman. Now, at seventy-nine, she walked with a staunch determination. Her silver-white hair had begun thinning, becoming so sparse on top that she had bought at the May Company a made-to-order hairpiece—white and silver-gray, with a streak of yellow. Each of her daughters learned to place it on her top knot. They agreed it looked like a crown, augmenting her complexion, which continued pink and radiant. Jennie loved flowers, particularly orange marigolds, and nowadays always wore a flower on her dress, sometimes real, sometimes not. Out of the house, she was seldom caught without a rose or artificial orchid pinned to her shoulder, and simple costume jewelry around her neck.

Instead of settling into quiet widowhood, surrounded by comforting friends and relatives, Jennie headed out into the world again, determined to finish what she and Andrew had begun. Despite her age, her mind was clear, and she still had plenty of energy. In the next fourteen years, she would make six trips around the world, visiting nearly fifty countries.

Jennie had four dreams: to promote Andrew's writings, which she felt had always needed wider publication; to continue distribution of his plaques, which were of such great use and benefit in the missionary field; to maintain the Waterloo Street property, which she regarded as a focus of God's work; and to ensure the perpetuation of the Go-Ye Fellowship. This last, she brooded over like a mother hen. At times, she thought others did not care for it as much as she did, and she feared for its survival.

In July, 1964, four months after Andrew's death, she returned to Brazil where the Panorama Conference Center, which was now complete on the banks of the Parana River, was holding its first interdenominational conference. Jennie threw herself into organizing and directing the conference. One hundred missionaries and pastors attended from all over Brazil. For Jennie, the conference was poignant with memories of Andrew. She saw many people whom they had known during their service there. Over the fireplace in the main dining hall hung his large plaque: "O magnify the Lord with me, and let us exalt His Name together." Seeing the graceful floral decoration, the letters spelling out the Scripture, she could almost feel him standing beside her again.

After the conference, she accepted numerous invitations to speak throughout Brazil and Argentina. Returning to Los Angeles with Nellie, who had at last resigned her ministry in Brazil, Jennie immediately scheduled visits to Go-Ye missionaries in Hawaii, Japan, Taiwan, Singapore, Malaysia, and India. Her sister Nellie, alarmed at these trips, exclaimed, "Why this great pressure that everything be done at once? Why this rushing here and there? Are you afraid death will overtake you before you can get accomplished all that you and Andrew planned together?"

"No, Nellie," Jennie answered, "I am not afraid of death. I am just moving as the cloud leads...."

As the reports came back to Nellie, she reported to the Go-Ye Fellowship, "They have taken to referring to our Jennie as 'Typhoon Jennie'. Evidently, she is being a true blessing everywhere she speaks."

In late 1964, the Smiths in India asked Jennie to come, settle down, and live with them. "I am not ready to settle down to just living," Jennie told her children. "I have work to finish and a message to give. God is pouring His Word into my heart. I must keep pouring out....Wherever I have stopped I have found a hungry world. How glad I am to have plenty of oil and meal. Like the widow of Elijah's land, I am making cakes...cakes for the multitude...."

Jennie exhibited a will and spirit that overwhelmed those she met. On one excursion into Malaysia with her son-in-law Kaare Wilhelmsen, she became closely acquainted with a Mrs. Harriet Shoemaker, a missionary lady thirty years her junior. For a time the two ladies occupied a camp trailer together. About daybreak Harriet was awakened by Jennie praying and praising God from her high bed in the trailer. Harriet later wrote, "Her joy was fed by streams from Heaven, and I never knew them to run dry. She was eighty when she challenged me to fasting and prayer. Her powers of endurance amazed me....She had assigned herself the task of learning three new verses a day. Her festive spirit was unforgettable."

Although Jennie understandably missed Andrew's harp and beautiful chalk drawings, she carried a small easel and flannel board to illustrate the gospel lessons. She did not pass up one opportunity to witness. "I am knee-deep in the harvest," she exclaimed to anyone who suggested she was doing too much. "I am accepting, as far as my strength goes, every door that is open even a crack. Oh, for a thousand tongues to sing my dear Redeemer's praise...."

Jennie made several trips to visit her daughter Esther and family in Ethiopia. One day an old grandmother living near the Russells' house broke her leg. As Jennie and her interpreter neared what looked like a tenement house, a neighbor approached her and said, "You can't tell the story of Jesus here. All of these folks are fighting with each other."

"Ha!" replied Jennie, "This is just the place. We have the cure for all this fussing and fighting." Setting up the flannel board, she started in.

Despite her trips abroad, Jennie continued to tape radio broadcasts for the audiences back home. In India, while visiting with Joe and Marietta, she prepared, with the assistance of the Buckwalters, missionaries with the Delhi stations of FEBC, two programs a day, six days a week, which she sent back to Los Angeles. When finally she returned to the Go-Ye in Los Angeles, she arranged for daily broadcasts over the KHOF FM radio program, "The Bible in Action."

In early 1967, Jennie persuaded her son Hubert, who was then working in Inter-Church Ministries in Chicago, to move to Los Angeles to head up the Go-Ye Fellowship and to oversee Andrew's various ministries of publication, art work, and mottoes, so that Jennie could be free to travel in the mission fields. Hubert and Rachel moved their family into the residence at 1307 Waterloo.

In July, 1969, Nellie died. She was ninety-four years old. It was one of the hardest trials Jennie ever endured. Nellie had practically raised her, and had been her constant companion in life. Her earliest memories were of Nellie holding her, comforting her, playing with her. Together, they had shared a vision of service to the Lord. Countless were the memories of "Tia Nellie" laboring in Mexico, Trinidad, and Brazil to bring the Good News to all who would hear it. Now, to see this dear sister lying emaciated, with sunken cheeks and eyes, and to hear her desperate, labored breathing in the final moments before death, was perhaps the most terrible thing Jennie ever faced.

The only surviving member of her family was now her brother Tom Clay. At age eighty-seven, he lived in Caliente, Nevada, where he published a small newspaper, *The Lincoln County Record*, in which he wrote blustering editorials lambasting what he regarded as the degenerate and corrupt values of the state (prostitution and gambling). Tom and Jennie didn't see each other much these days, although he wrote regularly and had come to Andrew's funeral.

Two months after Nellie's passing, Jennie started on another world trip, her fourth since Andrew's death. To her friends, she wrote, "My time clock, my sister Nellie, has slipped out of my arms into His. I feel to wrap myself up in my precious sister's mantle and continue my missionary journey...." The trip was planned to terminate in Des Moines in time for the wedding of her son, Bryant, to Lucille Jenkins. Lucille, whom Jennie called her "lovely queen," had been a missionary for thirty-four years in Liberia. Bryant's first wife, Lola Lee, had died the year before of cancer.

This time Jennie visited India, Ethiopia, Iran, Afghanistan, Pakistan, Saigon, Taiwan, Hong Kong, Tokyo, and Hawaii. In Kabul, Afghanistan, where Jean and Kaare Wilhelmsen had ministered, Jennie visited the church built through the efforts of the Christian community led by Christy Wilson. The church had been erected over the protests of the predominantly Muslim population. In memory of Andrew, Jennie placed in the church an oil painting depicting the Good Shepherd reaching down to rescue a sheep which had fallen into a rocky crevice.

From Kabul, she went on to visit her grandson, David Mitchell, Hubert's son, now thirty-eight and serving with his wife, Synnove, as a missionary in Pakistan. She wrote ahead to him: "Don't treat me as if I were old. I'm coming to serve. I can take at least one meeting a day." In fact, while at her grandchildren's house, an old British army barracks made of dried mud, she took two, sometimes three meetings a day. She also met several times with nomad tribesmen. One leader, Mabul Khan, of a Muslim Gypsy clan, invited her to eat with him and his leading men. The floor of his tent was covered with Persian carpets. As Jennie sat down on the floor, she realized her dress was too short for modesty. The Khan took one of his homespun blankets and draped it around Jennie so that she would not offend the men as they ate. The food was served on huge platters, around which the men sat in a close circle, dipping the food from the common plates with their fingers. Jennie joined in without hesitation, relishing the meal with gusto.

Before leaving, she related the Gospel message. Impulsively, she also shared something she had never before spoken of publicly. "I was born the daughter of a horse thief," she told them. The men, all skilled horsemen, gasped in astonishment. Like the American frontiersmen, they depended on horses for their livelihood, and they regarded horse thieves as little better than dogs.

"Is it true?" the Mabul Khan asked incredulously.

"Yes," Jennie answered with a chuckle, "the daughter of a horse thief!

I've been ashamed of this all my life, till in my eighties the Lord argued with me, 'Now, Jennie, that's just pride. You are nothing but a product of grace, so you might as well share it.' The daughter of a horse thief has become the daughter of a king!"

Leaning back, the Mabul Khan and his men regarded Jennie with new respect. The Khan said, "Surely, it is a miracle of grace!"

In 1971, Jennie left once more to visit her daughter Marietta in India. Here she met her granddaughter, Alice Jean Russell, the first child of Esther and Murray Russell, who had been raised in Ethiopia. Although the girl had an ambulatory handicap, she had just finished college and wanted to be a missionary. She and Jennie decided to form a missionary partnership and travel together throughout the Orient. "We'll be 'Paul' and 'Silas,'" said Jennie.

Jennie Mitchell and grandaughter Alice Jean Russell (Paul and Silas) at the baptismal service in India, 1971.

Alice Jean was totally committed to her grandmother, waiting on Jennie hand and foot, bowing to her every desire. She found Jennie exciting to be with, a "clown" who brought fun and cheer to everyone. She marvelled how Jennie could start up conversations with almost anybody. Relishing the exchange, Jennie zeroed in on a stranger's concerns like an old friend, which brought an instant rapport, an instant trust. Hang-ups, human stresses, and prayer requests were quickly treated with respect, and prayed for on the spot. In the middle of a conversation, Jennie would close her eyes and begin, "...And, now, Lord Jesus...." It was difficult to shock Jennie, and she received with equal equanimity reports of difficulties, accidents, and threatening circumstances. It was her nature to seek pleasantness and good humor. She turned from unpleasantness wherever she found it, whether in speech or action. She tried to diffuse harshness or crudity with laughter and good humor. When she preached now, tears flowed freely down her face. At every meeting, many came forward to have her lay hands on them for prayer. Wherever she went, people could not get over the fact that she was traveling around the world at eighty-seven years of age.

As "Paul" and "Silas" traveled in India, Nepal, Indonesia, Pakistan, and Afghanistan, they met many Christian groups who were succumbing to the overwhelming darkness of idolatry and opposition to the Christian message. "They just need to huddle round the Word, turn inward to God," said Jennie. "That's where their strength lies." She began organizing small clubs to promote unity and strength through positive and regular Christian witness. Each club was given a name which matched a Scripture lesson. Members signed their names to a roster, and a leader was appointed to keep the club active and in line with a Bible lesson. The Clubs' names were curious:

Youth Renewal Club	In Everything Give Thanks Club
Hallelujah Club	Writer's Club (Write your testimony)
One Next to Me Club	I'm very Important Club
Complete in Him Club	Rejoice Evermore Club
Do It Club	Gap Filler Club
Bless Club	Be Strong Club
My Very Best Club	Radio Club
Yes, Lord Club	Gather Up the Fragments Club
Victory Club	Power Club

For years afterwards, letters from around the world arrived at the Go-Ye Fellowship in Los Angeles telling of the renewed spiritual activity generated by these clubs.

In India, Jennie encountered her most frustrating situation, which derived, oddly, not from Indians, but from Western youngsters who had turned up at the youth center which Marietta and her husband, Joe, operated near the University of Delhi. Dropouts who had rejected the values and beliefs of their own culture, these young people had come by bus and plane from Europe and America, seeking what Jennie could only regard as strange gods and idolatrous beliefs. Most were ragged and malnourished, with sores on their bodies. Many used drugs. The Smiths had taken several into their home, feeding and doctoring them, and spending long hours conversing and studying the Bible together, striving to redirect their lives.

In the evenings, while the rain pounded on the roof, anywhere from five to fifteen young people sprawled on the living room floor "rapping" with each other, or with Joe or Marietta. Try as she might, Jennie could not get used to these quiet, leisurely, circuitous conversations interspersed with long periods of silence, during which people smoked, picked at the carpet, or stared silently ahead. Their demeanor was so low-key, so passive, their voices so nearly inaudible, that Jennie became agitated. She urged Marietta to just "preach the gospel." Alice got along with them better than Jennie.

In her prayers, Jennie complained, "Lord, I didn't come here to do nothing." Finally, given the opportunity to speak, Jennie vigorously passed out Scripture tracts, miniature Hallelujah slips with the instruction "Use these on your college campus!", and handmade paper crosses which she used to explain the significance of Christ's redemption of the world. Although they listened quietly, most remained indifferent, as if it were all somehow irrelevant.

Jennie and Alice travelled together for eight months, visiting twenty-five cities in three countries. Finally, Alice returned to work with her parents, Esther and Murray, who had transferred to Kenya after the Marxist takeover of Ethiopia. Later, Alice ventured back into Ethiopia as a Christian teacher and social service worker during the years of famine in that country.

In late 1974, Jennie made a final trip to Brazil. In Sao Paulo and Belo Horizonte, she looked into the faces of the brown-eyed Brazilians and shouted for joy, telling them they were made in God's image...that they were important to God and their individuality "would never be duplicated."

On June 1, 1975, she celebrated her ninetieth birthday. Her children and co-laborers planned a special celebration. Flowers arrived from children in far-off countries, and hundreds of cards came from well-wishers. At a reception in the Go-Ye compound, three hundred people enjoyed punch and cake. Wearing a pink dress and an orchid, Jennie invited the guests back "in another ten years to help celebrate my one hundredth birthday."

Jennie spent much of the next year at home on Waterloo Street. She started her day by opening the large front door on the warm California sunrise and inserting her plastic American flag in its holder on the front porch. In the last several years, the Waterloo Street neighborhood had changed. It now included a number of multi-ethnic families, Latinos, Thais, Pakistani, and Armenians. On nice days, Jennie sat on the porch and watched the people go by. Much of the time she sat inside by the front window in the sunshine with her Bible on her knees, surrounded by a clutter of letters, articles, and papers. She worked on her scrapbook which contained pictures of her children, grandchildren, and friends from six missionary trips around the world. She particularly enjoyed the pictures of herself and Andrew costumed in foreign garb, riding a variety of conveyances, from a borne-of-four-chair-dandy, to howdahs on the backs of elephants. Streams of history! Had it all actually happened?

She felt a loneliness now. She had always been subject to it, but since Andrew's death, the feeling had grown. Since childhood she had needed to be at the hub of things. It bolstered her identity. Her fear of isolation drove her to be always on the move. All her life she had been a transient, easily setting off, being farewelled, and then returning home to be welcomed. During these last years, she had flitted among her children, never lighting very long, breezing in and out. "I must get back to 1307," she'd say. Or if she'd get weary of the Waterloo Street house, she'd mention, "Keep the door latch open, I'm coming." She was careful not to wear out her welcome, realizing that even her children could take her only "in small doses." And so she visited here and there, trying never to stay too long, but enough to keep ahead of the loneliness.

Jennie could feel her body deteriorating. Regarding herself in the mirror, she noticed her diminishing size, and said to Rachel, Hubert's wife, "I seem to have shrunk." More than anything, she wanted to grow old gracefully. In every way she resisted aging. Although she walked with a cane now, she encouraged herself by joking, "Here comes Mrs. Sure-foot." To help her fading memory, she began reading more. She read twenty Bible chapters a day, plus other books and articles. She made long lists of names, people she had known in foreign countries and the Go-Ye Fellowship, trying to recall incidents and places.

The day came, however, when she needed aid in performing personal physical tasks. It was Rachel who helped her bathe. Some of Jennie's reserves had to be broken down, for it was against all her upbringing. However, she finally consented to the indignity, saying lightly to her daughter-in-law, "Aren't you getting into my territory now?"

Gradually, she began having to take orders from her daughters. This was hard on everyone. When Marietta made her promise not to walk downstairs without holding the rail, Jennie promised, "All right, Retta, girl, I will do that." Once, however, when Helen, weary of Jennie repeating a story, asked her abruptly not to tell it again, Jennie reacted in a way that her daughter was not prepared for. "Don't you ever talk to me like that again," Jennie scolded. "Not one of my children may ever speak to me like that. You may remind me, but I will not take that kind of talk."

Stunned, Helen said, "Please forgive my impatience, Mama. I spoke too bluntly. I'm sorry."

"Of course, I forgive you, Sweetheart," said Jennie immediately. "I forgive you."

Jennie had various ways of dealing with emotional hurt. For a long time, she had felt inferior because she hadn't been as logically minded as Andrew. One day, the Lord had told her, "I love you just as you are. I have chosen you." From that time on, she had tried never to wallow in self-pity, never to cry over her imperfections.

On an early Sunday morning in January, a group using the Go-Ye chapel tried to light the floor furnace. A burning match fell into the basement below, igniting some papers on a table. The fire was not discovered until it had a good start.

People ran for hoses. Jennie, tottering down the steps as fast as she could, attempted to go through the smoke into the chapel to rescue treasured items, but was pulled back. A young man, whose father had been a fireman, took quick action and got the Fire Department to the scene just in time to save the building. However, hundreds of Andrew's books, plaques, and papers were scorched, and many precious objects stained. Jennie was near collapse at the thought that the entire compound had almost gone up in flames.

In the fall of 1977, in her ninety-second year, Jennie became like a caged eagle. Her failing strength, however, did not permit what her spirit wanted to do. Frantic to be going and doing, she organized a patriotic prayer project. The purpose was to enlist 1001 Christians in united prayer groups to "turn America right side up." Enlisting the aid of Fern, the Go-Ye secretary, she mailed hundreds of letters to her family and Go-Ye constituents containing prayer requests for specific national leaders and groups. At the top of the list were President Jimmy Carter and Vice-President Walter Mondale, the President's staff, the Justices of the Supreme Court, Senators, Congressmen, the Cabinet, and "the Governor of your state and mayor of your city." Blank cards were enclosed for prayer partners to sign and return their prayer promise. Jennie decided that she must make one last tour of the USA to support this project. At the last minute, her children living in L.A. stepped in and persuaded her that the mailing campaign was sufficient. Jennie sighed. It was not sufficient, she knew, but she had not the strength to do otherwise.

One day, while walking with Margaret, the wife of her grandson, Daniel Mitchell, Jennie suddenly grabbed her hand and exclaimed, "Darling, the Lord told me today, 'Jennie, you must face death!' Just like that, He said, 'You must face death!'"

Jennie's longing had been never to die. Nellie, too, had had this feeling. In both sisters, there had been something that expected to live always. To Jennie, death was unreal, something to be put off indefinitely, something that would never happen. She seemed almost to have counted on an imminent Second Coming to rescue her from the ordeal of dying. Both she and Nellie were like soldiers who concentrated more on the battle than on a cessation of the battle. From this time on, as her strength began steadily failing, Jennie became more reconciled to the possibility of death.

In November, 1977, Esther invited her mother to Nairobi for a visit. Jennie could stay for a year and return when the Russells came home on their furlough. Esther was coming to the United States for the wedding of her daughter Jennifer, Jennie's namesake, in Greeley, Colorado. If Jennie would meet her there, they would fly back to Kenya on the plane together.

It was the opportunity Jennie had been waiting for. Alice Jean (Silas) travelled ahead from Kenya to accompany Jennie to Colorado. The two arrived in Greeley the day of the wedding and went directly to the church. As Esther was being ushered into the Chapel by her son John, she passed by all of the relatives and friends, including Jennie. This was nearly too much for Jennie, who hadn't seen her daughter for nearly a year. Leaning over the pews, Jennie tried to poke Esther with her cane. When it wouldn't reach, she sent Alice. Not to stop and greet her mother, even in the midst of a formal wedding! Why, whoever heard of such a thing?! Wasn't it a family affair, after all?

A week later, at Kennedy airport in New York, Jennie phoned Los Angeles to say goodbye to Hubert and Rachel. How good they had been to her all these last years. She felt she must talk to them one last time. Over the phone, crackling with static from the long distance connection, she heard Rachel say, "Mother, I love you."

Speaking slowly, Jennie replied, "You have shown it, Rachel, dear."

On the plane a blind, black woman sat just in front of Jennie. From time to time, Jennie heard snatches of her conversation: "Jesus..." and "....work for the Lord...."

"I want to talk with that lady," Jennie whispered to Esther. Exchanging seats, Jennie and the woman were soon sharing their experiences, gesturing with animation and exclaiming shouts of praise, completely unaware of the other passengers. One whole section of the plane listened as Jennie prayed aloud for her new friend.

Jennie breathed a sigh of relief as the British airliner, which had crossed Europe, the Mediterranean, and four thousand miles of Africa, finally landed in Nairobi, Kenya. Although she had made the ten-thousand-mile trip from New York all right, she now had difficulty breathing in the high altitude of Nairobi. She was looking forward to this time of rest with her grandchildren. The Russell home sat atop a green hill overlooking a lush valley, which Jennie found soothing and peaceful.

Soon after their arrival, however, she decided she couldn't "idle" any longer. She needed to teach and fellowship with the people. The Murrays fixed a flannelgraph board for her and gathered in the neighborhood children. Telling the story of Queen Esther, her animation enveloped the young listeners with a magic that held them spellbound. Soon after, she was happily sharing Esther's classes with native women and children.

With Christmas came the usual celebration and church functions. It was a Russell tradition to go carolling on Christmas morning. Jennie insisted on going along, although her feet were swollen. To ease her feet she wore large comfortable slippers. As a light rain fell, the carolers walked from house to house, singing until the doors were opened and they were invited in for fellowship. Later, one friend remarked to Esther, "I'll never forget the sight of your white-haired mother standing in her slippers in the rain singing Christmas carols."

Jennie enjoyed playing endless games of cards and Chinese Checkers with her grandchildren, Joy and Peter. When she lost her appetite at the dinner table, she slyly bargained with the children, "I'll eat one bite, if you'll finish it."

The loneliness, however, returned upon her at unexpected moments. At Christmas, she experienced an intense longing for Andrew, whom she missed now more than ever. Thus, the gift that completely overwhelmed her was one Murray discovered in the Keswick Book Store in Nairobi, just before Christmas – one of Andrew's plaster plaques: "I WILL NEVER LEAVE THEE NOR FORSAKE THEE."

Jennie kept part of her awareness on the Go-Ye Fellowship. Before retiring in the evening, she prayed with Esther for the worldwide Go-Ye family. Sitting on the bed, she went over the list of dear ones she didn't want to forget in prayer. To Esther, she related something about each person, who was as close to her, Esther realized, as her own family.

Jennie's last letter to the Go-Ye began:

> "My Dear and Precious Friends,
>
> "As my Father has sent me, so send I you with the same equipment...Go to Jerusalem and I will send the Holy Spirit and you will receive power to do greater works than I have done...Heal the sick...Cast out demons...Raise the dead! You will have tribulation in the world, but be of good cheer, I have overcome the world!....
> "You and I are now Kings and Priests...Joint-heirs with Christ. He gives faith, love, grace, joy, and peace! No wonder we are to God a sweet savor of Christ...."

Before leaving the United States, Jennie had had a premonition that she might not be returning. After Christmas, she wrote to Hubert in Los Angeles: "I have made plans with Esther that in case of my death....just bury me here in Kenya and do not ship the body home." Jennie had always wanted to be buried on the mission field. Kenya might be the fulfillment of that wish.

In early January, Murray Russell, who was associated with the World Vision ministry, left for a two-month project in the Philippines, planning to return in early March, after stopping in India to see Marietta and Joe. Esther, left alone to care for Jennie, worried about her mother's deteriorating condition.

The Russells employed a Kikuyu housekeeper and cook, named Julia. Except for a few words, she could not understand much English. In the mornings when Jennie hailed her with, "Well, Hallelujah, Julia," she would reply, "Well, Hallelujah, Mama!" Although neither could understand the other, Julia took to sitting with Jennie, accompanying her around the house, listening attentively to all that Jennie said, now and then making some comment in Swahili.

One morning around the first of March, just before Murray was expected back, Esther asked Julia to take Jennie for a short walk, "...just to the bridge and back." Julia, however, didn't get the directions right and led Jennie on a mile-long walk up and down the hill. It was too much for Jennie. At one point they had to go to a stranger's house to borrow a stool so Jennie could sit down and rest. Unable to flag down a car for a ride, they finally staggered home. Jennie rolled into bed very exhausted. The next day, it was apparent the ordeal had precipitated a crisis. Her body seemed to lose its delicate balance. She lost her appetite and couldn't eat. She became panicky. She exclaimed to Esther, "Oh, what shall we do?" To Julia, she pleaded, "Oh, please, Julia, come rub my neck. Oh, rub it some more...Julia, I am so very sick."

When the condition persisted, Esther decided to take Jennie to the hospital for examination and tests. It took all of her and Julia's strength to get Jennie into the back seat of the Russells' tiny Ford Escort. Jennie, resting her head on Julia, was in good spirits. She exclaimed, "Isn't this jolly! My head on Julia's bosom. What a comfort...!"

At the hospital, however, the white sheets of the high hospital bed filled Jennie with fear. She had always been afraid of hospitals and institutions. Their impersonality filled her with dread and impending doom. Hospitals and old folks' homes were places for those who needed ministering to. Jennie was a minister! Also, she was too home and family oriented to accept the impersonal attentions of nurses and orderlies. Esther hoped the doctor would provide some comfort.

However, the English woman doctor surveyed them with an impatient eye. She crisply ordered Esther and Julia from the examination room, making it perfectly clear that she could handle everything without the family present.

At the same time, she warned this "old lady" that she wouldn't tolerate any games.

Jennie spent ten days in the Nairobi hospital, being wheeled from here to there for tests and x-rays. The hours were long and tedious. She settled into a state of quiet desperation. Nursed mostly by native Kenyans, she tried to keep up her spirits by reaching out to the nurses and attendants ("Oh, what beautiful dimples you have! I'm collecting dimples!"). A family member sat constantly at the bedside, reading, writing a letter, trying to keep her company and maintain the pretense of the normal. Although her vital signs stabilized, she began refusing food. At times she appeared to lose her sense of reality. In an effort to focus her mother's awareness, Esther began talking of her ninety-third birthday, about six weeks ahead. This exercise helped bring Jennie's spirit under control. She had always needed a plan, something to look forward to. Despite this, one morning she whispered aloud, "I want to go and see Mr. A. E. Mitchell."

In answer to Esther's cable, Murray arrived from Manila, bringing Marietta from India. "Oh, Retta, Retta, you did come!" Jennie exclaimed when she saw her other daughter.

On March 10, the anniversary of Andrew's birthday, they took Jennie home. However, she was no longer the jolly, talkative woman who had been admitted to the hospital. Her heart had weakened perceptibly. She was unsmiling and silent. Her face was gaunt. The sparkle in her eyes was gone, and she stared ahead, seeming not to recognize any of them. The family took her home and tucked her into bed, and then, gathering round, sang her favorite chorus: "Hallelujah, hallelujah." Only then did she smile faintly.

Jennie lived another three weeks, occasionally speaking, but most of the time lying silently. When she did speak, it was evident that deep inside her sense of humor continued strong. To warm her feet, she wore wool socks. The wooden floors of the house had recently been waxed, and one morning, as Murray was putting her in the wheel chair, her socked feet slipped on the polished wood and they both fell in a heap on the floor. Jennie nearly slid under the bed. They all laughed. The next day, when Murray tried to move her again, she glanced up and said, "Would you like another dance?"

One morning she surprised them by telling an old joke: "Many years ago, Esther put a large, frozen Thanksgiving turkey into the washing machine to thaw out. She forgot it and dumped a whole load of washing over it. The machine went through all the cycles. At the end she found the turkey thawed and unharmed."

Toward the end of March, Jennie's condition deteriorated rapidly. The family took turns sitting at the bedside, waiting for the end. At night, they left

Esther Russell beside her mother's grave, Nairobi, Kenya, 1978.

a small night light on, and the door ajar. At any sound, one of the family went into her room. On March 29, a letter arrived from Jennie's brother, Tom Clay:

> "...Hello Sis, I love you and think you are beautiful.
>
> "Blood is thicker than water, and our blood has coagulated. Our mother Marietta said: 'I'll be with you always', and she is closer than when we were on her knee....
>
> "I am still Tom, and your blood-brother. Here is a kiss and a hug. Let's get on our stick horses for a little ride."

Esther read it to her mother, but Jennie did not respond. At six o'clock in the morning the next day, Marietta answered Jennie's call for "Water! Water!" Jennie could not, however, handle the drink. The family stood helplessly by, holding her hands. Presently, her pulse stopped. It was over. Jennie was gone.

"We wept," Esther wrote home. "Through our tears we thanked our Father for this life which had become so much a part of our own. We folded those hands that had comforted many. We closed those eyes which had never dimmed for nearly ninety-three years. We closed that strong mouth which had blessed so many with words of encouragement, that had blessed her children through long hours of intercession."

As two Kenyan men carried Jennie's body down the hall and outside to a waiting car, Julia, the housekeeper, folded Jennie's hands over her head in typical African fashion.

At the funeral the pallbearers were a representative blend of Kenyans, Ethiopians, grandchildren, and missionaries. For the benediction, the choir sang Jennie's favorite: "How Firm a Foundation."

The grave was under a bright red Flame tree in the small Langata Cemetery bordering the Nairobi game park. Marietta thought that Jennie would have delighted in the place. One could see a long ways across the plain, which appeared to stretch to eternity under the bright blue canopy of the African sky. The Kenyan word, "Langata," meant "savanna," or "prairie." Marietta thought it significant that Jennie, who had been born on a prairie, was now being laid to rest on one. For a moment, as the casket was being lowered, she thought she heard something quite impossible: meadowlarks singing! How could that be?

Epilogue

GRANDMA JENNIE COMES TO CHURCH:

A grandson's sermon

By the Rev. Arthur J. Landwehr May 14, 1978

First United Methodist Church, Evanston, Illinois

(Abridged transcription)

This morning we are going to celebrate Pentecost, Mother's Day, and Family Sunday because of Grandma Jennie.

Grandma Jennie wanted to be here this morning. She said so in a letter which I read to you on Easter Sunday morning. Her response was to an invitation to our 125th Anniversary next year. It went like this: "Dear Arthur and Avonna Lee, I'll be happy to be with you in the First Methodist. My heavenly Father is so carefully watching over this 92-year-old sheep. My life is full of blunders.

"How often I have yearned to live one life for practice and another when I've learned. Ha! The practice should be over at 92, and from now on this is for real. I think ten more years are enough. I must finish my course well. Deep love, Grandma Jennie."

A week after Easter one person said to me, "I'm looking forward to meeting Grandma Jennie. You must tell us more Grandma Jennie stories." There are more "Grandma Jennie" stories, but Grandma Jennie died that week. The disappointment of her announced death has been written on your faces as I have shared that fact with you. Yes, Grandma Jennie was a real person, the grandmother of my wife. You never knew when she was going to drop in for a visit with her jolly spirit and chuckling laughter. You never knew what she was going to teach you next.

When she was 86, she stopped in for a visit on her way around the world to visit her children, all of whom are missionaries. She was chuckling to herself as we were driving to O'Hare, and I wondered what was titillating her spirits that afternoon. She said, "You know, Arthur, it's a bit amusing to see my children struggling through old age."

She was born June 1, 1885, Jennie Clay, from Enterprise, Nebraska, near the Sioux Indian Reservation on the South Dakota border. Her parents were pioneers who lived in a sod house, raised cattle and horses on the prairies, withstood the tornado weather, winter snows, and collected cow chips for fuel for their stoves. Jennie was one of five children. Her elder brother, Tom, at 95 lives in Caliente, Nevada, where he is the owner-editor of the county newspaper, *The Record*. In 1892, they drove their cattle, horses and prairie schooner to Clayton, New Mexico, sold them and took the train to Denver, Colorado, and then on to Los Angeles. As a young girl, Grandma Jennie and her girl friend often rode her horse down Main Street from 2lst to City Hall.

She graduated from Normal School and became a teacher in the public schools. As a teenager she became very much involved in the Echo Park Methodist Church. The reality of the Gospel made a deep impression upon her. The years wore on, her commitment to teaching and to helping people grew and deepened.

Her dedication and charm attracted the attention of a man named Andrew E. Mitchell. He was an artist, a sculptor, a teacher, a philosopher. His wife, Sadie, had died leaving him with two boys, 14 and 11, and two girls, 9 and 6. The 14-year-old would turn out to be my wife's father.

They were married on May 12, 1920, and at age 35, she became the mother of four children who needed a mother's love and care. Later, two daughters were to be added to their home.

They were active in their church. It was in the days in which Methodism really believed that everybody who was a part of the church ought to be actively engaged in ministry. They didn't hire a staff to do their work for them. Everybody was a minister. Part of their ministry was going to the jails to care for the inmates, some of whom were eventually to be paroled to their home. They had an open-door policy.

Struggle came to Echo Park Methodist Church, as it does to many churches throughout the years. The Methodist Church was becoming too bureaucratic, according to A.E. Concern for people was being diminished. Disaffection grew.

Somewhere, A.E. and Grandma Jennie developed a missionary vision. They found some people who wanted to share the good news of God's love but had no financial support. So, with paint and canvas, A.E's artistic talent was put to use. Money was raised to send out missionaries from a missionary fellowship they developed from scratch. Before very long, 35 missionaries received support from Grandma Jennie and A.E. Mitchell's efforts.

The six children became missionaries in different denominations and all over the world. The places they have touched are many. Here are just a few. They've served in Iran, Pakistan, Japan, Hong Kong, Singapore, India, China, Turkey, Afghanistan, Trinidad, Sumatra, Brazil, Ethiopia, and Kenya, and surely some places have been overlooked.

In 1964 A. E. Mitchell died. A few months later at age 79, Grandma Jennie announced to the whole family that she had a global responsibility. "The world is my parish," a phrase most certainly linked to her Methodist orientation. So around the world she went, first to Ethiopia. She was a stout woman, a strong-looking woman with a formidable face and beautiful long hair, though I never saw just how long it really was. It was always tucked up in a neat bun on the back of her head.

She loved children and thought it was very important for every child to learn about the love of God. Wherever she was, whether it was in Ethiopia, or Brazil, she would, whenever the opportunity arose, share the good news. In Ethiopia she didn't understand the regulations of the village in which she was walking. She had a whole group of children gathered around her, and soon the police came. Can you imagine the police arresting a little old lady, 79, for telling children stories? She couldn't either.

As they hauled her off to jail, she began to tell the police about the loving goodness of God and of Jesus. The police didn't quite know what to do with her. Finally, her daughter was called and everything was explained. She really wasn't disturbing the peace. She was trying to tell children an awfully wonderful story.

I hadn't realized how much Grandma Jennie had gotten around. Three weeks ago, I was at the Lutheran Northwestern Seminary in St. Paul where we were involved as United Methodists in bilateral conversations with the Lutherans. Late at night I was in the rest room preparing myself for bed, when a very dark, short young man walked through the door. I looked at him through the mirror and asked him, "Where are you from?"

"Ethiopia," he smiled.

I said, "You don't happen to know a Murray Russell?" He smiled again. "He happens to be my wife's uncle, a Presbyterian minister."

He said, "Yes, I know him, he was my pastor."

"By the way, did you happen to know Grandma Jennie?"

He beamed from ear to ear. "Oh, Grandma Jennie, I knew her. She's a strong Christian woman," he said.

And I said, "Did you know Grandma Jennie died?" His face dropped as if part of the sun had just fallen out of place. I began to realize what a bit of sunshine she was to so many people.

Part of her deep concern as a grandmother was her responsibility to her family and to her grandchildren, especially the younger ones who had been deeply affected by the trauma of the 1960s. In her vocabulary were three words which she used to deal with most of life – Bless. That was a happy word of benediction – Bless. Bless. Bless.

A second word was Hallelujah. That word was used to fight battles. Grandma never moaned. Grandma never grumbled, but when Grandma knew that the test had to be met, her word was Hallelujah. And whenever things became very stressful, as the time when Grandpa was dying, it was HALLELUJAH, HALLELUJAH!!

One of her grandchildren (all of them were very well-educated) became involved in a group that decided to buy a farm and live communally. Grandma Jennie wasn't sure about this so she went out to the farm before they moved in. She sensed there was something wrong with the whole affair. The vibrations weren't right. She didn't like the idea of four families moving in together, and the kind of visionary entrapment that her grandchildren had gotten into.

She wrote on little pieces of paper, "Hallelujah," and put them in the cracks everywhere; in fence posts, in tree bark, in the children's room, in the cracks in the floor. Their daughter said recently, "Every time we turned around we found a piece of paper that said, 'Hallelujah ' on it and we knew that somebody thought something was deeply wrong with what we were doing. She was right. Our three years was a nightmare, and Grandma Jennie's walking all over that piece of property putting her 'Hallelujahs' there, I am sure, was a basic factor in us ever escaping a very demonic experience."

Her third phrase was "Isn't it jolly." "Isn't it jolly" was simply the normal state of affairs when the "blesseds" and "hallelujahs" had done their jobs. "Isn't it jolly" is the way it was to be. She believed that the one thing that would last throughout life and time itself was one's relationship to God. Her grandchildren could have educations, which they all did, but to miss this was to miss life itself.

So much of her life was shaped by the Echo Park Methodist Church. "The world is my parish," a quotation from Wesley, Methodism's founder, and the second Methodist emphasis, "freedom in the Holy Spirit" must have registered deeply with her. Some things she believed for sure.

She believed in the interaction between the seen and the unseen. Sometimes this took curious turns. She had the heaviest luggage of anybody I've ever known. It took both hands to lift her luggage. I asked her one day, "Grandma, what do you have in here?" She listed all of the things, lots of it electronic equipment so that she could tape messages here and there and everywhere.

"Well, Grandma, who lifts these bags when you get to the airport?"

She said crisply, "The Lord always helps." I thought of all of the Lord's army who must have helped carry those heavy burdens throughout the years.

She exercised her understanding of this inner-play between the seen and the unseen through prayer. I'll never forget the first few months of our marriage. There had been a big debate as to whether or not we ought to hold off our wedding so that Grandma Jennie could be there. We decided six months was just a little too long to wait.

After we were married, Grandma Jennie came for a visit. She wanted to meet me, and I knew that this was for sizing up. There we were, sitting in our basement apartment which I would say was rather modest, a few pipes dripping here and there, just to keep the basement on the humid side.

All of a sudden out of the clear blue, she said, "Children, (a word at that time I could not appreciate) God is a good God, and He wants the two of you to be well and happy. Now you can't be well here. We must ask God to move you." She bowed her head, and immediately we were in prayer. Two weeks later we were evicted. I stayed away from Grandma Jennie for quite a long time thereafter, and never asked her to pray.

She believed in Pentecost. Celebrating the presence of the Holy Spirit was the essence of life. Jesus was present because the Holy Spirit was the clone of Jesus. The real Jesus promised to come into human beings and empower them to do all kinds of wonderful good things as they lived out their lives.

She believed in being liberated. She used the word *FREE.* But liberation for her had three parts. First, liberation comes in being free from yourself. She knew the terrors of narcissism and self-centeredness.

Her last few weeks of life were spent in Nairobi, where she had gone to visit her daughter and son-in-law, who are Presbyterian ministers there. She had become very, very sick. Lovely Scottish nurses cared for her. One morning, when Allison bent over Grandma Jennie, who hadn't spoken for three or four days, Grandma Jennie opened her eyes wide, and in a strong voice asked, "Do you smoke?"

The nurse said, "Yes, I'm afraid I do."

"When did you get started doing that?" She continued.

"Good question," said Allison.

"Well, when you get to heaven, look me up." And Allison began to think– no condemnation in the old Methodist fashion of no smoking, no drinking. . . .Heaven was going to be a big place for Grandma Jennie. She could see heaven written on the most interesting faces, as she did here.

Secondly, God liberated her for service. She would have a lot to tell all of us about true freedom, especially those of us who think that freedom means doing what one wants to do in the spirit. That's not what freedom is. And she knew it.

True freedom was the ability to become motivated and moved to do what God needed to have done through one's life. There is only one freedom and that's the freedom to serve. Service is what gets passed on from one person to another, from one generation to the next.

And finally, this freedom, this liberation, produces joy. "It's jolly." Being a wife, a mother, a grandmother, a friend, a visionary, she believed that God put us into families to experience God's love. To experience the presence of the Holy Spirit so that we might learn what it is really to be children, not only of a family here, but the broader family, which is brought into existence by the grace of God.

Kamie, a teen-age poet of England says it well for Grandma Jennie:

What is it that the powers of darkness fear the most?
Next to the Father, Son and Holy Ghost?
'Tis not the fiery preacher, nor the man who has far trod,
But a close and loving family that's unified by God.

Yes, Grandma Jennie came to church! AMEN and AMEN.

Note: At the close of this unique sermon, there was a period of deep silence, and then the congregation broke into a spontaneous applause, quite unusual in a conservative collegiate congregation.

* * * * *

What Are Andrew and Jennie's Children Doing?

Bryant and **Lucille Mitchell** moved to Oregon after his retirement as General Chairman and Director of Foreign Missions for Open Bible Standard Churches. He lectures in Eugene Bible College, preaches, holds missionary rallies, and writes for Christian publications. In 1982 Bryant authored the book, *Heritage and Horizons*, the official history of Open Bible Standard Churches, and co-authored this book.

Hubert and **Rachel Mitchell** live in Los Angeles, California. After Jennie's homegoing, he succeeded his mother as president of the Go-Ye Fellowship. He founded Christians in Government in Los Angeles, authored the manual on Tele-Visitation, co-operates with the Billy Graham teams in their campaigns, and blesses many with the music of his voice and accordion, including the music he wrote for the song, "He Giveth More Grace."

Helen Mitchell Morken led a very active life as a missionary wife in Indonesia and Asia, and mother of six children. She passed away in June, 1983, after a three-year bout with cancer. Her husband, **David Morken**, lives in Lodi, California, with his wife **Wilma**. Although retired, he continues to preach in the USA and hold seminars for national pastors in foreign lands.

The present A. E. Mitchell children with their spouses in California, 1987.

Left to right with wives in front row: Murray and Esther Russell with daughter Joy (Jennie's youngest granddaughter), Bryant and Lucille Mitchell, Hubert and Rachel Mitchell, Joe and Marietta Smith, David and Wilma Morken.

Jean Mitchell Wilhelmsen served missions with her husband, **Kaare**, in India, Trinidad, and Afghanistan culminating with a ministry among the displaced Kazakhs in Iran, Turkey, and Germany under the Go-Ye Fellowship. She was a gifted writer and evangelist, and passed away in August, 1984, after the death of her husband in May, 1983.

Marietta Mitchell Smith and her husband, **Joseph**, retired after thirty-six years of missionary service in India under the board of the Brethren in Christ. They now live in Pennsylvania near Messiah College, founded by his grandfather, where they give special lectures. They also work with foreign students and spend part of their time in New York working with International Students, Inc, and Inter Varsity Christian Fellowship. She is co-author of this book.

Esther Mitchell Russell and her husband, **Murray**, live in Glendale, California, after serving twenty-three years as missionaries in Ethiopia and Kenya, Africa. Murray has just recently been retired by the Presbyterian Church under whom they have served. He continues interim pastoring and she is teaching English as a second language in schools and industry. They are also renewing the Gospel plaque business founded by her father, Andrew Mitchell.